DEDICATED TO COUNTLESS VICTIMS OF AVOIDABLE CANCER

UNREASONABLE RISK

HOW TO AVOID CANCER FROM COSMETICS AND PERSONAL CARE PRODUCTS:

THE NEWAYS STORY

By Samuel S. Epstein, M.D.

LIBRARY OF CONGRESS CATALOGING IN PUBLICATION DATA

ISBN 0-9715186-0-2

PUBLISHED BY ENVIRONMENTAL TOXICOLOGY, P.O. BOX 11170, CHICAGO ILLINOIS 60611, U.S.A.

FIRST ENGLISH EDITION
PRINTED BY PROLOGIC, PROVO, UTAH U.S.A.

TABLE OF CONTENTS

ACKNOWLEDGEMENTS

As Chairman of the Cancer Prevention Coalition, which conducted the research on which this monograph is based, I am pleased to acknowledge a wide range of sources of support for our mission in winning the losing war against cancer, and for providing citizens and consumers with information on avoidable and unknowing exposures to carcinogens in the totality of our environment. Apart from our growing and enthusiastic national and international membership, the Coalition has received generous support from Foundations including the Goldsmith, JMG, Gillian & Ellis Goodman, Tides, Gaia, Oestreicher, Cashman, Bioneers, HMR and Boston Fund, and Neways International besides other donors.

I would also like to express warm appreciation to members of the Coalition Executive and Board including: Dr. William Lijinsky, former Director Chemical Carcinogenesis, Frederick Cancer Research Center, Frederick, MD; Dr. Marvin Legator, Professor of Genetic Toxicology and Preventive Medicine, University of Texas, Galveston, TX: Dr. Quentin Young, past President of the American Public Health Association and Chairman of the Health and Medicine Policy Research Group; Barbara Seaman, co-Founder of the Womens' National Health Network; and Anthony Mazzocchi, Presidential Assistant to the Paper Allied Chemical and Energy Workers Union, AFL-CIO.

As importantly, I would like to acknowledge the group of sixty-five distinguished public health experts on cancer cause and prevention for endorsing my statement on "Losing the War Against Cancer; A Need for Public Policy Reforms," released at a February 4, 1992 Washington, D.C. press conference. These scientists included: past directors of three Federal agencies—Dr. Eula Bingham, former Assistant Secretary of Labor, Occupational Safety and Health Administration; the late Dr. David Rall, former Director of the National Institutes of Environmental Health Sciences and former Assistant Surgeon General USPHS; and Dr. Anthony Robbins, former Director of the National Institute for Occupational Safety and Health; Dr. Irwin Bross, former Director of Biostatistics, Roswell Park Memorial Institute, Buffalo, NY; Dr. Nicholas Ashford, MIT, Cambridge, MA; Dr. Vicente Navarro, Johns Hopkins University, Baltimore, MD; Dr. Thomas Mancuso, University of Pittsburgh; and the late Nobel Laureate, Dr. George Wald, Harvard University, Cambridge, MA. The interest and enthusiasm generated by this press conference was a major factor leading to the subsequent creation of the Cancer Prevention Coalition.

Others I would also like to thank include: Ralph Nader, for co-sponsoring my September, 1995 Cancer Prevention Coalition, Washington, DC press conference on the "Dirty Dozen" consumer products, launching the publication of The Safe Shopper's Bible; the indomitable Studs Terkel, for frequent invitations to discuss cancer politics and avoidable causes of cancer on his highly celebrated radio program series; and Michael Agrelius, Kate Cedergreen and Dr. Cole Woolley for most helpful editorial comments.

Warm commendation is also due to: Senator Ron Wyden (D-OR), for longstanding concerns on the dangers of cosmetic and toiletry ingredients; Senator E. Kennedy (D-MA), for his 1997 endorsement of the General Accounting Office report on carcinogenic ingredients in cosmetics; and Congresswoman J. Schakowsky (D-IL), for her recent bill (HR 1947) requiring warning labels on fragrances containing toxic ingredients.

As emeritus Professor of environmental and occupational medicine, I thank the University of Illinois Chicago School of Public Health for providing me with a hospitable base for teaching, scientific research, and public health policy initiatives on the causes and prevention of cancer.

Finally, writing this monograph, would have been hardly possible without the skilled administrative and editorial contributions of Julie Hlavaty, my highly efficient and dedicated office manager.

Cosmetic and personal care product industries worldwide are, for all intents and purposes, unregulated by government and essentially self-regulating. There are no requirements for pre-market ingredient and product safety testing. This virtual absence of regulation is disturbing as most people in developed countries use multiple personal care products, and to a lesser extent cosmetics, each day for a lifetime. This is even more alarming since the skin's role as a carrier more than a barrier has been well known for decades.

While nearly all nations require ingredient labeling, this is uninformative and tokenistic at best. The soup of complex chemical names of labeled ingredients, with few common names, is meaningless to consumers. The majority of toxicologists, public health and cancer prevention experts also have trouble deciphering these labels in the absence of any accompanying warning on the carcinogenic or other hazards of the named ingredients. Furthermore, few governments have taken even minimal regulatory action, specifically seizure or recall, against any product containing carcinogenic or otherwise hazardous ingredients, in spite of strongly supportive scientific evidence. This reckless regulatory abdication has encouraged mainstream industries to persist in marketing products that pose significant public health hazards. In this, they are powerfully supported by a global network of national trade associations. These associations work together in close collaboration, recently under the banner of "global harmonization", to anticipate and prevent any regulatory initiatives such as informative labeling.

Recognizing the serious and undisclosed carcinogenic hazards posed by a wide range of ingredients in mainstream industry consumer products, the author of this book co-authored The Safe Shopper's Bible in 1995. This book reviewed some 4,000 U.S. consumer products, including household products, cosmetics and toiletries, and provided detailed listings of the carcinogenic ingredients in individual products manufactured by named industries. Information was also provided on alternative safe products manufactured by non-mainstream industries. This book was thus designed to encourage consumers to vote with their shopping dollars and, in the absence of effective regulation, tilt the marketplace by rewarding safe alternative industries at the expense of indifferent mainstream industries.

In 1995, the author was unaware of the MLM industry, let alone Neways, to which there was no reference in The Safe Shopper's Bible. However, in the summer of 1997, the author received a promotional card from a Neways distributor in New Hampshire, named Mary Sanborn. Somewhat skeptically, the author requested specific information on the company's allegedly safe cosmetics and personal care products to review from a public health perspective. In response to Mary's follow-up call, the author expressed welcome surprise at the overall safety of Neways' products. Subsequent contact between the author and Neways management resulted in a series of discussions. These culminated in an ongoing collaboration between the company and the not-for-profit Cancer Prevention Coalition (1), directed to the identification and phasing out carcinogenic ingredients from their products.

Some six years have passed since The Safe Shopper's Bible was published, with no reference to Neways' safe cosmetics and personal care products. The author is now setting the record straight by writing this monograph, which recognizes the major contribution of Neways to product safety. Neways has set a groundbreaking example through major and precedential advances in phasing out carcinogenic ingredients from their cosmetics and personal care products. It is hoped that Neways' efforts will set an example for mainstream cosmetic and personal care product industries to phase out carcinogenic and otherwise toxic ingredients from their products.

CHAPTER ONE

HOW TO WIN THE LOSING WAR AGAINST CANCER

We are losing the winnable war against cancer. Over recent decades, the incidence of cancer in the U.S., and other major industrialized nations, has escalated to epidemic proportions (6, 9, 24). Lifetime risks of cancer in the U.S. are now approaching one in two for men and one in three for women; the estimated number of new cancer cases and deaths in 2001 are 1.3 million and 550,000 respectively. The overall increase in the incidence of all cancers in the U.S. white population since 1950 is about 60%, of which lung cancer, primarily attributed to smoking, accounts for about one quarter. A 1990 survey of major industrialized nations, including the U.S., Japan, the U.K. and other European countries, has similarly shown that non-smoking related cancers are responsible for about 75% of the overall increased incidence of cancer since 1950 (6). "In all the countries studied, mortality rates increased in persons over age 54 from cancer at some specific sites not linked to cigarette smoking, including multiple myeloma, cancers of the breast, brain, and other central nervous system sites, and myeloma, and for all cancer except lung and stomach." Over the same period, the incidence of non-smoking cancers in the U.S. increased approximately as follows: prostate cancer, non-Hodgkin's lymphoma and multiple myeloma, 200%; thyroid cancer, 155%; testis cancer, 120%; adult brain and nervous system cancer, 70%; female breast cancer, 60%; and childhood cancer, 35%. Similar trends are reflected in U.S. incidence rates from 1973 onwards (24).

More sharply increasing cancer rates have been reported in Japan (16, 27). From 1968-1997, mortality rates, age adjusted to account for increasing longevity, have changed approximately as follows: 300% increase in lymphatic leukemia and brain cancer in both sexes, and for kidney cancer in women; 100% increase in multiple myeloma in both sexes, kidney cancer in men, and breast cancer in women; 80% increase in ovarian cancer; and 60% increase in uterine cancer, as well as pancreatic cancer (the cancer from which Emperor Hirohito died) in both men and women. It may be noted that while the incidence of breast cancer in Japanese women is less than one half of that in western industrialized nations, it is rising so rapidly that it is expected to surpass that of stomach cancer to become the leading cause of cancer in women.

While cancer rates have escalated, our ability to treat and "cure" most cancers, with the notable exception of the relatively rare childhood and testicular cancers, contrary to general impressions, has remained largely unchanged for decades. Illustratively, the five-year survival rates for all cancers in the U.S. population from 1974 to 1990 increased from 49% to 54% for all races, and from 39% to 40% for blacks. Overall survival rates have scarcely improved since then (9).

The modern cancer epidemic cannot be explained away on the basis of increasing longevity, as incidence and mortality statistics are adjusted by age-standardization in the U.S. and other cancer registries to reflect these trends. Nor can the epidemic be largely attributed to faulty personal lifestyle factors. Although smoking is clearly the single most important cause of cancer, the incidence of lung cancer in U.S. men, but not women, is declining due to reduction in smoking, while the incidence of a wide range of non-smoking cancers is increasing at proportionately greater rates. Nor can the role of high fat diets be incriminated as a major cause of cancer, in sharp contrast to heart disease. Illustratively, breast cancer rates in Mediterranean countries are relatively low despite diets with up to 40% olive oil fat. Furthermore, epidemiological studies over the past two decades have consistently failed to establish any causal relationship between breast cancer and the consumption of fat *per se*, excluding consideration of meat and dairy fats which are heavily contaminated with carcinogenic pesticides and industrial pollutants. Finally, increasing cancer rates cannot be attributed to genetic factors which, at most, are directly implicated in well under 10% of all cancers. Furthermore, the genetics of human populations cannot possibly have materially changed within just the last few decades.

WHO'S RESPONSIBLE

What then is the predominant cause of the modern cancer epidemic? The answer is based on a strong body of scientific evidence incriminating the role of run-away technologies, particularly the petrochemical and nuclear industries. The explosive growth of these industries since the 1940s has, to varying degrees in different nations, outstripped the development of legislative and regulatory control. Resultingly, our total environment—air, water, the workplace, prescription drugs, consumer products (food, household products, and cosmetics and toiletries), has become pervasively contaminated with a wide range of industrial carcinogens, including persistent organic pollutants (POPs), such as organochlorine pesticides. **As a consequence, the public-at-large has been and continues to be unknowingly exposed to avoidable carcinogens from conception to death** (9).

The critical importance of environmental factors is well illustrated by a 1988 finding that adopted children whose adoptive parents died from cancer have as much as a five-fold increased risk of developing cancer themselves (25). These conclusions have been further and strikingly confirmed by the results of a recent large-scale study on 9,000 identical twins in Sweden, Denmark and Finland. The authors concluded:

"The overwhelming contribution to the causation of cancer in the population of twins that we studied was the environment. Even for cancers for which there is statistically significant evidence of a heritable component, most pairs of twins were discordant for the cancer— indicating that—the increase in the risk of cancer even among close relatives—is generally moderate" (20).

We are thus faced with an unparalleled crisis of international proportions. This crisis will be further exacerbated with the growing industrialization of relatively underdeveloped western European nations, notably Greece and Portugal, in addition to Third World countries.

How have those institutions charged with fighting the war against cancer responded to this crisis? The answer is badly, as they have been and remain largely indifferent to cancer prevention (9). In the U.S., the predominant complex of responsible institutions, known as the "cancer establishment", is comprised of the federal National Cancer Institute (NCI) and the private "charity" the American Cancer Society (ACS), together with its national network of funded university scientists and Comprehensive National Cancer Centers. The cancer establishment has massive resources at its disposal. The 2001 budget of the NCI is $3.8 billion, up from $220 million in 1971 when President Nixon declared the "War Against Cancer" in response to highly publicized pressure by the cancer establishment, coupled with demands for massively increased funding. President Nixon was promised that such funding would enable the "conquest of cancer" by 1987. The current budget of the ACS is about $700 million, with cash reserves and other assets approaching $1 billion (12).

The policies and priorities of the cancer establishment are still narrowly fixated on damage control— screening, diagnosis and treatment—and basic molecular research, with indifference to cancer prevention. For the ACS, this indifference reaches the level of overt hostility (9, 10, 12; Appendix 2A). These and other concerns relating to fiscal malpractice have led The Chronicle of Philanthropy, the authoritative U.S. charity watch dog, to charge that the ACS is "more interested in accumulating wealth than saving lives". ACS allocations for all primary prevention activities, primarily tobacco cessation programs and low-fat diets, are under 0.1% of its budget. NCI's budgetary allocation for occupational cancer, the most avoidable of all cancers and conservatively estimated to be responsible for about 10% of all U.S. cancer deaths in adults and children, is about 1%. The budget for research and outreach on African-American and other ethnic minorities, with their disproportionately high cancer rates, is also about 1% of NCI's budget; allocations for all primary prevention activities are well under 5%.

The U.S. cancer establishment's professional mindset and politically misshapen priorities are compounded by disturbing conflicts of interest, particularly for the ACS, with the cancer drug industry (Appendix 2A). As NCI's previous director Dr. Samuel Broder admitted, the NCI has become "what amounts to a governmental pharmaceutical company" (10). The establishment's myopic mindset is further illustrated by a succession of widely publicized misleading claims over the last four decades, to have turned "the tide against cancer," and to have discovered the latest "miracle" or "magic bullet" cancer drug. Such claims continue to be more optimistic than realistic.

Even more seriously, the poorly accountable U.S. cancer establishment has failed to provide Congress, regulatory agencies, notably the Food and Drug Administration (FDA), Environmental Protection Agency (EPA) and Occupational Safety and Health Administration (OSHA), and even more importantly the public with available scientific information on a wide range of avoidable carcinogenic exposures. Such information remains buried in government and industry files and in the scientific literature which is relatively inaccessible to the general public. As a result, corrective legislative and regulatory action has not been taken, and the public has been and still is denied its fundamental right-to-know of such information. This failure to disclose information has denied the public of the opportunity to take action to reduce its own risks of cancer.

The U.S., Canadian, U.K., Japanese, Australian and other cancer establishments worldwide, still explicitly rely on gerrymandered data and biased claims by industry-indentured academic and institutional apologists. Notable among these is the U.K.'s Sir Richard Doll, allegedly a leading expert on public health and cancer causation. As detailed in the world's leading public health journal, Doll has persisted in his attempts for over three decades to trivialize escalating cancer rates and to explain them away on the virtually exclusive basis of "blame-the-victim" or faulty lifestyle causation, coupled with "guesstimates" to the effect that pollution and industrial products account for only 3% of cancer mortality (9, 11). Reflecting his strong conflicts of interest, Doll is invidiously unique in his insistence that neither leaded petroleum, radiation from atom bomb tests, low-level radiation, diesel exhaust nor dioxins pose any public health hazards (11, 26).

Based on such evidence, the U.S., Canadian and U.K. cancer establishments have been charged with major responsibility for losing the winnable war against cancer. This serious charge against the NCI and ACS comes as no surprise, as the author raised it at a February 4, 1992 Washington, D.C. press conference on behalf of an *ad hoc* coalition of some 65 leading national U.S. experts in public health, preventive medicine and cancer prevention, including Nobel Laureates and past directors of three major federal agencies (9). These concerns are all the more serious in view of the strong influence that U.S. cancer establishment policies exert on other nations worldwide, and their mutually reinforcing and interlocking relationships. As disclosed at a recent press conference in London, the policies of the U.K. "cancer charities" are as gravely derelict and conflict ridden as those of the U.S. (Appendix 2B).

The mainstream media also share responsibility for losing the war on cancer. With roll-over enthusiasm over the last four decades, the media have breathlessly and uncritically greeted the latest claim for discoveries on "magic bullet" cancer cures as triumphs in the cancer war. This is in striking contrast with the media's usually limited and critical receptivity to information on avoidable causes of cancer. The mainstream media together with cancer establishments and petrochemical, cancer drug, and other industries form a powerful interlocking complex which has distorted international public policies to the extent of trivializing priority for cancer prevention in favor of damage control.

It should also be recognized that the majority of involuntary carcinogenic exposures also induce additional chronic toxic effects. These include reproductive, endocrine disruptive, neurotoxic and immunotoxic effects, for which there are no comparable systematic data on their incidence and related mortality trends. Cancer, in effect, represents a quantifiable measure of the adverse public health and environmental impacts of run-away industrial technologies, disinterested or complicit cancer establishments, and a roll-over media. As importantly, cancer also represents a paradigm of failed democratic decision-making processes. Thus, a reduction of cancer rates will most likely also be paralleled by a reduction in the incidence of other chronic environmentally-induced diseases.

HOW TO REVERSE THE EPIDEMIC

There is a wide range of interlocking personal and legislative initiatives that could be mobilized to reverse the escalating incidence of cancer, and reduce cancer incidence and mortality to the relatively low rates of the 1950's (9, 11, 24). These initiatives can be developed through a wide range of strategies. Of particular importance is personal action by shopping for safe products, thus tilting the market place in favor of safe alternative non-mainstream companies and industries at the expense of the unsafe mainstream. Such action can be extended by word of mouth, as well as by informing the general public at the local, community, regional and national levels of unrecognized and avoidable exposure to carcinogens in consumer products and the environment. The recent formation of local, regional and international Cancer Prevention Coalition offices provides a practical organizational basis for this initiative, which can be further extended to civic officials, and state and national representatives. However, direct or indirect legislative lobbying cannot be pursued under the auspices of the Coalition, or any other non-profit organization, as mandated by U.S. Internal Revenue Service regulations.

RIGHT-TO-KNOW

The right-to-know is, or should be, an inalienable and fundamental democratic principle with the probable exception of national security concerns. Industry claims of confidentiality and trade secrecy have often been, and still are, a serious deterrent to the recognition of potential risks from carcinogenic and otherwise toxic products and processes. There is an urgent need to develop international rules to restrict claims of confidentiality to what is unarguably essential to protect independently validated proprietary information, exclusive of any health considerations. All other information on the carcinogenic and otherwise toxic risks of a product, drug or process must be automatically and fully released to the public. It should, however, be emphasized that, with limited exceptions, the right-to-know in most nations is more honored by empty promises rather than action, or in the breach rather than performance.

There is a critical and overdue need to extend right-to-know requirements and legislation to the overseas operations, particularly in lesser developed countries, of U.S. corporations and those in other major industrialized nations. Such requirements should encompass occupational, environmental and human rights practices requiring all corporations to report on their operations in foreign countries. The greatest incentive to reduce the use of toxics is public knowledge of their identity and routes of avoidable exposure, particularly when safe alternatives are available. Right-to-know initiatives are thus among the most practical and potent political strategies in the war against cancer and against untested new products and technologies. Critical steps in this direction have already been developed in Europe with recent stringent requirements for labeling genetically-engineered foods.

It must be stressed, however, that responsible product labeling *per se* is inadequate, if not a travesty, unless accompanied by an explicit "Red Flag" warning of recognized cancer, health, environmental and occupational risks. Such warnings are also essential with regard to poorly defined or potential risks, such as is the case with genetically-engineered milk and foods. Furthermore, product label warnings should not be used as a justification for the authorization of new candidate carcinogens or for the continued use of carcinogenic products already in commerce. It must be stressed that product label warning is no substitute for a moratorium, product phase-out, or ban. Label warnings are not only discriminatory to uneducated and lower socio-economic population groups, but may even encourage industry to target such groups in order to penetrate national markets by price-regulation strategies.

Environmental Cancer: Citizens are entitled to full access to information from local and national governments on their avoidable carcinogenic exposures from air and water. Such information is likely to encourage industry to reduce environmental emissions and discharges of carcinogenic and toxic pollutants, and also to encourage more stringent governmental regulation. Every regional municipal authority should be required to provide consumers with a complete list of carcinogenic contaminants, their concentrations and detection levels in drinking water, together with each water bill. Similarly, every chemical, mining and nuclear industry should be required to disclose to local communities, regional and national governments a complete listing of all carcinogens, including intermediates and products, they process, manufacture and dispose. They should also be required to disclose the amounts of each carcinogen they discharge into surrounding air and water.

No industry should be allowed to operate unless it provides ongoing quantitative information on smokestack and fugitive atmospheric emissions of carcinogens in the air of its perimeter and the local community.

Occupational Cancer: In addition to the use of closed-system technologies, including local exhaust ventilation, to insure worker safety, workers and their representatives have inalienable rights to be given full information on the identity of all carcinogens with which they come in contact. This should be done through explicit product labeling and posting, and distribution of information included in the Material Safety Data Sheets (MSDS) of all carcinogens in raw materials, intermediates, impurities and finished products to which workers are exposed. Workers are also entitled to continuing quantitative information on levels of inhalation and skin exposure for each carcinogen. All such information should be made available to workers on a daily basis, and should also be reported to the responsible regulatory authorities.

Prescription Drugs: A recent survey of 241 high-volume U.S. prescription drugs reported that nearly half posed cancer risks based on carcinogenicity tests designed by industry, or government to prove safety. The carcinogenic effects of these drugs have been associated with low test dosages that are near or at therapeutic levels commonly used in treatment. These risks are compounded by the fact that prescription drugs are often administered individually or in various combinations to millions of patients, sometimes for decades or starting in childhood. One leading authority has claimed that prescription drugs may pose the single most important class of unrecognized and avoidable carcinogenic risks for the entire U.S. population (Moore, 1998).

To argue that such risks are more than justified by their very real benefits is to posit a false dilemma, especially in view of the fact that patients are rarely affirmatively and explicitly informed of these risks, and of the availability of safer and effective alternatives. Legislation is urgently required to ensure that the pharmaceutical industry provides clear and explicit advertising and labeling warnings on the carcinogenic effects of prescription and non-prescription drugs. Physicians should also be required to endorse these warnings and provide patients with information on safe and effective alternatives. Failure to do so should result in professional and legal accountability.

Consumer Products: Consumer product legislation is well overdue. All foods, grown with the application of carcinogenic pesticides should be clearly labeled with a cancer warning, the name of each carcinogenic pesticide and the concentrations of its residues. Of particular concern are the high residues of multiple carcinogenic pesticides in grains, vegetables and fruits. Recent estimates indicate that by the age of one year, cancer risks from residues of just eight common pesticides in 20 infant foods exceed the lifetime "acceptable" cancer risks, as estimated by the U.S. Environmental

Protection Agency. U.S. meat, from cattle implanted with sex hormones in feed lots to increase their body weight, should be clearly labeled as contaminated with residues of carcinogenic hormones. Also, U.S. milk, from cows injected with recombinant bovine growth hormone, rBGH, should be labeled as a genetically-engineered product, for which the public health hazards have been fully documented. Similarly, irradiation of food, including poultry, eggs, and produce, with doses up to some 1 billion times higher than that of a chest x-ray, should be prominently labeled as "irradiated", especially in view of their carcinogenic, mutagenic and nutritional risks. This requirement is in sharp contrast to efforts by industry, with enthusiastic complicity of the United States Food and Drug Administration and Department of Agriculture, to use labels with highly misleading and euphemistic absurdities, such as "cold or electronic pasteurization".

Ingredients of cosmetics and personal care products (CPCP) are generally identified on their labels by a long list of chemicals. However, this is meaningless to the overwhelming majority of consumers, let alone to expert toxicologists and cancer prevention professionals. This critically necessitates a "Red Flag" warning of the wide range of multiple carcinogenic ingredients, contaminants and precursors in most mainstream industry products. Similarly, the complete composition of all household products, including home, lawn and garden pesticides, should also be clearly labeled, together with cancer warnings for each listed carcinogenic ingredient. Consumer product legislation should require data and affidavits in support of alleged claims of safety for "organic" or other "natural" products. **Consideration should also be given to the granting of tax incentives to the manufacturers of safe alternative products.**

Mainstream industry consumer products—foods, beverages, cosmetics, toiletries, and household products—contain a wide range of undisclosed carcinogens in the form of ingredients, contaminants and precursors. These pose major, but generally unrecognized, avoidable risks of cancer.

Examples of carcinogens in 12 common consumer products known as "The Dirty Dozen" (Appendix 2C), none labeled with any cancer warning, are listed in Table 1.1. The gravity of these risks is illustrated by the following examples:

- Beef frankfurters: Children eating up to about a dozen each month are at an approximately 4-fold increased risk of brain cancer and 7-fold increased risk of leukemia. (This is due to the formation of a nitrosamine carcinogen, by the interaction of nitrite, used as a colorant, and natural amines in meat).

TABLE 1.1: THE (1995) DIRTY DOZEN PRODUCTS AND SAFE ALTERNATIVES*

FOOD

Beef Frankfurters - (e.g. Oscar Mayer Foods Corporation)

Unlabeled toxic Ingredients- *Benzene Hexachloride*, carcinogenic; *Dacthal*, carcinogenic: (Can be contaminated with dioxin); *Dieldrin*, carcinogenic; *DDT*, carcinogenic; *Heptachlor*, carcinogenic; *Hexachlorobenzene*, carcinogenic; *Lindane*, carcinogenic; *Hormones*, carcinogenic and feminizing; *Antibiotics*, Some are carcinogenic (e.g. Sulfamethazine).

Labeled Toxic Ingredient - *Nitrite*, Interacts with meat amines to form carcinogenic nitrosamines.

Note: Substantive evidence of causal relation to childhood cancer.

Whole Milk - (e.g. Borden or Lucerne)

Unlabeled Toxic Ingredients - *DDT*, carcinogenic; *Dieldrin*, carcinogenic; *Heptachlor*, carcinogenic; *Hexachlorobenzene*, carcinogenic; *Antibiotics*, Some are carcinogenic; *Recombinant Bovine Growth Hormone:* Evidence of breast, colon and prostate cancer risk.

HOUSEHOLD PRODUCTS

Ajax Cleanser - Colgate-Palmolive, Inc.

> **Unlabeled Toxic Ingredient** - *Crystalline Silica*, carcinogenic (by inhalation).

Zud Heavy Duty Cleanser - Reckitt & Colman, Inc.

> **Unlabeled Toxic Ingredient** - *Crystalline Silica*, carcinogenic (by inhalation).

Lysol Disinfectant Spray - Reckitt & Colman, Inc.

> **Labeled or Unlabeled Toxic Ingredient** - *Orthophenylphenol (OPP)*, carcinogenic.

Zodiac Cat & Dog Flea Collar - Sandoz Agro, Inc.

> **Labeled Toxic Ingredient** - *Propoxur*, carcinogenic.

Ortho Weed-B-Gon Lawn Weed Killer - Monsanto Co.

> **Labeled Toxic Ingredient** - *Sodium 2,4- Dichlorophenoxyacetic acid (2,4-D),* carcinogenic.

> **Note:** Substantive evidence of causal relation to lymphoma, soft tissue sarcoma, and other cancers.

COSMETICS and TOILETRIES

Talcum Powder - Johnson & Johnson, Inc.

Labeled Toxic Ingredient - *Talc*, carcinogenic.

Note: Substantive evidence of causal relation to ovarian cancer.

Cover Girl Replenishing Natural Finish Make-up (Foundation) - Procter & Gamble, Inc.

Labeled Toxic Ingredient - *BHA*, carcinogenic; *Talc*, carcinogenic; *Titanium Dioxide,* carcinogenic; *Triethanolamine (TEA),* Interacts with nitrites to form carcinogenic nitrosamines; *Lanolin,* Often contaminated with DDT and other carcinogenic pesticides.

Crest Tartar Control Toothpaste - Procter & Gamble, Inc

Labeled Toxic Ingredient - *FD & C Blue #1*, carcinogenic; *Saccharin*, carcinogenic; *Fluoride*, Possible carcinogen.

Alberto VO5 Conditioner (Essence of Neutral Henna) - Alberto-Culver USA, Inc.

Labeled Toxic Ingredient - *Formaldehyde*, carcinogenic; *Polysorbate 80*, usually contaminated with the carcinogen 1,4-dioxane; *FD &C Red #4*, carcinogenic.

Clairol Nice 'n Easy (Permanent Haircolor) - Clairol, Inc.

Labeled Toxic Ingredient - *Quaternium-15* (Formaldehyde releaser) carcinogenic; *Diethanolamine (DEA),* Interacts with nitrites to form a carcinogenic nitrosamine; *Phenylene-Diamines,* Includes carcinogens and other ingredients inadequately tested for carcinogenicity.

Note: Substantive evidence of causal relation to leukemia, multiple myeloma, non-Hodgkin's lymphoma and other cancers.

---

*Presented by the Cancer Prevention Coalition at a September 21, 1995 Washington, D.C. press conference,co-sponsored by Ralph Nader, launching publication of <u>The Safe Shopper's Bible</u> (Appendix 2C).

- Talc: Women, in the IR reproductive years, regularly dusting their genital area with talc after bathing or showering are at approximately 3-fold increased risk of developing ovarian cancer.

• Permanent hair color: Women using permanent or semi-permanent black or dark brown hair dyes are at increased risk for non-Hodgkin's lymphoma, multiple myeloma, chronic leukemia, and also breast cancer. In fact, there is growing evidence that use of these hair dyes accounts for about 20% of all non-Hodgkin's lymphomas in U.S. women.

REDUCTION OF TOXICS IN USE

Empowerment of the public with the right-to-know of avoidable and uninformed exposures to carcinogens is likely to stimulate grass roots demands. This is likely to result in strong legislative pressures for phase-out of toxics in use in the wide range of carcinogenic petrochemical products and processes, currently firmly embedded in commerce. Strategies based on toxics-use reduction however, are not only practical but also cost-effective. Such strategies include phasing out the manufacture, use and disposal of carcinogenic and otherwise toxic chemicals ingredients. This will lead to commercial development of safe alternative products and technologies.

Many such initiatives were strongly endorsed at the author's February 4, 1992 Washington, D.C. press conference, by some 65 leading national public health and cancer prevention experts. These initiatives include recommending reform of the U.S. cancer establishment, and reorienting its priorities to cancer prevention, with major emphasis directed to toxics-use reduction (9).

"In close cooperation with key regulatory agencies and industry, the NCI should initiate large-scale research programs to develop non-carcinogenic products and processes as alternatives to those currently based on chemical and physical carcinogens. This program should also include research on the development of economic incentives for the reduction or phase-out of the use of industrial carcinogens, coupled with economic disincentives for their continued use, especially when appropriate non-carcinogenic alternatives are available".

It should be stressed that toxics-use reduction is based on the principle of risk prevention in sharp contrast to "risk management" strategies, characterized by lower short-term costs and strongly favored by regulatory agencies and industry. These risk management strategies are also supported by a growing battery of handsomely funded indentured scientists and industry-funded think tanks, such as the Harvard Center for Risk Analysis, The Hudson, Cato and Competitive Enterprise Institutes, the American Policy Center, and the International Life Sciences Institute, which specialize in "risk assessment". Risk management accepts the inevitability of risk from industrial processes and products while claiming that such risks can be "managed" to levels variously described as "acceptable or insignificant or minimal". These claims are derived from highly dubious and possibly manipulated risk assessment mathematical formulas, which are shaped by predetermined financial or regulatory interests. Such assessments claim to predict minimal anticipated disease or mortality from any particular level of carcinogenic exposure or exposures.

Following a well-organized political campaign by environmental groups and favored by progressive industry, the Commonwealth of Massachusetts unanimously passed the "Toxics Use Reduction Act" in 1989 which created the Massachusetts Toxics Use Reduction Program. The Act is a specific form of pollution prevention that focuses on reducing the use of toxic chemicals, besides generation of hazardous waste, by improving and redesigning industrial products and processes. The Toxics Use Reduction Institute of the University of Massachusetts, Lowell, played an important role in developing the Act by providing education, training, research on new materials and processes, a technical library and information source, and specialized laboratories for evaluating safe alternative technologies. The notable achievements of this Act include: 1) reducing the generation of toxic wastes from 1989 to 1997 by 50 percent by reducing toxics use by 20 percent; 2) establishing toxics-use reduction as the preferred means for achieving compliance with federal and state environmental statutes; 3) promoting reduction in the production and use of toxic chemicals; 4) enhancing and strengthening the enforcement of existing environmental laws; 5) promoting coordination between state agencies administering toxics-related programs; and 6) sustaining and promoting the competitiveness of Massachusetts industry. The Massachusetts Act could also serve as a useful model for U.S. state, U.S. national and international legislation. Granting tax incentives for the urgent development of safe alternatives to toxic-based, conventional technologies, as well as tax penalties for failure to adopt available safe alternative technologies, might possibly encourage the active interest of mainstream industry in such initiatives. Nothing could be more appropriate for stimulating belated reform of the mainstream cosmetic and personal care product industry.

The relatively new trend to voluntary and economy-driven corporate environmentalism is already proving more potent than ideologically and legislatively-driven toxics use reduction. A major development in this trend is the selling of services and functions rather than products. For instance, the U.S. Atlanta-based Interface Inc. leases floor covering services and recycles old carpets which otherwise must be eventually incinerated or dumped in landfills. Similarly, Xerox now leases copiers and recycles old models. A parallel development is "Eco-efficiency and Pollution Prevention" (E2 P2) or "corporate environmentalism." This concept is typified by the growing investment of Royal Dutch Shell, Amoco and British Petroleum in renewable sustainable energy sources, including wind, solar power and fuel cells, and by extending product ranges to improved gasoline mixes. While cynicism from citizen groups may be reasonably anticipated, considering the past environmental track record of some of these companies, such initiatives should nevertheless be welcomed.

Additionally, the potentially mutual reinforcing role of legislative and market place pressures should be fully recognized in tilting the market place in favor of safe alternative industries.

A further example of the role of market place pressures that merits legislative recognition and support, relates to consumer products, including food, household products, cosmetics and toiletries. The growth of organic and non-toxic non-mainstream food products in U.S. markets has reached double digit annual figures over the last decade. The 1995 Safe Shopper's Bible rated approximately 4,000 conventional mainstream and safe non-mainstream products for undisclosed carcinogenic ingredients and contaminants. This action has already resulted in a significant market shift away from hazardous to safe alternative products, which are now becoming more popular and price competitive. Similar trends have also emerged in the safe alternative non-mainstream cosmetic and personal care product industry as evidenced by the rapid growth and success of companies, such as Neways International multilevel marketing and also Aveda/Estee Lauder retail international outlets.

Clearly, such health-driven marketplace pressures depend on a fully informed public, who recognize their **right-to-know** of involuntary and avoidable exposures to carcinogens in consumer products, air, water, and the workplace. Such knowledge and concerns have been recently reflected by the success of non-price competitive safe products. Illustrative are the booming sales of a leading sportswear manufacturer, Patagonia, which has completely converted to organic cotton by the use of well-established integrated pest management strategies. This is particularly important as cotton is the most pesticide-intensive U.S. crop, accounting for 10% of total national pesticide use. These concepts have been recently amplified and extended into a new paradigm for a system called "natural capitalism" or "environmental capitalism", which has set a landmark agenda for a rational, safe and ecologically sound concept of industrial development.

THE PRECAUTIONARY PRINCIPLE

Another important initiative in fighting the losing cancer war is an absolute prohibition of the introduction to commerce of new carcinogenic products and untested new technologies. Under the terms of the 1948 U.N. Universal Declaration of Human Rights the right to life, and its corollary right to health, is the first and most important of all fundamental rights recognized by many international conventions. Thus, implementary legislation is needed to mandate that considerations of life and health take absolute precedence over economics and trade.

The first line of defense against avoidable risks from carcinogenic and otherwise toxic exposures is an absolute prohibition of further increasing the burden of current exposures, due to the authorization of new candidate carcinogenic products and processes. Such a prohibition is based on the obvious **Precautionary Principle**, which is based on preventing new risks and that zero risk policies are essential for public and environment protection. As such, this Principle is particularly relevant to genetically-engineered food for which industry claims of safety are based on "trust us" assurances, rather than published scientific data. These claims are further invalidated by the extensive scientific evidence on the veterinary and public health hazards, particularly increased risks of breast, colon, and prostate cancers, from consumption of genetically-engineered, rBGH/BST, milk.

The Precautionary Principle was initially invoked by the EU in 1980 with regard to chlorofluorohydrocarbons, and again by the German government in 1994 at the Second North Sea Conference, in relation to marine dumping of toxic wastes. Such policies are clearly preferable to the deliberate acceptance of risks followed by attempts to "manage", rather than prevent such risks. Ineffective management, by reducing exposures to levels claimed "acceptable" by self-interested industry or complicit regulatory agencies, solves few real problems. Even recognizing the sovereign rights of each nation to set its own levels of sanitary protection, zero-risk policies must therefore constitute the standard principle, and not the rare exception, characteristic of current practice. In this connection, it may be noted that French President Jacques Chirac, at a 1998 meeting of the World Conservation Union, proposed to increase the powers of the United Nations Environment Program to avoid sovereignty disputes that hamper the global fight against pollution. President Chirac warned that countries around the world were holding on to an outdated idea of sovereignty, while environmental pollution ignored national borders.

The Precautionary Principle would thus mandate the categorical responsibility of industry to provide unequivocal evidence on the safety of all new candidate products and processes, thereby ensuring that they do not pose potential or recognized human or environmental risks. This principle further absolves citizens and regulatory agencies from the heavy burden for proving risks in response to industry challenges, and allows the banning of suspect products in circumstances of scientific uncertainty. The raw data, on the basis of which industry claims of safety are based, must be fully disclosed and evaluated by an independent agency with qualified representation of non-governmental organizations (NGO's) and their scientific consultants at industry's expense. This is essential to exclude bias or manipulation, for which there is a well documented and decades-old track record in a wide range of petrochemical and other industries (7, 8; Appendix 2D). A recent illustrative example is afforded by the review of 161 studies in the National Library of Medicine files on four heavily regulated industrial chemicals – formaldehyde, perchloroethylene, atrazine and alachlor. While only 14% of industry studies reported toxic or carcinogenic effects, such effects were disclosed in 71% of independent studies. The recent announcement by the U.S. American Chemistry Council (formerly known as the Chemical Manufacturers Association) of a $1 billion new safety testing program merits skepticism rather than reassurance. This is further compounded by the fact that the program is headed up by Dr. Roger McLennan, who has strained over the last decade, behind a façade of scientific objectivity, to disprove the overwhelming evidence on the cancer risks of diesel exhaust. Prior to that, McLennan worked for the Chemical Industry Institute of Toxicology whose major role has been to challenge or attempt to explain away evidence on the carcinogenicity of profitable industrial chemicals.

In 1997, the Swedish Chemicals Policy Committee, established by the Swedish Government in May, 1996, published a revolutionary document entitled "Towards A Sustainable Chemicals Policy". In their official report to the Government, the Committee embraced the fullest implementation of the Precautionary Principle ever proposed for policies regarding industrial chemicals. These policies will shift the burden of proof of safety away from the public to industry. Industry will have to produce detailed evidence that all new chemicals proposed for use pose no carcinogenic, mutagenic or endocrine disruptive adverse public health effects, and no adverse environmental impacts, including persistence and bioaccumulation. The new law will also ban persistent organic pollutants (POPs) and other persistent chemicals such as lead, and require the phasing out of chlorinated paraffins, such as plasticizers and flame retardants. Swedish companies will have five years to test the estimated 2,500 chemicals that they use in quantities over 1,000 tons per year for such effects. By 2010, chemicals used in lesser amounts will also have to be tested.

OTHER INITIATIVES

There are a wide range of other organizational initiatives which should also be recognized. These include demanding transparency, integrity and independence of key scientific institutions, designated expert committees and regulatory bodies, coupled with demands for public input into their decision making. The 1972 U.S. Federal Advisory Committee Act requires that the composition of regulatory agency advisory committees must reflect balanced and qualified representation of all concerned interests, and that meetings must be publicized in advance and open to the public. However, in practice, these requirements are more often honored in the breach than the observance.

Finally, consideration should be given to extending laws and penalties on white-collar crime, now generally applicable to crimes of economic motivation with adverse economic consequences, to crimes of economic motivation with adverse public health consequences. This consideration is consistent with a major legislative initiative proposed by the author some three decades ago (Appendix 2D). These could be levied against managers, executives and consultants of industries who knowingly manipulate, distort or suppress information on the environmental, occupational and consumer hazards of their products and processes.

CHAPTER TWO

CANCER RISKS FROM MAINSTREAM INDUSTRY PRODUCTS

As explained in Chapter One, unknowing and avoidable exposures to mainstream industry carcinogenic petrochemicals in the totality of the environment—air, water, the workplace, cosmetics and toiletries, besides other consumer products—are largely responsible for the escalating incidence of cancer over recent decades, and for the current cancer epidemic. There is little excuse or reason for continuing carcinogenic exposure, as methods for the detection of such risks have been well developed and widely available for decades.

According to Neways' recent conservative estimates, three personal care products are applied daily to infants and children, men use ten personal care products daily, and women use six cosmetics and thirteen personal care products each day (Table 2.1). Some products, particularly hand soaps, are used on several occasions each day. Assuming that the mainstream products used by most women each contain only two carcinogens, this would amount to over 40 different avoidable carcinogenic exposures daily. It is unthinkable that women would knowingly inflict such exposures on themselves if their routinely used products were labeled with explicit warnings of cancer risks. It is unbelievable that the Food and Drug Administration remains silent and recklessly abdicates regulatory responsibility, and that the cancer establishment remains disinterested and fails to advise Congress and consumers of these avoidable risks.

TABLE 2.1 TYPICAL PRODUCTS USED DAILY BY INFANTS AND CHILDREN, MEN AND WOMEN

INFANTS AND CHILDREN: PERSONAL CARE PRODUCTS
Hand soap
Shampoo
Toothpaste

MEN: PERSONAL CARE PRODUCTS
Body lotion
Body wash
Conditioner
Deodorant
Hair gel/mousse/pomade
Hair spray
Hand soap
Mouthwash
Shampoo
Toothpaste

WOMEN: PERSONAL CARE PRODUCTS
Body lotion
Body wash
Conditioner
Deodorant
Face lotion

Face soap
Hair gel/mousee/pomade
Hair spray
Hand lotion
Hand soap
Mouthwash
Shampoo
Toothpaste

WOMEN: COSMETICS
Blush
Eye shadow
Face powder
Foundation
Lipstick
Mascara

HOW TO DETERMINE CANCER RISKS

There are two separate lines of evidence for determining risks of cancer from exposure to industrial chemicals, products or manufacturing processes—the experimental and the epidemiological.

The experimental evidence is based on standardized tests in mice and rats; it should be noted that such tests on most industrial chemicals have been conducted by U.S. Federal agency programs at the taxpayers', rather than more properly at the industry's, expense. There is an overwhelming consensus in the informed independent scientific literature, as confirmed by expert bodies, including the World Health Organization's International Agency for Research on Cancer (IARC), that positive results of well designed animal tests create the strong presumption of human cancer risk. In fact, the IARC uses such evidence as the major basis for ranking human risks (15). This consensus is also reflected in U.S. and international legislative and regulatory precedents.

It should be emphasized that relatively few chemicals, less than 600, have been shown to be carcinogenic in rodent tests. Consequently, there is no basis whatsoever for the common but false industry claim that every chemical is carcinogenic when tested at high doses. In fact, doses used in animal tests are determined based on the absence of evidence of toxicity, such as weight loss, in long-term studies. Moreover, a high percentage of avoidable chemical causes of human cancer were first detected in animal tests, and subsequently confirmed in epidemiological studies. It may be noted that the results of most such positive animal tests were initially dismissed or challenged by the industries concerned. However, the validity of such findings have been subsequently confirmed by epidemiological studies, in some instances decades later.

Epidemiological studies depends on the ability to identify population groups exposed to a particular carcinogen or carcinogens, and then to compare their cancer rates with those in unexposed groups. Large scale epidemiological studies have been conducted on the effects of tobacco use, based on comparison of lung and other cancer rates in millions of nonsmokers and those who have smoked 1, 2, 3 or 4 packs of cigarettes daily. Smaller scale studies have been conducted on workers exposed to carcinogenic products or processes in a wide range of industries, compared to unexposed workers in the same or other industries, or to unexposed general population groups. Restrictedly, some general population studies have been conducted on clusters of people exposed in localized geographical locations to higher levels of environmental carcinogens in air or water than unexposed control groups. However, epidemiological studies are more difficult, if not impractical for the population-at-large, as most people are exposed to similar carcinogens in air, water, food, household products, and cosmetic and personal care products (CPCPs).

For these reasons, there are relatively few epidemiological studies on CPCPs. The majority of the population in industrialized nations use these products to varying degrees; therefore, there is no practical way for identifying and comparing exposed and nonexposed groups. However, notable exceptions include epidemiological studies on particular population sub-groups, such as consumers using talc or certain hair dyes, and professional cosmetologists.

SOURCE OF EVIDENCE ON CANCER RISKS OF COSMETICS AND PERSONAL CARE PRODUCTS

What is the source of evidence on the carcinogenicity of ingredients in CPCPs, and just how reliable is this? Evidence on the carcinogenicity of the multiple carcinogenic ingredients and contaminants in CPCPs is detailed in numerous sources. These sources include the following: a series of 78 IARC monographs published since 1972, each detailing different classes of industrial and other chemicals (15); some 500 National Institutes of Health Technical Report Series on individual carcinogens, based on rodent bioassay tests, initiated by the National Cancer Institute in 1968 and transferred in 1979 to the National Institute of Environmental Health Sciences (NIEHS) National Toxicology Program (NTP); the NTP's supposedly annual Report on Carcinogens, initiated in 1978 but only nine of which had been published by 2000, which summarizes evidence on a limited number of carcinogens identified in animal tests or human studies, and summaries of relevant regulations by the Food and Drug Administration (FDA) and other Federal agencies; numerous articles in scientific publications that are virtually inaccessible or incomprehensible to the general public, and which report the results of animal tests and human epidemiological studies on CPCP ingredients; compilation, analysis and interpretation of all existing evidence in fully referenced books and sources. These sources include: the 1980 Science Action Coalition's <u>Consumer's Guide to Cosmetics;</u> the author's books including the 1995 <u>Safe Shopper's Bible</u>, the 1998 <u>Breast Cancer Prevention Program,</u> and the 1998 <u>The Politics of Cancer, Revisited;</u> and a wide range of information from the Cancer Prevention Coalition (Appendix 1), and it's website www.preventcancer.com. Such information is designed for the general public and includes Cancer Alerts, Newsletters, Press Releases (Appendix 2), and Citizen Petitions to the FDA (Appendix 3). Wide dissemination of such documentation has been recently enhanced by the creation of a national and international network of CPC Offices (Appendix 4). Finally, evidence on the carcinogenicity of some CPCP ingredients and contaminants is admitted, although trivializing so, in the <u>Cosmetic Industry Review (CIR) Ingredient Compendium</u> (4), published annually by the Cosmetic, Toiletry and Fragrance Association (Chapter 3).

It should be emphasized that testing for carcinogenicity, besides related toxicity, of CPCPs must be conducted on the products' ingredients and contaminants, rather than on the whole products themselves. Tests on the latter would be too insensitive to detect the carcinogenic effects of individual ingredients and contaminants, let alone to determine which ingredients are responsible. This is especially critical in view of the relatively low concentrations of carcinogenic ingredients in any product. An additional concern is the small number of rodents used in standard test protocols. Thus, statements proclaiming "Not Tested On Animals" properly relate to the whole product, generally the cruel acute eye irritation (Draize) test in rabbits. These statements should not be misunderstood as implying that the product ingredients have not been tested for carcinogenicity, in the absence of which no assurances of safety would be possible.

CARCINOGENS IN COSMETICS AND PERSONAL CARE PRODUCTS

Most cosmetics and personal care products (CPCPs) manufactured and marketed by mainstream and multilevel marketing (MLM) industries are veritable "witches brews" of multiple known carcinogenic ingredients and contaminants. However, no such information is disclosed to the public.

Apart from a few complete products which themselves are carcinogenic, such as talc, there are two major classes of carcinogenic ingredients. The first class includes those ingredients that are carcinogenic themselves, which are known as the "frank" carcinogens. The second group are those "hidden" carcinogens that, while not carcinogenic themselves, may under certain conditions have carcinogenic properties. Over 40 carcinogens used in mainstream industry CPCPs are "frank" (Table 2.2), and over 30 are "hidden" (Table 2.3). While the identity of the "frank" carcinogens, besides other ingredients, is listed on the product labels, the alphabet soup of complex chemical names conveys no meaningful information whatsoever, on their cancer risks to unsuspecting consumers. Still less revealing are the "hidden" carcinogens to which there is no reference on ingredient listings. As such, their presence is unrecognized by the majority of chemists, toxicologists and cancer prevention experts, let alone consumers.

TABLE 2.2 "FRANK" CARCINOGENS
Benzyl Acetate*
Butylated Hydroxyanisole (BHA)
Butylated Hydroxytoluene* (BHT)
Butyl Benzylphthalate
"Coal Tar Dyes" (and Lakes)
    <u>D & C</u>
        Red 2, 3, 4, 8, 9, 10, 17, 19 & 33
        Green 5
        Orange 17
    <u>FD & C</u>
        Blue 1 & 2
        Green 3
        Red 4 & 40
        Yellow 5 & 6
        Blue 1, 2 & 4
    Diaminophenol
    Disperse Blue 1
    Disperse Yellow 3
    Nitrophenylenediamine
    p-Phenylenediamine* (following oxidation)
    Phenyl-p-phenylenediamine
    Crystalline Silica
    Diethanolamine (DEA)
    Dioctyl Adipate
    Ethyl Alcohol*
    Fluoride*
    Formaldehyde
    Glutaral
    Hydroquinone
    Methylene Chloride
    Polyvinyl Pyrrolidone
    Pyrocatechol
    Saccharin
    Talc
    Titanium Dioxide*

---

*Evidence of carcinogenicity is limited

TABLE 2.3 "HIDDEN" CARCINOGENS

CONTAMINANTS

    Aflatoxin: <u>in</u>, peanut oil and flour

    Arsenic and Lead: <u>in</u>, coal tar dyes, polyvinyl acetate, PEGs (polyethylene glycols)

    Chloroaniline: <u>in</u>, chlorhexidine

    Crystalline Silica: <u>in</u>, amorphous silicates

    DDT, Dieldrin, Endrin and other organochlorine pesticides: <u>in</u>, lanolin, hydrogenated cottonseed oil, quaternium-26

    DEA (diethanolamine): <u>in,</u> DEA-cocamide/lauramide condensates, quaternium-26

    1,4-Dioxane: <u>in</u>, ethoxylated alcohols, including PEGs, oleths, choleth-24, ceteareth-3, laureths, polysorbate 60 & 80, nonoxynol

    Ethylhexylacrylate: <u>in</u>, acrylate and methacrylate copolymers

    Ethylene Oxide: <u>in</u>, PEGs, oleths, ceteareth-3, laureths, polysorbate 60 & 80, nonoxynol

    Formaldehyde: <u>in</u>, polyoxymethylene urea

NITROSAMINE (NDELA) PRECURSORS

    Bromonitrodioxane

    Bronopol (2-bromo-2-nitropropane-1,3-diol)

    Diethanolamine (DEA)

    DEA-Cocamide, Lauramide & Oleamide condensates

    DEA-MEA/Acetame

    DEA-Sodium Lauryl Sulfate

    Diethanolamide-Cocamide, Lauramide & Oleamide condensates

    Metheneamine

    Morpholine

    Padimate-O (octyldimethyl para-amino benzoic acid)

    Pyroglutamic Acid

    Triethanolamine (TEA)

    TEA-Sodium Lauryl Sulfate

FORMALDEHYDE RELEASERS

    Bronopol

    Diazolidinyl Urea

    DMDM-Hydantoin

    Imidazolidinyl Urea

    Metheneamine

    Quaternium-15

    Sodium/Hydroxymethylglycinate

"Hidden" carcinogenic ingredients fall into four major groups:

- Common carcinogenic contaminants of otherwise non-carcinogenic ingredients

- Non-carcinogenic ingredients which, by interaction, are precursors of carcinogenic nitrosamines

- Non-carcinogenic ingredients which break down in the product itself or on skin to release the "frank" carcinogen formaldehyde

- Even less well recognized "hidden" carcinogenic ingredients are those in fragrances, scents and perfumes, also present in many household products, for which there are no requirements for any ingredient listing.

Most CPCPs contain a wide range of "frank" and "hidden" carcinogens. For example, permanent and semi-permanent black and dark brown hair dyes are a mix of a wide range of "frank" carcinogens, notably "coal tar dyes", and "hidden" ingredients, including formaldehyde releasers and ethoxylated alcohol detergents. Cosmetic talc is a unique "frank" carcinogen which is also the near exclusive ingredient of talcum powder (Appendix 2E & 3A).

GENOTOXIC CARCINOGENS

It should further be noted that seven of these "frank" carcinogens have also been shown to induce genetic damage in experimental animal or human studies summarized by the IARC, and for this reason these ingredients are classified as "genotoxic carcinogens" (Table 2.4). This is particularly important as even the mainstream petrochemical industry admits that there is no way for determining thresholds or safety levels for exposure to genotoxic carcinogens.

TABLE 2.4 GENOTOXIC CARCINOGENS
Aflatoxin
Arsenic
1,4-Dioxane
Ethylene Oxide
Formaldehyde
Lead
Nitrosodiethanolamine

CARCINOGEN "PROMOTERS"

Apart from "frank" and "hidden" carcinogens, there are other non-carcinogenic ingredients and products, which under certain conditions can promote or enhance the effects of unrelated carcinogenic exposures. These include sodium lauryl sulfate, alpha-hydroxy acids, and chemical sunscreens.

EXAMPLES OF CARCINOGENS IN COSMETICS AND PERSONAL CARE PRODUCTS

Diethanolamine

One common ingredient of CPCPs is diethanolamine (DEA), which is both a "hidden" and "frank" carcinogen. By the mid-1970s, it was discovered that DEA, used by metal workers as a surfactant or detergent in cutting fluids, reacted with nitrite preservatives to form the potent carcinogen nitrosodiethanolamine (NDELA) in a process known as nitrosation. A similar interaction occurs between the closely related ingredients triethanolamide and diethanolamide fatty acid condensates and nitrites. It was subsequently recognized that DEA, commonly used in CPCPs, also interacts with nitrite preservatives or contaminants in any product, or with nitrogen oxides in the air, to form NDELA on the skin (Appendix 2F & 3B).

In 1979, FDA published a notice in the Federal Register warning the industry of the dangers of NDELA and recommending the phase-out of DEA and TEA from mainstream products. However, to all intents and purposes the U.S. industry has remained unresponsive, apart from trivializing risks of NDELA and adding inhibitory ingredients in tokenistic efforts to reduce nitrosation. In striking contrast, the German government issued a formal recommendation to the industry in 1987 to discourage the continued use of DEA and TEA.

In November 1997, it was discovered that DEA itself is also a "frank" carcinogen. Studies reported by the NTP showed that painting mouse skin with DEA, or its cocamide or lauramide fatty acid condensates, induced liver and kidney cancer (Appendix 2G). The carcinogenicity of the condensates was attributed to their contamination with free DEA in concentrations ranging from 0.5 to 8.5 percent.

1,4-Dioxane

A wide range of CPCPs, including shampoos, hair conditioners, cleansers, lotions, and creams, as well as household products such as soaps and cleaning fluids, contain ethoxylated alcohol surfactants or detergents such as polysorbates (Tweens) and laureths. These ingredients are generally contaminated with high concentrations of the volatile 1,4-dioxane, which is both readily inhaled and absorbed through the skin. The carcinogenicity of 1,4-dioxane in rodents was first reported in 1965 and subsequently confirmed in 1978; the predominant cancers were nasal in rats and liver in mice. Epidemiological studies on dioxane-exposed furniture makers also found suggestive evidence of excess nasopharyngeal cancers. On the basis of such evidence, the Consumer Product Safety Commission concluded that "the presence of 1,4-dioxane, even as a trace contaminant, is a cause of concern." These avoidable risks of cancer in numerous CPCPs and household products are inexcusable, particularly as dioxane is readily removed from surfactants during their manufacture by a simple process known as "vacuum stripping." The same process is also effective in removing ethylene oxide, another volatile and potent carcinogen, from ethoxylated detergents.

Talcum Powder

By the early 1960s it was recognized that dusts and powders similar to talc and asbestos could migrate to the ovaries from the contaminated genital area of asbestos workers. These findings were associated with a high mortality of ovarian cancer in female asbestos workers. Subsequent studies from 1982 onwards have shown some threefold increase in the incidence of invasive ovarian cancer following frequent genital exposure to cosmetic grade talc in talcum powder (Appendix 2E & 3A). In contrast, a recent report published in the Journal of the National Cancer Institute and based on the Harvard Nurses Health Study, concluded that the perineal use of talc only "modestly" increased the risks of invasive ovarian cancer. This report however, is highly flawed by defects such as its very short follow-up of 15 years and its exclusion of women using talc before their first pregnancy, when risks are known to be much greater than later in life.

Given the fact that some 20 percent of U.S. women regularly dust their genital areas, sanitary pads, or diaphragms with deodorizing talcum powder, and that ovarian cancer is one of the most lethal cancers in U.S. women, striking over some 25,000 and killing 14,000, annually, it is most reprehensible that both FDA and industry have been totally unresponsive. The FDA has neither banned talcum powder nor required industry to label it with explicit warnings, and nor has industry taken such voluntary action. This is all the more surprising in view of the fact that starch-based powder, a safe, cheap and effective substitute, is readily available. In 1994, the Cancer Prevention Coalition filed a Citizen Petition to the FDA requiring immediate labeling of talcum powder products with warnings of ovarian cancer risks (Appendix 3A). After lengthy delays, the petition was denied on "limited availability of (agency resources)", and later on allegedly scientific grounds.

Another unrelated risk of talcum powder is its use as a dusting powder in infants. This can result in inhalation of significant amounts of powder resulting in acute or chronic lung irritation (pulmonary-talcosis) and even death. It may also be noted that in 1993 the NTP reported evidence on the induction of lung cancer and rare adrenal cancers in rats exposed by inhalation to cosmetic grade talc.

Hair Dyes

It is estimated that 35 percent of women and 10 percent of men in the U.S., Japan and Europe use hair dyes. Black and dark brown permanent and semi-permanent dyes contain a wide range of "frank" and "hidden" carcinogens. These include "coal tar" dyes, surfactants including DEA and TEA, ethoxylated alcohols, and formaldehyde releasers (Table 2.5). There is strong evidence associating frequent and prolonged use of these dyes with major risks of relatively rare cancers, particularly chronic leukemia, multiple myeloma, Hodgkin's disease and non-Hodgkin's lymphoma. It is estimated that use of these dyes accounts for over 20 percent of all non-Hodgkin's lymphoma in women, in whom incidence levels have escalated by some 200 percent since the 1950s (9). While a highly flawed 1994 American Cancer Society publication attempted to trivialize cancer risks from hair dyes, it did however recommend "removal of carcinogens from hair dyes and appropriate labeling of hair coloring products" (Appendix 4). There is also suggestive epidemiological evidence from the 1970s associating prolonged use of these dyes with excess risks of breast cancer; a December 1999 publication in Cancer Causes and Control confirmed this association for premenopausal breast cancer.

Furthermore, there is substantial evidence from over a dozen epidemiological studies on the excess risks of bladder cancer in cosmetologists and hairdressers, particularly men, as well as non-Hodgkin's lymphoma and ovarian cancer in women. Cosmetologists regularly use permanent and semi-permanent black or dark brown hair dyes, in addition to a wide range of other exposures, including to hairsprays, aerosols, solvents and formaldehyde preservatives. Cosmetology is a high-risk occupation.

TABLE 2.5 "FRANK" AND "HIDDEN" CARCINOGENIC INGREDIENTS IN PERMANENT AND SEMI-PERMANENT DARK HAIR DYES

INGREDIENT	HAZARD
"COAL TAR" DYES	
CI disperse Blue 1	Carcinogenic
D&C Red 33	Carcinogenic
HC Blue No. 1	Carcinogenic
Para-phenylenediamine	Carcinogenic when oxidized
DETERGENTS/SOLVENTS	
Diethanolamine/Triethanolamine	Combine with nitrite to form carcinogenic

	nitrosamines
Diethanolamine	Carcinogenic
Cetearaths and Laureths	Contaminated with the carcinogens 1,4-dioxane and ethylene oxide

HUMECTANTS

| Polyethylene glycol | Contaminated with the carcinogens ethylene oxide and 1,4-dioxane |

PRESERVATIVES

DMDM-hydantoin	Release carcinogenic formaldehyde
Imidazolidinyl urea	Release carcinogenic formaldehyde
Quaternium 15	Release carcinogenic formaldehyde

Fragrances

As emphasized in The Safe Shopper's Bible, fragrances in mainstream CPCPs, soaps, and other household products are leading causes of allergy, sensitization, and irritation. Fragrances and perfumes are also poorly recognized but important sources of indoor air pollution. In addition, the synthetic nature of most perfumes and fragrances may pose a toxic hazard through avoidable carcinogenic exposure.

The National Institute of Occupational Safety and Health has reported that the fragrance industry uses up to 3,000 ingredients, predominantly synthetic, some 900 of which were identified as toxic. However, the industry is not required to disclose any information on fragrance ingredients due to trade secrecy considerations. The FDA supports this non-disclosure on the grounds that "consumers are not adversely affected—and should not be deprived of the enjoyment" of these products.

An analysis of six different mainstream perfumes by Scientific Instrument Services, released in November 1998, identified over 800 ingredients with distinctive patterns for each product. These ingredients include a wide range of volatile and semi-volatile organic chemicals which are thus significant contributors to indoor air pollution (Appendix 2H).

Following repeated consumer complaints of irritant, respiratory and neurological effects from exposure to Calvin Klein's Eternity eau de parfume, as documented in FDAs 1995 Annual Report on Listing Consumer Complaints for Cosmetic Products, the Environmental Health Network of California commissioned its chemical analysis by two independent laboratories, Scientific Instrument Services and the industry's Huber Research, a member of the Research Institute of Fragrance Materials Laboratory. The toxicity of the majority of the 41 identified ingredients have been poorly characterized. Other ingredients are known to cause a variety of toxicological effects, including neurotoxic and respiratory, by skin absorption and inhalation. More importantly, two ingredients, butyl acetate and butylated hydroxytoluene are carcinogenic, as admitted on the chemical industry's Material Safety Data Sheets. On the basis of these results, the Environmental Health Network, supported by the Cancer Prevention Coalition, filed a Citizen Petition to the Food and Drug Administration in May 1999 requiring that the perfume be declared "Misbranded" (Appendix 2H), and requiring warning labels on all fragrances which are marketed without prior safety testing. The FDA has not yet responded to the Petition, although legislation (HR 1947) was recently introduced in the U.S. Congress requiring warning labels of fragrances (Chapter Four).

Ethyl Alcohol

There is strong epidemiological evidence on the causal association between drinking alcoholic beverages and cancers of the mouth, pharynx, esophagus, lungs and liver. More limited evidence has also shown associations between long-term use of high alcohol (more than 25 percent) mouthwashes and risks of mouth and pharyngeal cancers, including among non-drinkers and non-smokers. However, an objection has been made to such evidence on the grounds that people who regularly use high alcohol mouthwashes may do so because of problems of odor or bad taste from pre-existing chronic causes of oral irritation which may themselves be pre-cancerous. Prudence, however, clearly justifies avoidance of alcohol containing mouthwashes.

Alpha-Hydroxy Acids

Alpha-hydroxy acids (AHAs) are a wide range of non-carcinogenic salts and esters of lactate and glycolate ingredients in skin conditioning and exfoliating products used personally, in salons or for medical purposes. They are readily absorbed through the skin, especially at low pHs, and also increase absorption of carcinogenic and other ingredients.

AHAs are not only skin irritants, but they act by removing a very superficial layer of the skin, known as the stratum corneum, which absorbs ultraviolet radiation (UVR) from sunlight and tanning lamps. Clinical testing has clearly shown that UVR induces a statistically significant increase in the incidence of sunburn cells (SBCs) in skin pretreated with AHA. Apart from increasing risks of sunburn, use of AHA products is likely to increase risks of skin cancer, particularly malignant melanoma which can be lethal, even if diagnosed and treated at early stages.

Sunscreens

Concern is also mounting on the risks of malignant melanoma from the prolonged use of chemical sunscreens, particularly on children, in contrast to physical sunblocks such as zinc oxide. Sunscreens encourage prolonged sun exposure by preventing sunburn, while protecting against non-lethal skin cancer due to long wave ultraviolet (UVA) radiation. However, most sunscreens allow transmission of the more dangerous short wave (UVB) radiation responsible for the highly lethal malignant melanoma. For this reason, some sunscreens now carry a warning label that, even with proper use: "U.V. exposure can still lead to skin cancer". However, modern "High Intensity" sunscreens, with skin protection factors (SPF) over 15, may protect against both UVA and UVB.

As reported in New Scientist Magazine (April 2001), by researchers from the University of Zurich Institute of Pharmacology and Toxicology, five common ingredients in sunscreens, besides lipsticks, are estrogenic. These ingredients—benzophenone-3(Bp-3), homosalate (HMS), 4-MBC, octyl-methoxycinnamate (OMC), and octyl-dimethylPABA (OD-PABA)—increase breast cancer cell division and induce cancer protein production in laboratory experiments. Additionally, 4-MBC, OMC and Bp-3 increase uterine growth when fed to immature rats. More disturbingly, painting rat skin with 4-MBC at concentrations similar to those found in sunscreen products, significantly increases uterine growth before puberty.

UNIQUE CANCER RISK FROM COSMETICS AND PERSONAL CARE PRODUCTS

Mainstream industry CPCPs are the single most important, yet generally unrecognized, class of avoidable carcinogenic exposures for the overwhelming majority of citizens in the U.S. and other major industrialized nations. The reason for these unique risks reflects a complex of individual and interactive factors.

Interaction Between Different Carcinogenic Ingredients

Serious as is the absorption of any single carcinogenic ingredient, particularly from large areas of skin, this is relatively trivial compared to the lifetime absorption of a variety of ingredients, totaling some 70, in multiple CPCPs (Tables 2.2 and 2.3). While the effects of numerous carcinogens are minimally additive, there is limited evidence that they are likely to be multiplicative or synergistic.

Prolonged Duration of Exposure

Exposure to carcinogenic CPCP ingredients is lifetime, from birth to death, for different products. In fact, exposure precedes birth from maternal skin absorption at the earliest stages of pregnancy. Furthermore, apart from wash-off products, most others are applied to and remain on the skin for prolonged periods of time.

High Permeability of Skin

The skin is highly permeable to carcinogenic and other toxic ingredients, especially following prolonged exposure. A 1989 study showed that 13 percent of the carcinogenic preservative butylated hydroxytoluene (BHT) and 50 percent of the carcinogenic pesticide DDT, which often contaminate the common non-carcinogenic ingredient lanolin, are rapidly absorbed through human skin. Even more disturbing is evidence that the permeability of skin to carcinogens may be greater than that of the intestines. In evidence presented at 1978 Congressional hearings, the absorption of nitrosodiethanolamine (NDELA) formed by the nitrosation of DEA, is over 100 times greater from the skin than by mouth. This is particularly important as consumption of the closely related carcinogen, diethylnitrosamine, in nitrite-preserved bacon has been associated with up to 4- and 7-fold increased risks of childhood brain cancer and leukemia, respectively.

Incredibly, the mainstream industry and regulatory authorities appear unaware of the high permeability of skin or choose to ignore this critical concern. Revealingly one Canadian industry, Lander Company, Scarboro, Ontario, labels its Cocoa Butter product as "Fast Absorbing". This product contains three carcinogens, diazolidinyl urea, TEA and polysorbate 20.

Effect of Wetting Agents on Skin Permeability

The permeability of skin to carcinogens, besides other toxic ingredients, is further increased by the concomitant presence of wetting agents or surfactants, probably the most common class of ingredients in the majority of CPCPs. There are two major classes of surfactants that include the relatively gentle or "non-ionic" surfactants MEA and DEA, and the harsh ionic detergents like sodium lauryl sulfate (SLS). The harsh detergents are strongly irritant depending on their concentration and the duration of exposure. The Cosmetic Ingredient Review (CIR) 2000 Compendium admitted that SLS "causes severe epidermal changes—of the skin of mice—(indicating) a need for tumor-enhancing activity assays" (4). The Compendium further admitted that SLS containing products are "designed for brief discontinued use, following which they are thoroughly rinsed from the surface of the skin." As reported in model studies published in 2000 by the Danish Institute of Public Health (22, 23), a single 24-hour exposure of SLS to human skin damages skin protein and causes prolonged disruption of "the skin barrier integrity of the skin," to allow the penetration of carcinogens such as nickel and chromate. Thus, skin absorption of carcinogenic ingredients could be greatly increased by SLS type detergents.

Bypassing Detoxifying Enzymes

Carcinogens in CPCPs pose greater cancer risks than does food contaminated with carcinogenic pesticides and other industrial carcinogens. Carcinogens taken in by mouth are absorbed from the intestines into venous blood which then reaches the liver. Once in the liver, carcinogens can be detoxified to varying degrees by deactivating (P53) enzymes before reaching the rest of the body. In striking contrast, carcinogens absorbed through the skin bypass the liver and reach the general blood circulation without this protective detoxification.

HYPERSENSITIVITY OF THE FETUS, INFANTS AND YOUNG CHILDREN

There are numerous experimental studies demonstrating the much higher sensitivity to chemical carcinogens of young animals when compared to adults. For instance, adult mice are totally resistant to the carcinogenic effects of aflatoxin, which induces liver cancer in 100 percent of infant mice. Similarly, benzopyrene induces ten times higher the incidence of liver cancer in infant mice when compared to adult mice. Vinyl chloride and diethylnitrosamine induce 40 and 15 times, respectively, the incidence of liver cancer in infant rats when compared to adults. Similarly a related nitrosamide carcinogen induces 50 times the incidence of brain cancer in infant rats compared to adult rats.

As reported in 1989 by the IARC, administration of a variety of carcinogens to rabbits in late pregnancy induces kidney and nervous system cancers in their offspring. Prenatal exposure of rats to diethylstilbestrol, a synthetic estrogenic-type hormone known to be a potent carcinogen since the 1940's, induces vaginal and cervical cancers in their young female progeny. This is strikingly consistent with the diagnosis from 1971 onwards of rare vaginal cancers in young girls whose mothers were treated during pregnancy with the same hormone for "complications of pregnancy", allegedly due to hormonal deficiency.

Some 30 U.S. and international studies have confirmed the high incidence of cancers in children whose parents were exposed to a variety of chemical carcinogens in the workplace during pregnancy (9). Also, an increased incidence of brain cancer and leukemia has been reported in children whose mothers were exposed to nitrosamine carcinogens in nitrite-preserved meats during pregnancy. These findings are relevant to the striking 35 percent increase in the incidence of childhood cancers since 1950, and the 20 percent increase in the incidence of brain and nervous system cancers since 1973 (24). A 1989 report by the Natural Resources Defense Council concluded that a high percentage of U.S. preschool children are likely to develop cancer in later life as a result of consumption of fruits and vegetables commonly contaminated by some eight pesticides (9).

The increased susceptibility of infants and young children to a wide range of carcinogens has been fully recognized for well over two decades. This reflects limited physiological capability to detoxify chemical carcinogens due to their immature liver enzymes. Another reason for the increased susceptibility of infants and young children is due to the fact that their cells are dividing more rapidly than adults. Thus, there is a greater probability that carcinogens will cause DNA mutations in cells of the young and initiate the development of delayed cancers in adult life.

While the hypersensitivity of children to carcinogens has been long recognized, surprisingly this does not extend to their avoidable carcinogenic exposures from numerous carcinogens in common CPCPs such as shampoos and lotions. This was revealingly illustrated in 1994 when Child Magazine selected a book entitled Raising Children Toxic Free by Drs. Needleman and Landrigan as "One Of The Ten Best Parenting Books Of The Year". Although these doctors are leading pediatricians and experts on toxic chemicals, the book ignores toxic and carcinogenic risks of personal care products except for a brief reference to lead in some hair dyes.

CHAPTER THREE

INDUSTRY TRADE ASSOCIATIONS

Founded in 1894, the Cosmetic, Toiletry and Fragrance Association (CTFA) is the leading U.S. trade association for the multibillion dollar cosmetics and personal care product industry, representing the great majority of CPCP sales (3). CTFA also represents the industry's interests at the local, state, national, and international levels. CTFA active members are manufacturers and distributors of cosmetic, fragrance, and personal care products. Associate members are suppliers of ingredients, raw materials and packaging.

CTFA's major mission is "to protect the freedom of the industry to compete in a fair marketplace", while assuring the effectiveness of its products. CTFA also claims to assure the safety of industry's products "by voluntary self-regulation and reasonable governmental requirements." CTFA pursues a highly aggressive political agenda, at national and state levels, with emphasis against what it considers to be "unreasonable or unnecessary labeling or warning requirements". Recent examples include blocking an "unneeded New York bill—to require cancer warning labels on cosmetic talc powder." A broader initiative has been directed to defeating various recent state bills requiring what CTFA dismisses as, "new and unnecessary warnings" for cosmetics and personal care products (3).

The Association is also very active in the international arena, working in close cooperation with the European Trade Association (COLIPA), the Japanese Cosmetic Industry Association (JCIA) and the Japanese Government on a wide range of issues including the following:

- Commenting on proposed regulatory changes worldwide.

- Developing an international database.

- Organizing "Mutual Understanding Conferences."

- Dealing with global trade issues and barriers.

- Harmonization and regulatory reform. A notable achievement has been influencing the Japanese government to deregulate its very restrictive pre-market approval system to one more similar to that in the U.S. As of April 2001, the new system has opened up the Japanese market to new cosmetic products, provided they do not contain any of the few ingredients on their prohibited or negative list.

CTFA SAFETY TESTING GUIDELINES, 1991

CTFA first began publishing its Technical Guidelines in the CTFA Cosmetic Journal in 1969. Since then, CTFA technical committees and staff have updated the Guidelines, the latest version of which, however, is now about ten years old (2).

The Guidelines emphasize that "responsibility for ensuring the safety of cosmetic products rests with the manufacturer and/or distributor. Product manufacturers should first consider the need for safety testing, taking into account various factors, including the available toxicological test and other data on individual ingredients in the product (and on products similar in composition to the product being evaluated) before undertaking any testing program." Protocols for ingredient testing, either individually or in composites at their highest product concentrations, are presented for: primary skin, eye and mucous membrane irritation; sensitizing potential; photosensitization; percutaneous toxicity; oral toxicity; and inhalation toxicity. However, all these are short-term tests, the longest duration of which is only 90 days for subchronic oral toxicity. The protocols make no reference, whatsoever, to chronic toxicity and carcinogenicity testing. In fact, the word "carcinogenicity" is conspicuous by its absence in the Guidelines. However, a section on "Evaluation of Cosmetic Products" cursorily admits that the "potential for chronic toxicity should be considered in the evaluation of safety."

The Food and Drug Administration (FDA) was so impressed by these Guidelines that it decided to rely on them rather than develop formalized Good Manufacturing Practice regulations. In 1983, Arthur Hull Hayes, Jr., M.D., then FDA Commissioner, publicly enthused: "—your trade association published Technical Guidelines well before we even mentioned regulations or guidelines. I am persuaded that they are of excellent quality". Unbelievably so, the FDA's position and reliance on these Guidelines remains unchanged today.

CTFA LABELING MANUAL, 1997

This provides updated information on FDA's labeling requirements under the Fair Packaging and Labeling Act (FPLA), and the Food, Drug and Cosmetics Act (FDCA). The Manual states that the "industry takes pride in its reputation for providing safe products while requiring minimum use of government resources."

Conspicuous in the Manual is the absence of any reference to the carcinogenicity of product ingredients. A meaningless exception is the reference to two carcinogenic coal tar dyes which had been banned since 1978. For other "coal tar" dyes, the Manual relies on the Hair Dye Exemption clause of the FDCA which allows their use provided there is a warning to the effect that these dyes may "cause skin irritation in certain individuals—."

The Compendium is published annually by the CTFA. The 2000 publication provides information on 917 cosmetic ingredients, including information on hundreds for which it is claimed that there are no published scientific data. Based on its review of the 917 ingredients, the Compendium concluded (4):

- Nine ingredients were found to be unsafe (1%).

- Data on 110 ingredients were insufficient to support safety (12%).

- Another 302 ingredients were found safe for use with qualifications (33%).

- For 496 ingredients, these were found to be safe as used (54%).

Thus, the CIR, the industry's own expert review committee, admits that 119, over 10 percent of its products ingredients, are unsafe or that their continuing use is unsupported by safety data. Included in those ingredients that, subject to highly contrived qualifications, are allegedly "safe for use", are "frank" carcinogens such as formaldehyde and diethanolamine, and a wide range of "hidden" carcinogens (Tables 2.2 & 2.3). The latter include: the formaldehyde releaser, diazolidinyl urea; 1,4-dioxane and ethylene oxide contaminants in ethoxylated alcohols; and nitrosamine precursors, including bronopol and diethanolamine (DEA). The CTFA's very prompt attempts to challenge evidence on the carcinogenicity of such carcinogenic ingredients and contaminants are naïve rather than creative. Responding to the NTP's December 1997 draft report documenting the evidence on the carcinogenicity of DEA and its fatty acid condensates following skin painting of mice, the CTFA submitted comments alleging several problems with the studies. These included: use of an ethanol solvent as a potential confounding factor; the potential for oral ingestion of DEA; claims of undefined "serious limitations in analytical chemistry"; and "inadequate time available for proper review of the studies". While these objections were considered by the NTP, its conclusions remained unchanged in the final July, 1999 report.

The Compendium endorses the use of carcinogenic ingredients or contaminants provided their concentrations in any finished product are below arbitrarily defined "limitations," which are established in the absence of any attempted rationale (4). This reflects unawareness, or self-interested denial, of the overwhelming consensus in the scientific literature and regulatory precedents that there is no basis for assigning safe limits or thresholds for carcinogens. The uncritical belief of "safe" thresholds for carcinogens is also inconsistent with the now general scientific acceptance, even by the mainstream chemical industry, of the absence of thresholds for carcinogens that also induce genetic damage in human or other mammalian test systems; such carcinogens are known as genotoxic. It may be noted that several CPCP carcinogens are also genotoxic (Table 2.4).

The Compendium makes a confusing exception to its allowable use of carcinogens below "concentration limitations" for Nonoxynol, an ethoxylated surfactant commonly used in hair dyes and colors. Nonoxynol is usually contaminated with the potent genotoxic carcinogen ethylene oxide at levels up to 35 parts per million (milligram/liter). A summary Table states that Nonoxynols are "safe as used in rinse-offs: safe at less than 5 percent in leave- ons." The text warns of the need to ensure that the use of Nonoxynol containing "cosmetic products should not result in ethylene oxide exposures above 0.1 milligrams daily," while reassuring that the small amounts of ethylene oxide in cosmetics "were not considered sufficient to pose a carcinogenic risk."

The Compendium also authorizes the use of DEA amines, amides and their condensates under conditions that supposedly preclude nitrosation and thereby prevent the formation of nitrosamine carcinogens. This is an unrealistic condition as nitrosation can occur from the interaction between amine or amide precursors, in the absence of nitrite ingredients, and with nitrite contaminants in the finished product or atmospheric nitrogen oxides on the skin.

Apart from the risks of any individual carcinogenic ingredient, the CIR appears unaware of the additive, let alone synergistic, risks from prolonged exposures, prenatally to death, of multiple carcinogenic ingredients in a variety of CPCPs.

THE INTERNATIONAL FRAGRANCE ASSOCIATION (IFRA)

The International Fragrance Association, founded in 1973, is an international organization of over 100 fragrance manufacturers representing 15 nations, including the U.S., South America, Europe, Australia and the Far East. Fragrances are very big business and represent nearly 50 percent of all prestige beauty dollars now spent in the U.S. Fragrances are also extensively used in a wide range of other products potentially involving skin contact. These include: household cleaning products, including aerosols; detergents; shoe polishes; carpet powders; and liquid refills for air fresheners. Particularly high levels of fragrances may also be used in non-skin contact products. These include: air fresheners; insecticides; toilet blocks; candles; plastic articles, other than toys; and liquid fuels.

The primary objective of IFRA is to safeguard the self-regulatory practices, policies and status of the industry by the development of a Code of Practices and safety guidelines. These objectives include:

- Maintaining a credible self-policing system based on the Code of Practices

- Establishing usage guidelines for fragrances on the basis of available scientific data, recognizing however, that these are not binding on any nation or company

• Monitoring legislative trends worldwide and assuring their consistency to avoid the development of trade barriers

A fragrance use may, in theory rather than in practice, be restricted by IFRA on grounds including: use in products at higher than recommended concentrations; sensitization; neurotoxicity; phototoxicity; photosensitization; undefined biological effects; carcinogenicity; and inadequate data.

THE TRACK RECORD OF IFRA

The self-regulatory status of the fragrance industry and its highly secretive practices, including failure to disclose ingredient identity (17), creates the potential for self-interested and abusive malpractice. This is all the more serious in view of the following concerns: there is no pre-approval process for ingredient safety; available evidence on fragrance ingredient safety testing is both limited and highly questionable; there is no consideration of inhalation beside dermal exposure; and there is no consideration of interactive effects between the numerous ingredients in perfumes or fragrances. These concerns are illustrated by reference to the grossly inadequate toxicological data on Calvin Klein's Eternity eau de parfum (Chapter 2; Appendix 2H).

THE RESEARCH INSTITUTE FOR FRAGRANCE MATERIALS (RIFM)

RIFM is an international non-profit organization created by IFRA in 1966 to conduct research on fragrance ingredients and to assure their safety. An "independent" board of toxicologists, pharmacologists, and dermatologists from outside the fragrance industry makes evaluation of ingredient safety. Their findings are presented to IFRA's Scientific Advisory Board, which may or may not accept and act on them. Of over 5,000 ingredients used in the fragrance industry, approximately 1,300 have so far been evaluated by the RIFM. The data are then published in Food and Chemical Toxicology on the basis of which IFRA then formulates safety guidelines. The reliability of these data and guidelines are, however, questionable as illustrated by reference to RIFM's publication on musk ambrette which failed to report its severe phototoxicity and neurotoxicity. Reflecting the "trade secrets" status of fragrances, there is no labeling or any other public disclosure of their ingredients. Nor is there any disclosure of the qualifications and possible conflicts-of-interest of its members.

CHAPTER FOUR

REGULATION

Based on a review of international legislation, it is clear that the cosmetic and personal care product industry worldwide is essentially self-regulating. There are no regulatory requirements for premarket testing of ingredients and products. Nor, with few exceptions, such as children's bubble baths and hair dyes, are there any requirements for labeling products with warnings of carcinogenic or otherwise toxic hazards. Regulations for 72 nations are summarized in a recent Cosmetic, Toiletry and Fragrance Association publication, based on information from 46 international contributors, among whom Amway MLM is disproportionately highly represented (5).

With the deregulation of the Japanese cosmetic industry on April 1, 2001, most countries now share very similar regulations on product efficacy and safety. While there are some differences in the way cosmetics are defined and labeled, and in the number of ingredients that are prohibited or restricted, most countries rely exclusively on industry to ensure their safety, even though their published regulations misleadingly emphasize governmental concern and priority for consumer safety. In fact, all such regulations are more honored in the breach rather than in the observance. Furthermore, while most countries maintain listings of prohibited or restricted ingredients (Table 4.1), very few such listings include any of numerous "frank" and "hidden" carcinogenic ingredients (Tables 2.2-2.4) which are still in common international use. This contrasts with Neways products, which contain none of these ingredients, with the exception of some "coal tar" dyes which are being phased out.

TABLE 4.1: PROHIBITED AND RESTRICTED CARCINOGENIC INGREDIENTS

CARCINOGENIC INGREDIENTS	COUNTRIES							
	US	AU	CA	EU	JA	KR	MX	UK
Acid green 1				▒				▒
Acid orange 3								
Aflatoxin								
Arsenic			■	■		■		■
Benzyl acetate*								
Blue 1, 2, 4								
Bromonitrodioxane			■					
Bronopol								▒
Butyl benzylphthalate								
Butylated hydroxyanisole								
Butylated hydroxytoluene*								
Chloroaniline								
Crystalline silica								
D&C Green 5								
D&C Red Nos. 2, 3, 4, 8, 9, 10, 17, 19, 33								
D&C Orange 17								
DDT								■
DEA								
DEA-cocamide, lauramide & oleamide condensates								
DEA-MEA/Acetame								
DEA-Sodium Lauryl Sulfate				▒				▒
Diaminophenol								
Diazolidinyl urea								
Dieldrin								
Dioctyl adipate								
1,4-Dioxane	■		■			■		■
Disperse Blue 1								
Disperse Yellow 3						■		
DMDM-hydantoin								
Ethyl alcohol*								
Ethylene oxide			■			■		■
Ethylhexylacrylate								
FD&C Blue Nos. 1 & 2	■							
FD&C Green No. 2	■							
FD&C Green No. 3								
FD&C Red Nos. 4 & 40								
FD&C Yellow Nos. 5 & 6								
Fluoride			■	■				▒
Formaldehyde					■			
Glutaral								■
Hydroquinone			■			■		■
Imidazolidinyl urea				■				
Lead								
Metheneamine								
Methylene chloride			▒					
Morpholine								■
Nitrophenylenediamine								
Organochlorine pesticides								
Padimate-O								
Payroglutamic acid								
p-Phenylenediamine*								▒
Phenyl-p-phenylenediamine								
Polysorbate 60 & 80								
Polyvinyl pyrrolidone								
Pyrocatechol								
Quaternium-15 & 26						■		
Saccharin								
Sodium/hydroxymethylglycinate								
Talc				▒				
TEA								
TEA-Sodium Lauryl Sulfate								
Titanium dioxide*								

Country Code
US = United States, AU = Australia, CA = Canada, EU = European Union, JA = Japan, KR = Korea, MX = Mexico, UK = United Kingdom

Symbol Key
* -- Evidence for carcinogenicity is limited

■ -- Use of ingredient is prohibited
▒ -- Use of ingredient is restricted

"Restricted use of ingredient" includes:
- limited amount of ingredient allowed in final product
- limited age group for which product may be used
- requirements for label warnings or disclaimers

51

The regulatory policies and practices of the FDA are reviewed here in detail in view of the common misconception that the Agency is highly protective of the health and welfare of consumers, and is a "gold standard" for other countries. However, there are more similarities than differences between regulations in the U.S. and other nations worldwide.

The legislative framework for regulating cosmetic and personal care products, whether manufactured in the U.S. or imported, is based on the Food, Drug and Cosmetic (FD&C) Act and its United States Code (USC) amendments, (21 USC, Chapter 9). Other regulations are also found in the Code of Federal Regulations (21 CFR, Subchapter G). Products are also regulated under the Fair Packaging and Labeling (FP&L) Act (13).

DEFINITION

Cosmetics and personal care products are classified together. Any product containing ingredients that are also drugs or have some type of therapeutic effect, including hormone creams, sun-tanning products, deodorants and anti-dandruff shampoos, must comply with the drug and cosmetic provisions of both Acts. While soap is defined separately from other cosmetics and personal care products, it is regulated in the same way as other cosmetics.

> The term "cosmetic" means articles intended to be rubbed, poured, sprinkled, or sprayed on, introduced into, or otherwise applied to the human body or any part thereof for cleansing, beautifying, promoting attractiveness, or altering the appearance, and articles intended for use as a component of any such articles; except that such term shall not include soap.

REGULATION

According to the USC, cosmetics are deemed adulterated or unfit for use in the following circumstances: A cosmetic shall be deemed to be adulterated:

> (a) If it bears or contains any poisonous or deleterious substance which may render it injurious to users under the conditions of use prescribed in the labeling thereof, or under such conditions of use as are customary or usual, except that this provision shall not apply to coal-tar hair dye, the label of which bears the following legend conspicuously displayed thereon: ``Caution—This product contains ingredients which may cause skin irritation on certain individuals and a preliminary test according to accompanying directions should first be made. This product must not be used for dyeing the eyelashes or eyebrows; to do so may cause blindness", and the labeling of which bears adequate directions for such preliminary testing. For the purposes of this paragraph, the term ``hair dye" shall not include eyelash dyes or eyebrow dyes.

(b) If it consists in whole or in part of any filthy, putrid, or decomposed substance.

(c) If it has been prepared, packed, or held under unsanitary conditions whereby it may have become contaminated with filth, or whereby it may have been rendered injurious to health.

(d) If its container is composed, in whole or in part, of any poisonous or deleterious substance which may render the contents injurious to health.

(e) If it is not a hair dye and it is, or it bears or contains, a color additive which is unsafe within the meaning of this title.

Supposedly, products that are adulterated must not be sold in the U.S. or its territories, and are subject to FDA enforcement. However, the USC does not provide a list of "poisonous or deleterious" substances which are overtly prohibited from use.

Manufacturers in the United States, and those importing cosmetics into the U.S. are requested to voluntarily register their products with the FDA, as follows:

> The owner or operator of a cosmetic product establishment which is not exempt under the USC, and engages in the manufacture or packaging of a cosmetic product is requested to register for each such establishment, whether or not the product enters interstate commerce. This request extends to any foreign cosmetic product establishment whose products are exported for sale in any State.

The FD&C Act requires ingredients to be labeled on the inside and outside of containers and wrappers; the FP&L Act also requires listing on the outside container. However, the FD&C Act does not require pre-market testing of product ingredients, so that the burden-of-proof on the dangers of any personal care or cosmetic ingredient, as well as their efficacy, is the responsibility of the Federal Government. As FDA Commissioner Edwards emphasized in 1972:

"It is fundamental that no manufacturer of a consumer product has the right to place that product on the market without first substantiating its safety.—In the case of a cosmetic, the FD&C Act does not require approval by the FDA prior to marketing, but it necessarily contemplates that the manufacturer has obtained all data and information necessary and appropriate to substantiate the product's safety prior to marketing."

However, the track record proves that FDA's assumption of industry's fundamental responsibility is both naïve and unwarranted. The FD&C Act gives the FDA unqualified authority to declare a product "misbranded" if there is evidence that its safety has not been substantiated, or if there is evidence that the product contains harmful ingredients. Once misbranded, the FDA has also full authority to take regulatory action, including requiring a formal "warning" label, product recall and seizure. Nevertheless, the FDA has very rarely exercised this option, no matter how dangerous the product and its ingredients.

The FDA has developed a list of nine prohibited individual or classes of ingredients, six of which are toxic and three of which are carcinogenic.

Prohibited Ingredients

1. Zirconium – containing complexes in aerosol products, as they can induce granulomas in the lung.

2. Hexachlorophene, because of its neurotoxicity; however, this ingredient may still be used in the absence of "an alternative (effective) preservative".

3. Mercury compounds, because of their neurotoxicity.

4. Chlorofluorocarbon propellants, although they may still be exported.

5. Dithionol, as it can cause photosensitivity.

6. Halogenated salicylanilides, as they can induce photosensitivity.

7. Chloroform, "because of its animal carcinogenicity and likely hazard to human health".

8. Vinyl chloride as an ingredient in aerosol products, "because of its carcinogenic effects on humans and animals".

9. Methylene chloride, "because of its animal carcinogenicity and likely hazard to human health".

In addition to these three carcinogens, in accordance with the 1960 Color Additive Amendments of the FD&C Act, FDA prohibits the use of color additives found to induce cancer in animals or humans.

Apart from the nine prohibited ingredients, FDA claims that it monitors three common contaminants in other ingredients. Nitrosamines, 1,4-dioxane and pesticide residues (Table 2.3), are monitored to ensure that no more than "trace levels" are present in any product. These claims, however, are more tokenistic than real.

While the FDA expressed concerns about nitrosamine contamination of cosmetics in the 1979 Federal Register, it still has taken no regulatory action against common nitrosamine precursors (Appendix 3B). This oversight is particularly incriminating in light of recent evidence on the carcinogenicity of DEA, one of the most common nitrosamine precursors (Appendix 2G). Moreover, it has been known since 1978 that ethoxylated (non-ionic) detergents, such as PEG and polysorbates, are contaminated with 1,4-dioxane at levels as high as 100 ppm. It has also been well known that 1,4-dioxane is easily and cheaply removed from detergent ingredients by vacuum stripping. Nevertheless, FDA has still taken no regulatory action against 1,4-dioxane-contaminated detergents or against any common carcinogenic pesticide residues, especially those present in lanolin. In this connection, it may be noted that the industry has voluntarily discontinued use of the following three ingredients: Methylcoumarin (6-MC), as it can induce photosensitivity; Musk Ambrette, as it can induce photosensitivity and neurotoxicity; Acetylethyltetramethyltetraline (AETT), as it can induce serious neurotoxicity besides coloring internal organs.

MOUNTING CRITICISM OF THE FDA

Criticism of the FDA's regulatory abdication has been increasing for well over two decades; however, such criticism has had virtually no impact. A 1978 report to Congress by the non-partisan General Accounting Office warned of approximately 100 ingredients in cosmetic products, which had been listed by the National Institute of Occupational Safety and Health in their Registry of Toxic Effects of Chemical Substances (RTECS) data base "as suspected carcinogens" (14). In addition, 24 listed ingredients "are suspected of causing birth defects, and 20 may cause adverse effects on the nervous system including headaches, drowsiness and convulsions". The report also stressed that "many improvements in FDA's regulations could be made under its existing authority". Such improvements could include: taking "regulatory action against violative manufacturers"; restricting the "use of hazardous cosmetic ingredients"; requiring "appropriate precautionary labeling"; and establishing "tests to be used in evaluating cosmetic safety". These warnings were reiterated in 1989 by Congressman Ron Wyden (D-OR), Chairman of the House Committee on Regulations and Business Opportunities, who expressed grave concerns about a wide range of cosmetic and toiletry ingredients still remaining on the RTECS listing. Wyden criticized FDA for reckless failure to have taken any regulatory action against these ingredients.

In spite of such criticisms, in 1997 FDA proposed a reform bill that ignored and still further exacerbated the risks of cosmetics and personal care products. Included in the FDA proposals was a broad and sweeping pre-emption of States' rights to regulate any aspect of labeling (Appendix 5). FDA furthermore proposed its own exemption from requirements of the National Environmental Policy Act, requiring issuance of formal statements on possible adverse environmental impacts of the industry's ingredients and products. FDA's proposal evoked strong criticism by Senator Edward Kennedy (D-MA) in a September 10, 1997 Statement to the Senate (Appendix 5, 6). Senator Kennedy's warned that, as recently reported by the General Accounting Office, "more than 125 ingredients available for use as cosmetics are suspected of causing cancer", that others may cause convulsions and still others "are suspected of causing birth defects". Senator Kennedy also made strong reference to the Cancer Prevention Coalition's 1994 Petition to the FDA, warning on risks of ovarian cancer from the use of talc, and requesting the Agency to require cancer warning labels on talc products (Appendix 3A). FDA has still not responded other than formally to this petition, apart from other Coalition press releases and petitions (Appendix 2 &3). Detailed analysis of FDA's reckless regulatory abdication is further documented in books, including the 1974 The Legislation of Product Safety, the 1995 The Safe Shopper's Bible, and the 1998 The Politics of Cancer, Revisited.

Responding to growing concerns on the dangers of fragrances, particularly in view of their undisclosed ingredients (Appendix 2H), Rep. Jan Schakowsky (D-IL) re-introduced a bill (HR 1947), co-sponsored by Reps. Shelley Berkley (D-NV) and Chaka Fattah (D-PA), to the House Commerce Committee on May 22, 2001, which has been referred to the Subcommittee on Health. This bill, cited as the "Safe Notification and Information for Fragrances Act" (SNIFF), called for amending the FD&C Act to require labels to include fragrance names and warnings of any known toxic or allergic ingredient. While highly commendable, the SNIFF bill unwarrantedly assumes discretionary responsibility of the industry. More seriously, this bill fails to recognize that toxicity data are inadequate or even non-existing for a wide range of fragrance ingredients.

FDA'S RESPONSE

FDA has recently responded to growing and grave criticisms by trivializing and sanitizing them, or with expressions of serious concern. Unfortunately, none of these concerns have been reflected in the Agency's policies and regulatory actions. FDA has also mounted a series of damage control initiatives, which are more deceptively tokenistic than effective.

On December 9, 1999, FDA's Office of Cosmetics Fact Sheet of the Center for Food Safety and Applied Nutrition announced that it "takes the results of the 1997 NTP study on the carcinogenicity of DEA, very seriously and has made the assessment of public health risks as one of its highest priorities for the cosmetic program". However, FDA has failed to take any regulatory action to date. Similarly, FDA warned that a high percentage of cosmetics and personal care products contain carcinogenic nitrosamine contaminants in its March 30, 2000 Office of Cosmetics Fact Sheet. However, in this same Fact Sheet, the FDA admitted that such "contaminants raise concerns", as well known for over three decades. The Fact Sheet also extended this warning to 1,4-dioxane, another potent carcinogenic contaminant of ethoxylated detergents found in a wide range of products, also well known for over three decades. Nevertheless, FDA has still taken no regulatory action against either of these avoidable carcinogens or warned unsuspecting consumers.

Meanwhile, the FDA has reassuringly invited the multibillion dollar cosmetic industry to register its products and ingredients in a "Voluntary Cosmetic Registration Program". The stated objective of this program is to offer the industry advance notice when it is found to be "inadvertently" using unsafe ingredients, thus "avoiding risks of detention or recall due to ingredient-related violations". Such risks appear minimal at worst, especially in view of the fact that the FDA has unbelievably allocated only two officials to deal with critical national concerns of labeling and consumer warnings.

AUSTRALIA

The framework which regulates cosmetic and personal care products is found in the 1989 National Industrial Chemicals (NIC) Act. Labeling regulations are located in the 1974 Trade Practices Act.

DEFINITION

Australian law establishes only one classification for cosmetics and personal care items. They are all identified as Cosmetics in accordance with the 1989 NIC Act.

> "Cosmetic means a product applied to a person's body for the purpose of its cleansing or care, colouring it, influencing its smell, or otherwise changing its appearance or smell, without affecting its structure or functions."

REGULATION

The 1989 NIC Act regulates cosmetic ingredients under the direction of the National Occupational Health and Safety Commission (NOHSC). The Act also requires that all chemicals used in Australia, regardless of purpose or industry (apart from agricultural & veterinary chemicals, medicines and medicinal products and food additives), be approved by the NOHSC prior to their use or import into Australia. Because of this, Australia maintains an "approved" ingredients list, rather than a prohibited ingredients list as is the case in most countries. This places a greater burden on the producer of cosmetics, as each ingredient must either be on the approved list, or prior approval must be obtained from the Commission.

There is no requirement for industry to undertake safety testing on a finished product, provided that all its ingredients are found on the "approved" list. However, companies are responsible for their products, and must be able to prove safety and efficacy, should the NOHSC so request. Finally, cosmetic products do not require any special packaging unless they contain a dangerous substance, as specified in the "Standard for the Uniform Scheduling of Drugs and Poisons".

CANADA

The Food and Drugs (F&D) Act is the legislation governing cosmetics and personal care items. Labeling regulations are detailed in the Consumer Packaging and Labeling Act. There are also numerous other regulations governing cosmetic and personal care products.

DEFINITION

Canadian law establishes only one classification for cosmetics and personal care items, which are all identified as Cosmetics. Cosmetics include all products for hair, nails, face, lips, lotions and shampoos. Cosmetics are defined as "any substance or mixture of substances, manufactured, sold or represented for use in cleansing, improving or altering the complexion, skin, hair or teeth and includes deodorants and perfumes." This definition includes soap.

REGULATION

The Public Safety Bureau, under the direction of Health Canada, is charged with the regulation of cosmetics and personal care products. According to the F&D Act, cosmetics are considered unsafe and unsuitable for sale if found to be unclean, adulterated or in some way injurious to humans. The Act states: No person shall sell any cosmetic that:

(a) has in or on it any substance that may cause injury to the health of the user when the cosmetic is used according to the directions on the label or accompanying the cosmetic, or for such purposes and by such methods of use as are customary or usual therefor;

(b) consists in whole or in part of any filthy or decomposed substance or of any foreign matter;

(c) was manufactured, prepared, preserved, package or stored under unsanitary conditions.

Where a standard has been prescribed for a cosmetic, no person shall label, package, sell or advertise any article in such a manner that it is likely to be mistaken for that cosmetic, unless the article complies with the prescribed standard.

No person shall manufacture, prepare, preserve, package or store for sale any cosmetic under unsanitary conditions.

Additionally, the F&D Act allows the Assistant Deputy Minister of Health Canada to ensure the quality and safety of cosmetics in Canada by allowing them to request random samples for testing. The Cosmetic Regulations of the F&D Act states:

EVIDENCE OF SAFETY OF COSMETICS

The Assistant Deputy Minister may, in writing, request the manufacturer of a cosmetic to submit to him, on or before a specified day, evidence to establish the safety of the cosmetic under the recommended conditions of use of the cosmetic or when used under such methods of use as are customary or usual therefor.

Where the manufacturer of a cosmetic is requested by the Assistant Deputy Minister pursuant to subsection (1) to submit evidence of the safety with respect to a cosmetic, the manufacturer shall cease to sell that cosmetic after the day specified in the request unless he has duly submitted the evidence requested.

Where the Assistant Deputy Minister is of the opinion that the evidence submitted by a manufacturer pursuant to subsection (1) is not sufficient, he shall notify the manufacturer in writing to that effect and the manufacturer shall not thereafter sell the cosmetic unless:

(a)he has submitted further evidence to the Assistant Deputy Minister; and

(b)he has been notified in writing by the Assistant Deputy Minister that the further evidence is sufficient.

Health Canada maintains a prohibited list of those ingredients that are forbidden, and a restricted list of those that are allowed with restriction of quantities and types of uses. As long as a cosmetic product does not contain ingredients found in these lists and meets regulations outlined above, it may be sold in Canada.

Ingredients that have been identified as carcinogenic, and which have been expressly prohibited from use in cosmetic products include arsenic, bromonitrodioxane, 1,4-dioxane, ethylene oxide, fluoride, formaldehyde, and lead. However, this restriction does not apply to common carcinogenic contaminants in ingredients. Chemicals, which have been restricted to specific amounts or in specific mixtures, include methylene chloride and morpholine.

According to the CTFA, in Canada the, "disclosure of ingredients is still not required on the package of cosmetic products" (5).

EUROPEAN UNION (OTHER THAN THE U.K.)

Directive 76/768/EEC (European Economic Communities) was adopted to give clear guidance on the requirements a safe cosmetic product must fulfill to freely circulate within the European Union (EU), without pre-market authorization. It thus aims to guarantee the safety of cosmetic products, and places the responsibility of safety and efficacy on the producer or importer.

DEFINITION

According to the Directive, a cosmetic product is defined as such:

A "cosmetic product" shall mean any substance or preparation intended to be placed in contact with the various external parts of the human body (epidermis, hair system, nails, lips and external genital organs) or with the teeth and the mucous membranes of the oral cavity with a view exclusively or mainly to cleaning them, perfuming them, changing their appearance and/or correcting body odours and/or protecting them or keeping them in good condition.

The directives regulating cosmetic safety are prepared and enforced by the Commission of the European Communities (EC) and the Scientific Committee on Cosmetic Products and Non-Food Products.

According to the Directive, there is no pre-market control for cosmetic products at Member State or EU levels. While this indicates that pre-market testing is not required by EU member states, Ministries of Health of individual states may, at their discretion, adopt additional requirements, if justified on grounds of public health protection. This includes testing or the submission of information regarding safety and efficacy. Such information shall consist of the following pursuant to the Directive:

(a) the qualitative and quantitative composition of the product; in the case of perfume compositions and perfumes, the name and code number of the composition and the identity of the supplier;

(b) the physico-chemical and microbiological specifications of the raw materials and the finished product and the purity and microbiological control criteria of the cosmetic product;

(c) the method of manufacture complying with the good manufacturing practice laid down by Community law or, failing that, laid down by the law of the Member State concerned; the person responsible for manufacture or first importation into the Community must possess an appropriate level of professional qualification or experience in accordance with the legislation and practice of the Member State which is the place of manufacture or first importation;

(d) assessment of the safety for human health of the finished product. To that end the manufacturer shall take into consideration the general toxicological profile of the ingredient, its chemical structure and its level of exposure. Should the same product be manufactured at several places within Community territory, the manufacturer may choose a single place of manufacture where that information will be kept available. In this connection, and when so requested for monitoring purposes, he shall be obliged to indicate the place so chosen to the monitoring authority/authorities concerned;

(e) the name and address of the qualified person or persons responsible for the assessment referred to in

(d). That person must hold a diploma as defined in the Directive in the field of pharmacy, toxicology, dermatology, medicine or a similar discipline;

(f) existing data on undesirable effects on human health resulting from use of the cosmetic product;

(g) proof of the effect claimed for the cosmetic product, where justified by the nature of the effect or product.

The EU regulates the safety of cosmetic products, through the Directive which states:

> A cosmetic product put on the market within the Community must not cause damage to human health when applied under normal or reasonably foreseeable conditions of use, taking account, in particular, of the product's presentation, its labeling, any instructions for its use and disposal as well as any other indication or information provided by the manufacturer or his authorized agent or by any other person responsible for placing the product on the Community market. The provision of such warnings shall not, in any event, exempt any person from compliance with the other requirements laid down in this Directive.

The Directive regulates product safety by limiting the amounts of certain preservatives, UV filters and coloring agents which may be used in cosmetics.

The EU maintains a prohibited list of approximately 420 ingredients, including those identified as potentially carcinogenic, notably arsenic and lead. More than 60 ingredients have been restricted to specific amounts or in specific mixtures. These include hair dyes, Acid green 1, diaminophenol, fluoride, formaldehyde, hydroquinone and talc.

JAPAN

Prior to April 1, 2001, cosmetics were regulated under the Pharmaceutical Affairs Law (PAL). However, a three-year deregulation plan is now in effect which abolishes pre-market licensing requirements, and establishes new cosmetic standards. These include listings of prohibited and restricted ingredients, approved sunscreens and preservatives, as well as new labeling requirements (5).

DEFINITION

Under Article 2 of the Pharmaceutical Affairs Law, the term cosmetic applies to "items intended to be used by means of rubbing, sprinkling or by similar application to the human body for cleaning, beautifying, promoting attractiveness and altering the appearance of the human body, and for keeping the skin and hair healthy, provided that the action of the article on the human body is mild."

The Pharmaceutical and Medical Safety Bureau (PMSB) under the direction of the Ministry of Health, Labor and Welfare (MHLW), regulates cosmetics in Japan.

The PMSB establishes one classification for cosmetics and personal care items, all of which are identified as "Cosmetics". Cosmetics include all products for hair, nails, face, lips, lotions, and shampoos.

The most important aspect of the Japanese deregulation is that responsibility for ensuring the safety of cosmetic products has now been shifted from the MHLW to the industry. As the U.S. and EU both allow companies to produce and supply cosmetic products under their own responsibility, the recent PAL amendments create a greater degree of harmonization between all three markets.

As with the U.S. and EU, importing companies are required to submit notification to the MHLW that they intend to sell a product in Japan. The industry must also assure the safety of all product ingredients and keep files supporting safety data. Although mandatory product testing of cosmetics is no longer required, safety data must be made available to the MHLW upon request. However, the new amendments do not designate a specific format or outline for the safety data. Thus, what may be considered sound documentation and data by the producer may not be acceptable as such by the MHLW.

Also, companies producing cosmetic products, theoretically, must continuously analyze and update their safety data and strive to provide appropriate safety information to their customers. They must also report to the MHLW any information they may uncover which indicates the potential danger or safety risk of any ingredient.

The majority of recognized product ingredients used are now controlled by two "Negative Lists". One list strictly prohibits 30 different ingredients, including formaldehyde, while the other sets limits and restrictions on the use of certain ingredients, including "coal tar" dyes, formaldehyde-releasing preservatives, and ultraviolet light absorbers.

KOREA

Product regulations are defined in the Food and Drug (F&D) Act. However, there are also other laws dealing further with regulations.

DEFINITION

Korean law establishes only one classification for cosmetics and personal care items. All such products are identified as "Cosmetics". These include all hair, nails, face, lips, lotions, and shampoos products, other than those intended for therapeutic use.

REGULATION

The Department of Drug Evaluation of the Korean Food and Drug Administration (KFDA), under the Direction of the Ministry of Health and Welfare (MOHW), is charged with the regulation of cosmetics and personal care items. The MOHW maintains listings of prohibited and restricted ingredients.

Korea maintains a prohibited ingredients list of approximately 400 ingredients. Another list of restricted ingredients is also maintained. These lists identify ingredients that are expressly forbidden including hydroquinone, and also those that are allowed with restrictions of quantities and types of uses. These lists are not generally available in English, so most U.S. companies rely on the advice of local consultants or legal firms regarding product formulation.

A number of ingredients that have been identified as potentially carcinogenic, and which are expressly prohibited from use in cosmetic products in Korea include: arsenic, 1,4-dioxane, ethylene oxide, hydroquinone, and lead. Chemicals, which have been restricted to specific amounts or in specific mixtures, include diazolidinyl urea, DMDM-hydantoin, formaldehyde, imidazolidinyl urea, and quaternium 15.

Product import requirements are very complex. Once adequate review has been made to ensure that any product ingredient is not "restricted", together with extensive information, the product is then provided to the KFDA for testing. However, this testing is restricted generally to only six weeks.

The manufacturer or marketer of cosmetic products is required to maintain data on safety and efficacy. As with Japan, this shifts most responsibility for product safety of a product from the KFDA and MOHW to the industry. Again, there is no required format for such data, creating potential ambiguity for the industries concerned. However, warning statements for certain products are prescribed under "Enforcement of Cosmetic Law, Article 14". Generally, these warnings are more extensive than those required in the U.S. or EU (5).

MEXICO

Product regulations are found in the General Law of Health. There are numerous locations where cosmetic and personal care regulations, including on labeling, may be found. The list of prohibited and restricted ingredients for cosmetics and personal care products is found in the 1988 Diario Oficial.

DEFINITION

Mexican law establishes only one classification for cosmetics and personal care items. They are all identified as Productos de Perfumería y Belleza (Products of Perfume and Beauty). The law defines cosmetics as:

> Products of Perfume and Beauty are those products whose purpose it is to modify the natural odor of the body, that preserve or improve personal appearance, are used for personal cleanliness or are repellants for external use.

REGULATION

The Goods and Services Branch, under the direction of the Secretaria de Salud (Secretariat of Health), is charged with the regulation of cosmetics and personal care items. Mexico maintains a list of 43 prohibited ingredients, and 91 restricted ingredients, including preservatives, colorants, and UV filters, which are a composite of the U.S. and EU lists. However, these listings do not include any carcinogenic ingredients.

The import and sales requirements for Products of Perfume and Beauty are very simple. Once adequate review by the manufacturer has been made to ensure that a product complies with the restricted ingredients list, a notice must be sent to the Goods and Services Branch listing the product in the Mexican government's records before it can be marketed.

The Secretariat does not require safety or efficacy testing. It is expected that any company selling such a product would ensure the safety of its own products and maintain a safety data file on individual products and ingredients. The Mexican government reserves the right to test products as they see fit, although it is not standard practice.

The Procuraduria Federal del Consumidor (Federal Procurator for Consumers), reviews and approves labels before they may be used. In general, Mexico requires that all label information must be in Spanish, of equal or greater size and location as other languages. The net content and ingredients must also be clearly legible. All therapeutic claims on efficacy are strictly forbidden.

UNITED KINGDOM

As a Member State of the European Union (EU), British cosmetic legislation implements the EU Cosmetics Directive via The 1996 Cosmetic Products (Safety) Regulations (CPSR), and its amendments. Labeling regulations are detailed in the EEC and Commission Directive.

DEFINITION

According to the CPSR, a cosmetic is defined as:

> …any substance or preparation intended to be applied to any part of the external surfaces of the human body (that is to say, the epidermis, hair system, nails, lips, and external genital organs) or to the teeth or buccal mucosa wholly or mainly for the purpose of cleaning, perfuming or protecting them or keeping them in good condition or changing their appearance or combating body odour or perspiration except where such cleaning, perfuming, protecting, keeping, changing or combating is wholly for the purpose of treating or preventing disease.

REGULATION

The Trading Standards Office, under the direction of the Health Department, is charged with the regulation of cosmetics and personal care items. However, the Department of Trade and Industry (DTI) has issued a guide to the CPSR and assumes oversight of the sale of cosmetics in the U.K.

The United Kingdom does not require pre-market testing of cosmetic and personal care products. Any company selling a cosmetic product is responsible for ensuring the safety of its own products. As with Mexico, the U.K. reserves the right to test products as they see fit, although it is rare for the government to do so.

Generally, the U.K. requires that products be safe when applied under normal and "reasonably foreseeable" conditions. This safety requirement does not cover consumer misuse, but requires the manufacturer to carefully regulate the safety of the cosmetic products they produce. Also, should a manufacturer wish to use a substance that is normally restricted, but which is not found on the prohibited/restricted ingredients lists, authorization must first be acquired from the Department of Health.

The import requirements for cosmetics are simple. Once adequate review has been made to ensure that a product complies with the restricted ingredient list, a notice must be sent to the Department of Trade and Industry. This notice must include a Notification of Supply, a list of ingredients, a Certificate of Analysis along with the Method of Manufacture and safety data for each ingredient. All the documentation required for notification must be maintained by the distributor in a file referred to by the U.K. as a "Product Information Package". The product is then ready for general marketing.

The United Kingdom maintains a prohibited ingredients list. This document lists those ingredients that are forbidden and those that are allowed with certain restrictions. While the U.K. does specifically ban or restrict certain ingredients as noted on their prohibited ingredients list, regulation 4(2)(a) allows products to contain traces of banned substances if they could not be reasonably removed during or after manufacture. Specific ingredients which are banned from use in cosmetics include coloring agents, preservatives and UV filters which are listed in the prohibited ingredients lists. However if a preservative or UV filter is not listed, the Secretary of State may authorize its use, following a request by the manufacturer.

Certain cosmetic ingredients in the United Kingdom have been identified as potentially carcinogenic, and have been expressly prohibited from use in cosmetic products. These include: arsenic, DDT, 1,4-dioxane, ethylene oxide, hydroquinone, lead and morpholine. Ingredients which have been restricted to specific amounts or in specific mixtures include Acid green 1, diaminophenol, fluoride, formaldehyde and p-phenylenediamine. While the U.K. specifically bans or restricts these ingredients, products are allowed to contain "traces" of banned substances if they cannot be "reasonably removed during or after manufacture".

INGREDIENT LABELING WORLDWIDE

Most major industrialized nations now require ingredient labeling, even though this is minimally informative in the absence of appropriate warnings. Disturbingly, the CTFA states that "disclosure of ingredients is still not required on the package of cosmetic products" in Canada, and also that "there is no requirement for full ingredient labeling" in Korea (5). More seriously, if not universally, products in hotels, condominiums, public washrooms, and schools, as well as free samples, are generally unlabeled. Additionally, unlabeled products manufactured by small "rogue" industries are not uncommon.

Most governments, the International Labor Organization, and trade unions require that workers involved in the manufacture or processing of chemicals be provided with basic and relevant information on standardized Material Safety Data Sheets (MSDS). Copies of these MSDS documents must also be made available to the appropriate regulatory authority as well. Information required on each MSDS includes the name(s) of the chemicals involved, chemical concentrations in any product, permissible atmospheric and exposure levels, toxicity and carcinogenicity data, and safety precautions.

The cosmetic industry however, fails to comply with this basic obligation for cosmetic registration (5). The Japanese government does require submission of MSDS for specific ingredients. However, the U.S. only requires that manufacturers should keep MSDS records, but do not require their submission to regulatory agencies. Thus, Japanese and U.S. workers theoretically, at least, have access to ingredient toxicity that is denied to product consumers. Most nations however, fail to require the cosmetic manufacturing industry to supply this information to workers and government agencies alike.

Most consumers still take the safety of mainstream industry personal care and cosmetic products for granted. In general, consumers see no reason to distrust this multibillion dollar global industry, supported by powerful international trade associations (Chapter 3) and regulatory agencies (Chapter 4), especially in view of the silence of cancer and public health institutions (Chapter 1).

The 1995 Safe Shopper's Bible was the first major challenge to these false assurances of safety. The book details the very wide range of carcinogens in named products of named industries, none of whom have attempted to refute or challenge these revelations. The Safe Shopper's Bible also provides information on safe alternative non-mainstream products and industries, mainly with restricted availability, to which the reader is referred. However, The Safe Shopper's Bible omitted two major safe alternative industries, notably Aveda with its international retail outlets, and Neways International (MLM), of which the author then had no knowledge. However, following the author's chance encounter with a Neways distributor in 1997 and subsequent discussions with the company's management, it became apparent that Neways and the Cancer Prevention Coalition shared common goals. The Cancer Prevention Coalition and Neways decided to join efforts to conduct a detailed and ongoing analysis of all ingredients in Neways cosmetics and personal care products in order to identify any ingredients posing potential carcinogenic hazards. Neways has responded constructively and promptly banned all such ingredients, with the exception of a few which are being phased out, and replaced with safe alternatives.

BACKGROUND

Neways is a privately held company founded by Tom and Dee Mower. By background, Tom is a chemist with some two decades of experience in manufacturing industrial chemicals, including those used in floor cleaners. Tom has strong management experience as former CEO of Superior Technologies. Recognizing the carcinogenic and toxic hazards of a wide range of these industrial chemicals, he was disturbed to discover that many were also commonly used in cosmetics and personal care products. Tom was so disturbed that in March 1987 he and Dee created a new company in Salem, Utah, dedicated to marketing safe personal care products, particularly for hair, face and skin.

By 1993, this new company had grown by leaps and bounds, with some 600 local resident employees. Tom and Dee then renamed the company Neways International, again incorporated in Utah. By 1994, Neways developed interest in cosmetics which developed to the extent that Dee created a Leslie DeeAnn division specializing in a full range of cosmetic products.

Neways is now a global company manufacturing a full range of personal care and cosmetic products, in addition to nutritional supplements. The company markets its products through an international chain of multi-level marketing distributors, grossing hundreds of millions of dollars in sales annually. Besides the U.S. and Canada, these nations include the United Kingdom, Australia, Japan, Korea, New Zealand, Mexico, the Czech Republic, Hong Kong, Malaysia, Russia and the Ukraine. Key to Neways' success and rapid growth is its strong emphasis on and dedication to product safety, as well as educating its distributors on scientific information and developments.

Ideology and motivation apart, Neways' success reflects an interlocking complex of themes. Dominant is the realization by health conscious consumers and citizens of the failure of regulatory agencies worldwide to protect their health and safety. Consumers are also gradually sensing the regulatory agencies' indifference and ineptitude in deference to powerful industry pressures. This is coupled with the dawning realization that market place pressures may be more effective than regulation in promoting product and environmental safety. This is particularly well exemplified in the U.S. organic food industry, which has grown by up to 20% annually over the last decade, as consumers have gradually realized the extent of food contamination with carcinogenic and neurotoxic pesticides. However, this realization still lags behind for cosmetics and personal care products. Neways is meeting this challenge by educating its distributors to inform consumers about the safety of its products in striking contrast to those of mainstream industries.

SAFETY INITIATIVES

Since the founding of Neways International, the Mowers have directed high priority to the development of safe cosmetics and personal care products, which pose no risks of cancer and other hazards to unsuspecting consumers. With this objective, the Mowers have progressively reformulated their products so that with few exceptions they contain no "frank" or "hidden" carcinogenic ingredients, which are commonly found in mainstream industry products (Tables 2.2 and 2.3). The "hidden" carcinogens fall into three broad categories: carcinogenic contaminants of non-carcinogenic ingredients; non-carcinogenic ingredients that break down to form or release carcinogens; and non-carcinogenic ingredients or contaminants that interact with each other to create carcinogens. Another important initiative has been the development of safe fragrances.

BANNING OR PHASING OUT CARCINOGENIC INGREDIENTS

Shortly after the company was incorporated in June, 1987, the Independent Cosmetic Manufacturing and Distributors, Inc. reported that none of the company's products contained carcinogenic or toxic reproductive ingredients as listed in California's (Proposition 65) 1985 regulations. This endorsement was further reflected in a wide range of new products, introduced and marketed over the succeeding years, none of which contain any of the following carcinogenic ingredients:

- Ethyl alcohol (in mouthwashes)

- Fluoride (in toothpaste and cosmetics)

- Formaldehyde (in any products)

- Talcum powder (in all products)

- Methyl methacrylate (in nail products)

Additionally, Neways banned sodium lauryl sulfate, a harsh cationic detergent, from all its products. While this ingredient is itself non-carcinogenic, it damages the skin to such an extent as to substantially increase absorption of any other carcinogenic ingredients (Chapter 2).

In March 1998, Neways eliminated DEA and TEA, mild non-ionic surfactants or wetting agents from all their products. This action promptly followed the November 1997 preliminary report by the National Toxicology program that DEA, and its fatty acid condensates, such as lauramides, induced liver and kidney cancer besides accumulating and concentrating in the brain and other organs, following repeated application to the skin of mice (Appendix 2G and 6). This action was also important in view of prior evidence that DEA and TEA are precursors of carcinogenic nitrosamines by interacting with nitrite ingredients/contaminants in products or on the skin (Appendices 2F and 3B). As of January 2001, Neways decided to commence a phase-out of a few synthetic coloring agents from their cosmetic products.

REFORMULATION OF PRODUCTS TO ELIMINATE OR PHASE OUT "HIDDEN" CARCINOGENS

Besides eliminating the carcinogenic precursors DEA and TEA, Neways has eliminated other "hidden" carcinogens (Table 2.3). Notable among these are the potent carcinogens 1,4-dioxane and ethylene oxide that contaminate the widely used and relatively gentle non-ionic ethoxylated surfactants. These include PEGs, polysorbates, laureths and cetearaths, all of which are now certified as "dioxane-free" in Neways products. As of January 2001, Neways decided to phase out diazolidinyl urea that, while non-carcinogenic itself, breaks down in products or on the skin to release carcinogenic formaldehyde.

Fragrances are widely used in cosmetics, and to a lesser extent in personal care products and household products. The numerous fragrance ingredients in cosmetics, often over 100, are undisclosed on product labels on grounds of trade secrecy. This would not be unreasonable if their ingredients were safe. However, the limited available data on fragrances reveals that these products are a virtual witches brew of ingredients for which: no, or minimal, toxicology or carcinogenicity data are available. In addition, the available data are too inadequate to assure safety; and, there is clear evidence of a wide range of carcinogenic or other chronic toxic effects (Appendix 2H). Also, fragrances are one of the most common causes of allergic and sensitization effects, besides contributing to indoor air pollutants in view of their high volatility. The toxicological effects of cosmetic fragrances were brought to attention in May 2001, when legislation (HR 1947) requiring warning labels on fragrances was introduced into the U.S. Congress (Chapter Four).

Neways uses very few fragrances, only five, in its personal care products, and none in its cosmetics. Moreover, these few fragrances contain less than ten ingredients, most of which are floral and herbal, together with a few non-toxic synthetic ingredients. As of January 2001, Neways decided to phase out the few remaining fragrances from all its products.

A further recent important initiative has been the phasing out of the use of a common industrial ingredient, dibutyl phthalate from Neways' line of nail polishes. This action is based on the well-documented grounds of its reproductive toxicity, apart from its identification in the urine of adult women exposed to phthalate ingredients in mainstream cosmetics (Appendix 2I).

THE CANCER PREVENTION COALITION

The Coalition's major contribution to Neways' product safety has been largely directed to identifying carcinogenic ingredients, including "hidden" carcinogens, in all Neways cosmetic and personal care products. All such ingredients have been, or are being, phased out and replaced by safe alternatives. Another priority of the Coalition has been with regard to fragrance safety. The Coalition has also accepted invitations to participate at Neways national and international conventions at which the principles and details of product safety have been explained.

Besides investigating and explaining the hazards of multiple "frank" and "hidden" carcinogens in mainstream industry products, in contrast with those of Neways, the CPC has also emphasized two additional themes. First, Neways distributors are playing a significant public health role as foot soldiers in fighting the losing war against cancer by providing consumers with information on avoidable and otherwise uninformed exposure to carcinogens in common consumer products. Second, citizens have an inalienable and politically unchallengeable right-to-know of information, which still remains largely buried in government and industry files and in the relatively inaccessible scientific literature, on carcinogenic and other avoidable hazards in consumer products that pose serious risks to consumers' health and lives. Recognizing these critical considerations, Neways and its independent distributors have taken an active role in organizing local and regional CPC offices in the U.S., Canada and internationally (Appendix 7), as well as supplying these CPC offices with information on the Coalition's mission and broad range of resources. In all these wide-ranging activities, Neways, its independent distributors, and CPC have worked together closely in pursuit of mutual goals and objectives to reduce avoidable and involuntary exposure to carcinogens in consumer products, and to reduce the escalating incidence of cancer.

CPC would like to thank Neways staff for their contributions to this chapter and elsewhere in the book, including: Ian Campbell, Ben Jolley, Rod Hansen, Kerry Garrett, Jonathan Boyle, Margie Aliprandi, Neways independent distributor and CPC Board Member, for her enthusiastic help in organizing national and international Coalition Offices.

Finally, the author thanks Neways management and staff for assistance in assembling information on the company's products for this monograph. The author is further grateful to: Mike Agrelius, Kate Cedergreen, Will Halterman, Dr. Cole Woolley and Susan Hamilton.

CHAPTER SIX:

INGREDIENTS IN NEWAYS PERSONAL CARE AND COSMETIC PRODUCTS

Neways currently markets 44 personal care and 77 cosmetic products that contain a total of 355 ingredients (Table 6.1). The personal care products contain 264 ingredients (Table 6.2), while the cosmetics contain 121 ingredients (Table 6.3); 28 of all these ingredients are common to both product categories (Table 6.4). Information on product usage by category, gender and age groups, as well as their availability in the U.S. and seven other countries is detailed in Table 6.5.

It should be emphasized that the overwhelming number of Neways products contain no "frank" or "hidden" carcinogenic ingredients (Chapter Two, Tables 2.1-2.3). A small number of carcinogenic or otherwise toxic ingredients, "coal tar dye" lakes, dibutyl phthalate and ammonium lauryl sulfate, are being phased out or have been scheduled for phase out (Tables 1-3 & 5). The five fragrances that are currently used in nine personal care products contain less than ten predominantly herbal or floral ingredients, and are also being phased out.

It should also be noted that ethoxylated (non-ionic) surfactant or detergent ingredients in all products are now uniquely certified as "dioxane-free" as they have been vacuum stripped for this purpose. This process also removes ethylene oxide, which is another volatile carcinogen.

Table 6.1: INGREDIENTS IN NEWAYS PERSONAL CARE and COSMETICS PRODUCTS

Acesulfame potassium
Acetyl tyrosine
Acetylated lanolin
Acrylated oligomer photosynthesizers
Acrylated urethanes
Acrylates copolymer
Acrylates/octylacrylamide copolymer
Ahnfeltia concinna extract
Algae extract
Aliphatic urethane acrylate
Alkyl acrylate copolymer
Allantoin
Aloe barbadensis extract
Aloe vera
Aloe Vera extract
Ammonium chloride
Ammonium cocoyl isethionate
Ammonium lauryl sulfate
Anacystis nidulans extract
Apple extract
Apricot extract
Arginine
Arnica extract
[Aromatic fragrance]
Ascorbyl methylsilanol pectinate
Avocado oil unsaponifiables
Basil extract
Beeswax
Benzil dimethyl ketal
Bergamot extract
Betaglucan
Biotin
Bismuth oxychloride
Black iron oxide
Boron nitride
Burdock extract
Calcium glycerophosphate
Calcium pantothenate
Calendula extract
Camphor
Candelilla cera (candelilla wax)
Caprylyl pyrrolidone
Caranauba wax
Carbomer
Carnauba wax
Casein hydrolysate
Cassia betaglucan
Cellulose gum
Centella asiatica phytosome
Cera alba (beeswax)
Ceramide 6 (dioxane free)
Cetearyl alcohol
Cetearyl glucoside
Cetrimonium chloride
Cetyl alcohol
Cetyl dimethicone
Cetyl ester
Cetyl hydroxyethylcellulose
Cetyl laurate
Cetyl triethylammonium dimethicone copolyol phthalate
Chamomile extract
Chamomile oil
Chlorophyllin-copper complex
Chloroxylenol
Chocolate flavour
Cholecalciferol
Citric acid
Citrulline
Citrus extract
Cocamidopropyl betaine

Cocamidopropyl hydoxysultaine
Coconut extract
Cocophosphatidyl PG-dimonium chloride
Copper acetyl tyrosinate methylsilanol
Coriander extract
Corn oil
Cross-linked elastin
Cucumber extract
Curcuma longa (Curcuminoids)
Curcuma longa extract
Cyanoacrylate ester
Cyclomethicone
[D&C Red # 7 Ca lake]
[D&C Red #30 lake]
[D&C Red #33 Al lake]
[D&C Red #34 Ca lake]
[D&C Red #6 Ba lake]
[D&C Red #7 Ba lake]
[D&C Red #7 Ca lake]
[D&C Red #7 lake]
[D&C Yellow #5 Al lake]
Decyl glucoside
Decyl polyglucose
Deionised cold water
[Dibutyl pthalate]
Dicetyldimonium chloride
Dihydroxyacetone
Diisopropyl adipate
Diisopropyl sebacate
Diisostearoyl trimethylolpropane siloxy silicate
Dimethicone
Dimethicone copolyol (beeswax)
Dimethicone/vinyl dimethicone crosspolymer
Dimethiconol fluoroalcohol dilinoleate
Dimethyl isosorbide
Dioctyl sodium sulfosuccinate
Dipotassium glycyrrhizate
Disodium cocoamphodiacetate
Ergotheoneine
Erythrulose
Ethyl acetate
Ethyl alcohol
Ethyl ester of PVM/MA copolymer
Eucalyptus extract
Farnesol
Farnesyl acetate
[FD&C Yellow #5 Al lake]
Ferric ferrocyanide
Flavor
[Fragrance]
Geranium extract
Ginkgo biloba extract
Ginko biloba dimeric flavonoid phytosomes
Ginseng extract
Glucosamine HCL
Glucose/glucose oxidase/lactoperoxidase
Glycerine
Glyceryl abietate
Glyceryl caprate (coconut extract)
Glycol distearate
Glycolic acid
Grape seed extract
Grapefruit extract
Grapefruit powder
Green Tea extract
Guava extract
Hair keratin amino acids
Henna extract
Hibiscus extract
Homosalate

Honeysuckle extract
Hops extract
Horsetail extract
Hydoxyethylcellulose
Hydrated silica
Hydrogenated castor oil
Hydrogenated coco-glycerides
Hydrogenated palm oil
Hydrogenated polyisobutene
Hydrogenated rice bran wax
Hydrolyzed milk protein
Hydrolyzed mucopolysaccharides
Hydrolyzed soy protein
Hydroxyethycellulose
Hydroxy-2-methyl-1-phenyl-1-propanone
Hydroxypropyl guar
Hydroxypropyl methylcellulose
Iron oxide
Isodecyl neopentanoate
Isoparaffin, C13-14
Isopropyl palmitate
Isostearyl alcohol
Isostearyl neopentanoate
Jojoba esters
Kiwi extract
Lanolin
Lappa extract
Laurel extract
Laureth-7 (dioxane-free)
Lauroyl lysine
Lauryl lactate
Lauryl palmitate
Lavender extract
Lecithin
Lemon extract
Licorice extract
Linoleic acid
Lycasin 85% (hydrogenated starch hydrolysate)
Lysine PCA
Macadamia nut oil
Magna-T gum base
Magnesium ascorbyl phosphate
Magnesium carbonate
Magnesium silicate
Magnesium stearate
Magnoliaceae extract
Mandarin flavour
Mandarin oil
Mango extract
Matricaria extract
Menthyl anthranilate
Methyl anthranilate
Methylchloroisothiazolinone
Methylisothiazolinone
Methylparaben
Methylpropane diol
Methylsilanol carboxymethyl theophyline alginate
Methylsilanol hydroxyproline
Methylsilanol hydroxyproline aspartate
Methylsulfonylmethane (MSM)
Mica
Mica/iron oxide
Mica/iron oxide/titanium
Mica/lauroyl lysine
Micellar casein
Micrococcus lysate
Mulberry Root extract
Myristyl alcohol
Myristyl lactate
Myrrh extract

Natural vanilla flavor
N-butyl acetate
Neem seed oil
Nettle extract
Niacinamide
Nitrocellulose
Nova-T gum base
Nylon
Oat extract
Oat flour
Octocrylene
Octodecyl neopentanoate
Octyl methoxycinnamate
Octyl palmitate
Octyl salicylate
Octyldodecanol
Octyldodecyl neopentanoate
Odor destroying fragrance
Oleyl alcohol
Orange blossom extract
Orange extract
Oriental mushroom extract
Ornithine
Oxido reductases
Palm oil
Palmitoyl hydrolized wheat protein
Panthenol
Panthenyl triacetate
Papaya extract
Peppermint oil
Perfluoropolymethylisopropyl ether
Phenoxyethanol
Phospholipids
Phytosphingosine
Plantain extract
Polyacrylamide
Polyalkylmethicone
Polyester acrylate oligomer
Polyester acrylates
Polyquaternium-10 (dioxane free)
Polyquaternium-11 (dioxane free)
Polysorbate 60 (dioxane free)
Polysorbate 80 (dioxane free)
Progesterone
Propylene carbonate
Propylparaben
PVP
PVP/eicosene copolymer
PVP/hexadecene copolymer
Pyridoxine dicaprylate
Quillaja extract
Reactive polyester diacrylate
Red iron oxide
Red raspberry leaf extract
Retinol
Retinyl palmitate (vitamin A)
Rice peptides
Rosacea extract
Rose hip oil
Rosemary extract
Saccharide isomerate
Safflower oil
Sage extract
Sambucus extract
Sandlewood extract
SD Alcohol 40
SD Alcohol 40B
Shea butter
Silica
Silk amino acids

Sodium behenoyl lactylate
Sodium borate
Sodium C12-15 pareth-15 sulfonate (dioxane free)
Sodium C14-16 olefin sulfonate
Sodium carboxymethyl betaglucan
Sodium citrate
Sodium coco sulfate
Sodium isostearoyl lactylate
Sodium lauroyl sarcosinate
Sodium methyl cocoyl taurate
Sodium PCA
Sodium stearoyl lactylate
Sorbitol
Sorbitol liquid
Sorbitol powder
Soybean (glycine soja) protein
Spirea extract
Spiriulina extract
Stabilized chlorine dioxide
Stearalkonium chloride
Stearalkonium hectorite
Stearic acid
Stearyl glycyrrhetinate
Stearyl heptanoate
Stevia powder
Sucralose
Sugar Cane extract
Sunflower seed extract
Sunflower seed oil (Helianthus annus)
Sweet almond oil
Talc
Tangelo extract (orange oil)
Tangerine extract
Tetrahexydecyl ascorbate (Vitamin C)
Thyme extract
Titanium dioxide
Tocopheryl acetate (vitamin E)
Toluene
Tricontanyl PVP
Tridecyl neopentanoate
Triethyl citrate
Trilaurin
Tripropylene glycol diacrylate
Tutti-frutti flavor
Tween-60 (polysorbate 60--dioxane free)
Ultramarine
Umber 7065
Urea peroxide
VA/butyl maleate/isobornyl/acrylate copolymer
Vanilla
Vanilla extract
Vegetable protein extract
Vitamin A
Vitamin E (Tocopherol)
Vitamin E (D-alpha-Tocopheryl acetate)
Water (purified)
Watercress extract
Wheat amino acids
Wheat starch (modified)
Wild cherry extract
Wild yam extract
Willowbark extract
Wintergreen flavor
Witch hazel distillate
Xanthan gum
Xylitol
Yarrow extract
Yarrow flowers extract
Yeast cell derivatives
Yeast extract

Yellow iron oxide
Ylang Ylang extract
Zinc dimethicone
Zinc gluconate
Zinc oxide

Total Ingredients: 355

Designations
[ ] -- Brackets connote that the enclosed
ingredient is being phased out.

Table 6.2: INGREDIENTS IN NEWAYS PERSONAL CARE PRODUCTS

Ingredient	Products
Acesulfame potassium	**Dental Aids:** *NDK Gum*
Acetyl tyrosine	**Conditioners:** *2nd Chance* **Styling Aids:** *Super Booster*
Acrylates copolymer	**Styling Aids:** *Finishing Touch*
Acrylates/octylacrylamide copolymer	**Suncare:** *Lipceutical*
Ahnfeltia concinna extract	**Beauty Aids:** *Retention Plus*
Algae extract	**Lotions:** *Skin Enhancer*
Allantoin	**Beauty Aids:** *Bio-Mist Activator* **Shaving:** *Close Shaving Gel* **Soaps:** *Milky Cleanser* **Suncare:** *Sunbrero*
Aloe barbadensis extract	**Shampoo:** *2nd Chance*
Aloe vera	**Beauty Aids:** *Endau Progesterone Cream, Retention Plus* **Deodorants:** *Subdue* **Hair Sprays:** *Free Flex* **Lotions:** *Skin Enhancer* **Shaving:** *Close Shaving Gel* **Soaps:** *Milky Cleanser, Refresh, TLC* **Suncare:** *Neways Tanning Oil, Rebound, Sunbrero*
Aloe Vera extract	**Lotions:** *NightScience* **Suncare:** *Lipceutical, Tanacity*
Ammonium chloride	**Bubble Baths:** *Indulge* **Shampoos:** *2nd Chance, Silken, Ultimate* **Soaps:** *1st Impression, Refresh*
Ammonium cocoyl isethionate	**Shampoos:** *2nd Chance, Silken* **Soaps:** *1st Impression, Extra Gentle*
Ammonium lauryl sulfate	**Shampoos:** *2nd Chance*
Anacystis nidulans extract	**Lotions:** *Skin Enhancer*
Apple extract	**Beauty Aids:** *Lightning Drops*
Apricot extract	**Soaps:** *Extra Gentle*
Arginine	**Conditioners:** *2nd Chance* **Styling Aids:** *Super Booster*
Arnica extract	**Beauty Aids:** *Snap Back* **Shampoos:** *Silken*
[Aromatic fragrance*]	**Beauty Aids:** *Wrinkle Drops* **Conditioners:** *Exuberance* **Bubble Baths:** *Indulge* **Styling Aids:** *Finishing Touch, Free Flex, Sassy, Sculpting Gel*
Ascorbyl methylsilanol pectinate	**Suncare:** *Sunbrero*
Basil extract	**Shampoos:** *Ultimate* **Soaps:** *Extra Gentle, Refresh*
Bergamot extract	**Conditioners:** *2nd Chance* **Shampoos:** *2nd Chance, Silken* **Shaving:** *Close Shaving Gel*
Betaglucan	**Lotions:** *NightScience, Skin Enhancer*
Biotin	**Conditioners:** *2nd Chance* **Styling Aids:** *Super Booster*
Burdock extract	**Conditioners:** *2nd Chance* **Styling Aids:** *Super Booster*
Calcium glycerophosphate	**Toothpastes:** *Ultrashine Radiance*
Calcium pantothenate	**Conditioners:** *2nd Chance* **Styling Aids:** *Super Booster*
Calendula extract	**Shampoos:** *Ultimate* **Suncare:** *Rebound, Tanacity*
Candellila wax	**Suncare:** *Lipceutical*
Caprylyl pyrrolidone	**Shampoos:** *Silken* **Styling Aids:** *Free Flex*
Caranauba wax	**Suncare:** *Lipceutical*
Carbomer	**Toothpastes:** *Whiten*
Casein hydrolysate	**Dental Aids:** *NDK Gum*
Cassia betaglucan	**Suncare:** *Rebound*
Cellulose gum	**Toothpastes:** *Radiance, Ultrashine Radiance*
Centella asiatica phytosome	**Beauty Aids:** *Snap Back*

Ceramide 6 (dioxane free)	**Beauty Aids:** *Retention Plus*
Cetearyl alcohol	**Lotions:** *Barrier Cream* **Suncare:** *Body Bronze, Sunbrero*
Cetearyl glucoside	**Beauty Aids:** *Imperfection Lotion* **Suncare:** *Body Bronze, Rebound*
Cetrimonium chloride	**Conditioners:** *Exuberance* **Styling Aids:** *Replenishing Mist*
Cetyl alcohol	**Beauty Aids:** *Endau Progesterone Cream, Retention Plus* **Conditioners:** *Exuberance* **Lotions:** *NightScience, Skin Enhancer, Tender Care* **Suncare:** *Lipceutical*
Cetyl hydroxyethylcellulose	**Lotions:** *Barrier Cream, Skin Enhancer*
Cetyl triethylammonium dimethicone copolyol phthalate	**Shaving:** *Close Shaving Gel*
Chamomile extract	**Beauty Aids:** *Endau Progesterone Cream* **Lotions:** *NightScience*
Chlorophyllin-copper complex	**Toothpastes:** *Ultrashine Radiance*
Chloroxylenol	**Beauty Aids:** *Lash Enhancer*
Cholecalciferol	**Beauty Aids:** *Wrinkle Garde*
Citric acid	**Dental Aids:** *NDK Gum*
Citrulline	**Conditioners:** *2nd Chance* **Styling Aids:** *Super Booster*
Citrus extract	**Beauty Aids:** *Lightning Drops*
Cocamidopropyl betaine	**Shaving:** *Close Shaving Gel*
Cocamidopropyl hydoxysultaine	**Bubble Baths:** *Indulge* **Shampoos:** *2nd Chance, Silken, Ultimate* **Soaps:** *1st Impression, Refresh*
Coconut extract	**Suncare:** *Neways Tanning Oil*
Cocophosphatidyl PG-dimonium chloride	**Shaving:** *Close Shaving Gel*
Copper acetyl tyrosinate methylsilanol	**Suncare:** *Great Tan*
Coriander extract	**Deodorant:** *Subdue*
Corn oil	**Beauty Aids:** *Wrinkle Garde*
Cross-linked elastin	**Beauty Aids:** *Retention Plus, Wrinkle Drops*
Cucumber extract	**Beauty Aids:** *Lightning Drops*
Curcuma longa (Curcuminoids)	**Shampoos:** *Ultimate*
Curcuma longa extract	**Lotions:** *Skin Enhancer*
Cyclomethicone	**Lotions:** *NightScience* **Suncare:** *Neways Tanning Oil, Sunbrero*
d-Alpha tocopheryl (vitamin E)	**Suncare:** *Neways Tanning Oil*
Decyl glucoside	**Beauty Aids:** *Bio-Mist Activator* **Suncare:** *Great Tan*
Decyl polyglucose	**Beauty Aids:** *Lightning Drops* **Shampoos:** *Silken, Ultimate* **Shaving:** *Close* **Soaps:** *1st Impression, Extra Gentle, Milky Cleanser*
Dicetyldimonium chloride	**Shampoos:** *Exuberance*
Dihydroxyacetone	**Suncare:** *Body Bronze, Great Tan*
Diisopropyl sebacate	**Suncare:** *Neways Tanning Oil*
Diisostearoyl trimethylolpropane siloxy silicate	**Suncare:** *Lipceutical*
Dimethicone	**Beauty Aids:** *Endau Progesterone Cream, Retention Plus, Snap Back* **Lotions:** *Barrier Cream, Skin Enhancer, Tender Care* **Suncare:** *Body Bronze, Great Tan, Rebound, Sunbrero, Tanacity*
Dimethicone copolyol	**Conditioners:** *2nd Chance* **Styling Aids:** *Free Flex, Sassy, Sculpting Gel, Super Booster*
Dimethicone/vinyl dimethicone crosspolymer	**Lotions:** *NightScience*
Dimethiconol fluoroalcohol dilinoleate	**Lotions:** *Barrier Cream*
Dimethyl isosorbide	**Beauty Aids:** *Endau Progesterone Cream*
Dioctyl sodium sulfosuccinate	**Styling Aids:** *Finishing Touch*

Dipotassium glycyrrhizate	**Beauty Aids:** *Imperfection Lotion*　**Lotions:** *NightScience, Skin Enhancer*　**Suncare:** *Rebound*
Disodium cocoamphodiacetate	**Shampoos:** *Ultimate*　**Soaps:** *1st Impression*
Ergotheoneine	**Beauty Aids:** *Retention Plus*　**Lotions:** *NightScience*　**Lotions:** *Rebound, Skin Enhancer*
Erythrulose	**Suncare:** *Body Bronze, Great Tan*
Ethyl ester of PVM/MA copolymer	**Styling Aids:** *Free Flex, Sassy*
Eucalyptus extract	**Deodorant:** *Subdue*
Farnesol	**Beauty Aids:** *Imperfection Lotion*
Farnesyl acetate	**Beauty Aids:** *Imperfection Lotion*
Flavor	**Mouthwashes:** *Eliminator*　**Toothpastes:** *Radiance*
[Fragrance*]	**Beauty Aids:** *Retention Plus*
Geranium extract	**Conditioners:** *2nd Chance*　**Shampoos:** *2nd Chance, Silken*　**Shaving:** *Close*　**Styling Aids:** *Replenishing Mist*
Ginko biloba　dimeric flavonoid phytosomes	**Beauty Aids:** *Snap Back*
Ginko biloba　extract	**Beauty Aids:** *Lash Enhancer, Super Booster*
Ginseng extract	**Beauty Aids:** *Super Booster*　**Conditioners:** *2nd Chance*　**Soaps:** *Refresh*
Glucosamine HCL	**Conditioners:** *2nd Chance*　**Styling Aids:** *Super Booster*
Glycerine	**Dental Aids:** *NDK Gum*　**Toothpastes:** *Radiance, Whiten*
Glycol distearate	**Shaving:** *Close Shaving Gel*
Glycolic acid	**Beauty Aids:** *Wrinkle Drops*
Grape seed extract	**Beauty Aids:** *Retention Plus*
Grapefruit extract	**Soaps:** *1st Impression*
Green Tea extract	**Beauty Aids:** *Lightning Drops*
Guava extract	**Suncare:** *Neways Tanning Oil*
Hair keratin amino acids	**Conditioners:** *Exuberance*　**Styling Aids:** *Replenishing Mist, Sassy*
Henna extract	**Shampoos:** *Ultimate*
Hibiscus extract	**Soaps:** *1st Impression*
Homosalate	**Suncare:** *Neways Tanning Oil*
Honeysuckle extract	**Lotions:** *Barrier Cream*　**Shaving:** *Close Shaving Gel*　**Soaps:** *1st Impression*
Hops extract	**Bubble Baths:** *Indulge*　**Shampoos:** *Ultimate*
Horsetail extract	**Shampoos:** *Ultimate*　**Soaps:** *Refresh*
Hydoxyethylcellulose	**Styling Aids:** *Sculpting Gel*
Hydrated silica	**Toothpastes:** *Radiance, Ultrashine Radiance*
Hydrogenated polyisobutene	**Beauty Aids:** *Wrinkle Garde*　**Suncare:** *Neways Tanning Oil*
Hydrolyzed milk protein	**Beauty Aids:** *Bio-Mist Activator*
Hydrolyzed mucopolysaccharides	**Beauty Aids:** *Bio-Mist Activator*　**Conditioner:** *2nd Chance*　**Styling Aids:** *Replenishing Mist*
Hydrolyzed soy protein	**Conditioners:** *2nd Chance*　**Styling Aids:** *Super Booster*
Hydroxyethylcellulose	**Conditioners:** *Exuberance*
Hydroxypropyl guar	**Shaving:** *Close Shaving Gel*
Hydroxypropyl methylcellulose	**Soaps:** *Extra Gentle*
Isodecyl neopentanoate	**Suncare:** *Neways Tanning Oil*

Ingredient	Products
Isoparaffin, C13-14	**Beauty Aids:** *Imperfection Lotion, Snap Back* **Soaps:** *Milky Cleanser, TLC* **Suncare:** *Great Tan, Rebound, Sunbrero, Tanacity*
Isostearyl alcohol	**Suncare:** *Lipceutical*
Kiwi extract	**Shampoos:** *2nd Chance*
Lappa extract	**Beauty Aids:** *Imperfection Lotion*
Laurel extract	**Bubble Baths:** *Indulge*
Laureth-7 (dioxane-free)	**Beauty Aids:** *Imperfection Lotion, Snap Back* **Soaps:** *Milky Cleanser* **Suncare:** *Great Tan, Rebound, Sunbrero, Tanacity, TLC*
Lauryl lactate	**Suncare:** *Neways Tanning Oil*
Lavender extract	**Conditioners:** *2nd Chance* **Lotions:** *NightScience* **Shampoos:** *2nd Chance, Silken* **Shaving:** *Close Shaving Gel* **Styling Aids:** *Replenishing Mist*
Lecithin	**Beauty Aids:** *Endau Progesterone Cream, Lightning Drops* **Dental Aids:** *NDK Gum* **Lotion:** *NightScience* **Suncare:** *Rebound, Tanacity*
Lemon extract	**Beauty Aids:** *Lightning Drops* **Shampoos:** *Silken*
Licorice extract	**Beauty Aids:** *Lightning Drops*
Linoleic acid	**Cleansers:** *TLC*
Lycasin 85% (hydrogenated starch hydrolysate)	**Dental Aids:** *NDK Gum*
Macadamia nut oil	**Suncare:** *Tanacity*
Magna-T gum base	**Dental Aids:** *NDK Gum*
Magnesium ascorbyl phosphate (vitamin C)	**Beauty Aids:** *Lightning Drops*
Magnoliaceae extract	**Lotions:** *Skin Enhancer*
Mango extract	**Soaps:** *Extra Gentle Cleanser* **Suncare:** *Body Bronze*
Matricaria extract	**Bubble Baths:** *Indulge* **Shampoos:** *2nd Chance, Ultimate*
Menthyl anthranilate	**Lotions:** *Skin Enhancer*
Methyl anthranilate	**Suncare:** *Neways Tanning Oil*
Methylchloroisothiazolinone	*Refresh*
Methylisothiazolinone	*Refresh*
Methylparaben	**Beauty Aids:** *Endau Progesterone Cream, Imperfection Lotion, Lightning Drops, Replenishing Mist, Retention Plus, Snap Back, Wrinkle Drops* **Bubble Baths:** *Indulge* **Conditioners:** *2nd Chance* **Lotions:** *NightScience, Skin Enhancer, Tender Care* **Soaps:** *Milky Cleanser, TLC* **Styling Aids:** *Sculpting Gel, Super Booster* **Suncare:** *Body Bronze, Great Tan, Neways Tanning Oil, Rebound, Sunbrero, Tanacity*
Methylpropane diol	**Beauty Aids:** *Lightning Drops* **Deodorants:** *Subdue* **Lotions:** *Barrier Cream, NightScience* **Suncare:** *Body Bronze*
Methylsilanol carboxymethyl theophyline alginate	**Suncare:** *Body Bronze*
Methylsilanol hydroxyproline aspartate	**Beauty Aids:** *Snap Back*
Methylsulfonylmethane (MSM)	**Lotions:** *Tender Care*
Micellar casein	**Toothpastes:** *Ultrashine Radiance*
Micrococcus lysate	**Lotions:** *NightScience* **Suncare:** *Rebound, Tanacity*
Mulberry Root extract	**Beauty Aids:** *Lightning Drops*
Myristyl alcohol	**Conditioners:** *Exuberance*
Myrrh extract	**Beauty Aids:** *Imperfection Lotion, Lash Enhancer* **Deodorant:** *Subdue* **Soaps:** *TLC*
Natural vanilla flavor	**Dental Aids:** *NDK Gum*
Nettle extract	**Shampoos:** *2nd Chance, Silken* **Styling Aids:** *Super Booster*
Niacinamide	**Beauty Aids:** *1st Impression, Lash Enhancer* **Conditioners:** *2nd Chance* **Styling Aids:** *Super Booster*
Nova-T gum base	**Dental Aids:** *NDK Gum*
Oat extract	**Lotions:** *Skin Enhancer*
Octocrylene	**Suncare:** *Neways Tanning Oil, Sunbrero*

Octodecyl neopentanoate	**Suncare:** *Sunbrero*
Octyl methoxycinnamate	**Styling Aids:** *Finishing Touch, Free Flex* **Suncare:** *Body Bronze, Great Tan, Lipceutical, Neways Tanning Oil, Suinbrero*
Octyl palmitate	**Beauty Aids:** *Endau Progesterone Cream* **Lotions:** *Skin Enhancer, Tender Care* **Suncare:** *Body Bronze*
Octyl salicylate	**Suncare:** *Body Bronze, Great Tan, Neways Tanning Oil, Lipceutical*
Octyldodecyl neopentanoate	**Lotions:** *Barrier Cream*
Odor destroying fragrance*	**Deodorants:** *Subdue*
Orange blossom extract	**Soaps:** *Extra Gentle Cleanser*
Orange extract	**Conditioners:** *2nd Chance* **Shampoos:** *2nd Chance, Silken* **Shaving:** *Close Shaving Gel*
Oriental mushroom extract	**Lotions:** *NightScience*
Ornithine	**Shampoos:** *2nd Chance* **Styling Aids:** *Super Booster*
Oxido reductases	**Lotions:** *Skin Enhancer*
Palm oil	**Beauty Aids:** *Snap Back* **Suncare:** *Great Tan, Lipceutical*
Palmitoyl hydrolized wheat protein	**Suncare:** *Rebound*
Panthenol	**Conditioners:** *2nd Chance, Exuberance* **Shampoos:** *2nd Chance* **Soaps:** 1st Impression **Styling Aids:** *Finishing Touch, Free Flex, Replenishing Mist, Super Booster* **Beauty Aids:** *Lash Enhancer*
Panthenyl triacetate	**Beauty Aids:** *Imperfection Lotion*
Papaya extract	**Soaps:** *1st Impression*
Peppermint oil	**Toothpastes:** *Ultrashine Radiance*
Perfluoropolymethylisopropyl ether	**Lotions:** *Barrier Cream*
Phenoxyethanol	**Beauty Aids:** *Bio-Mist Activator, Endau Progesterone Cream, Imperfection Lotion, Lash Enhancer, Lightning Drops, Retention Plus, Snap Back, Wrinkle Drops* **Bubble Baths:** *Indulge* **Conditioners:** *2nd Chance, Exuberance* **Lotions:** *NightScience, Skin Enhancer, Tender Care* **Soaps:** *Milky Cleanser, TLC* **Styling Aids:** *Replenishing Mist, Sculpting Gel, Super Booster* **Suncare:** *Body Bronze, Great Tan, Neways Tanning Oil, Rebound, Sunbrero, Tanacity*
Phospholipids	**Beauty Aids:** *Wrinkle Drops*
Phytosphingosine	**Beauty Aids:** *Retention Plus*
Plantain extract	**Beauty Aids:** *Imperfection Lotion*
Polyacrylamide	**Beauty Aids:** *Imperfection Lotion, Snap Back* **Soaps:** *Milky Cleanser, TLC* **Suncare:** *Great Tan, Rebound, Sunbrero, Tanacity*
Polyalkylmethicone	**Lotions:** *Barrier Cream*
Polyquaternium-10 (dioxane free)	**Styling Aids:** *Sculpting Gel*
Polyquaternium-11 (dioxane free)	**Conditioners:** *2nd Chance* **Styling Aids:** *Sculpting Gel, Super Booster*
Polysorbate 60 (dioxane free)	**Conditioners:** *2nd Chance Conditioner*
Polysorbate 80 (dioxane free)	**Beauty Aids:** *Wrinkle Drops* **Conditioners:** *2nd Chance Conditioner*
Progesterone	**Beauty Aids:** *Endau Progesterone Cream*
Propylparaben	**Beauty Aids:** *Endau Progesterone Cream, Imperfection Lotion, Lightning Drops, Retention Plus, Snap Back, Wrinkle Drops* **Bubble Baths:** *Indulge* **Conditioners:** *2nd Chance* **Lotions:** *NightScience, Skin Enhancer, Tender Care* **Soaps:** *Milky Cleanser, TLC* **Styling Aids:** *Replenishing Mist, Sculpting Gel, Super Booster* **Suncare:** *Body Bronze, Great Tan, Lipceutical, Neways Tanning Oil, Rebound,*
PVP	**Styling Aids:** *Sculpting Gel*
PVP/hexadecene copolymer	**Lotions:** *Barrier Cream* **Suncare:** *Sunbrero*
Pyridoxine dicaprylate	**Lotions:** *NightScience, Skin Enhancer* **Suncare:** *Rebound*
Quillaja extract	**Shampoos:** *Ultimate* **Soaps:** *Extra Gentle*
Red raspberry leaf extract	**Beauty Aids:** *Bio-Mist Activator*

Retinol	**Lotions:** *NightScience*
Retinyl palmitate (vitamin A)	**Beauty Aids:** *Imperfection Lotion, Retention Plus, Wrinkle Garde* **Conditioners:** *2nd Chance* **Styling Aids:** *Super Booster* **Suncare:** *Neways Tanning Oil*
Rice peptides	**Lotions:** *NightScience*
Rosacea extract	**Lotions:** *Skin Enhancer*
Rose hip oil	**Beauty Aids:** *Retention Plus, Wrinkle Garde* **Lotions:** *NightScience, Skin Enhancer, Tender Care* **Suncare:** *Rebound, Tanacity*
Rosemary extract	**Shampoos:** *2nd Chance, Silken* **Soaps:** *Refresh* **Styling Aids:** *Replenishing Mist* **Suncare:** *Rebound, Tanacity*
Saccharide isomerate	**Lotions:** *NightScience, Skin Enhancer* **Suncare:** *Rebound*
Safflower oil	**Suncare:** *Lipceutical*
Sage extract	**Deodorant:** *Subdue* **Shampoos:** *2nd Chance, Silken* **Soaps:** *Refresh* **Styling Aids:** *Replenishing Mist*
Sambucus extract	**Soaps:** *Refresh*
Sandlewood extract	**Styling Aids:** *Replenishing Mist*
SD Alcohol 40	**Styling Aids:** *Free Flex, Sassy*
Shea butter	**Soaps:** *TLC*
Silk amino acids	**Soaps:** *Milky Cleanser, TLC* **Styling Aids:** *Finishing Touch, Sassy*
Sodium behenoyl lactylate	**Beauty Aids:** *Endau Progesterone Cream, Retention Plus* **Lotions:** *NightScience, Skin Enhancer, Tender Care*
Sodium borate	**Soaps:** *Milky Cleanser*
Sodium C12-15 pareth-15 sulfonate (dioxane free)	**Bubble Bath:** *Indulge* **Shampoos:** *Silken* **Soaps:** *1st Impression, Extra Gentle*
Sodium C14-16 olefin sulfonate	**Bubble Baths:** *Indulge* **Shampoos:** *2nd Chance, Silken, Ultimate* **Shaving:** *Close Shaving Gel* **Soaps:** *1st Impression, Refresh*
Sodium carboxymethyl betaglucan	**Suncare:** *Rebound*
Sodium citrate	**Beauty Aids:** *Lightning Drops*
Sodium coco sulfate	**Toothpastes:** *Ultrashine Radiance*
Sodium isostearoyl lactylate	**Bubble Baths:** *Indulge* **Shampoos:** *2nd Chance* **Shaving:** *Close Shaving Gel* **Soaps:** *Refresh*
Sodium lauroyl sarcosinate	**Toothpastes:** *Radiance*
Sodium methyl cocoyl taurate	**Soaps:** *Refresh*
Sodium PCA	**Beauty Aids:** *Bio-Mist Activator* **Lotions:** *Tender Care* **Soaps:** *Milky Cleanser, TLC*
Sodium stearoyl lactylate	**Lotions:** *Barrier Cream*
Sorbitol	**Beauty Aids:** *Endau Progesterone Cream, Snap Back* **Lotions:** *NightScience, Skin Enhancer, Tender Care* **Shaving:** *Close Shaving Gel* **Soaps:** *Milky Cleanser* **Suncare:** *Rebound* **Toothpastes:** *Radiance, Ultrashine Radiance*
Sorbitol liquid	**Dental Aids:** *NDK Gum*
Sorbitol powder	**Dental Aids:** *NDK Gum*
Soybean (glycine soja) protein	**Lotions:** *Skin Enhancer*
Spirea extract	**Bubble Baths:** *Indulge*
Spiriulina extract	**Lotions:** *NightScience, Skin Enhancer* **Suncare:** *Rebound*
Stabilized chlorine dioxide	**Mouthwashes:** *Eliminator* **Toothpastes:** *Radiance, Ultrashine Radiance*
Stearalkonium chloride	**Conditioners:** *Exuberance*
Stearic acid	**Beauty Aids:** *Endau Progesterone Cream, Retention Plus* **Lotions:** *Barrier Cream, NightScience, Skin Enhancer, Tender Care* **Suncare:** *Lipceutical*
Stearyl glycyrrhetinate	**Beauty Aids:** *Retention Plus*
Stevia powder	**Dental Aids:** *NDK Gum*
Sucralose	**Toothpastes:** *Ultrashine Radiance*
Sugar Cane extract	**Beauty Aids:** *Lightning Drops*

Sunflower seed extract	**Lotions:** *Skin Enhancer* **Suncare:** *Lipceutical*
Sweet almond oil	**Beauty Aids:** *Endau Progesterone Cream* **Lotions:** *Barrier Cream, Tender Care* **Soaps:** *Milky Cleanser* **Suncare:** *Body Bronze*
Tangelo extract (orange oil)	**Shampoos:** *Ultimate* **Soaps:** *Extra Gentle, Refresh*
Tangerine extract	**Beauty Aids:** *Bio-Mist Activator* **Conditioners:** *2nd Chance* **Shampoos:** *2nd Chance, Silken* **Shaving:** *Close Shaving Gel*
Tetrahexydecyl ascorbate (Vitamin C)	**Beauty Aids:** *Retention Plus* **Lotions:** *Skin Enhancer* **Suncare:** *Neways Tanning Oil*
Thyme extract	**Beauty Aids:** *Imperfection Lotion*
Titanium dioxide	**Dental Aids:** *NDK Gum*
Tocopheryl acetate (vitamin E)	**Beauty Aids:** *Lightning Drops, Wrinkle Garde*
Triethyl citrate	**Styling Aids:** *Finishing Touch, Free Flex*
Trilaurin	**Suncare:** *Lipceutical*
Tutti-frutti flavor	**Dental Aids:** *NDK Gum*
Tween-60 (polysorbate 60--dioxane free)	**Dental Aids:** *NDK Gum*
Urea peroxide	**Toothpastes:** *Whiten*
VA/butyl maleate/isobornyl/acrylate copolymer	**Styling Aids:** *Free Flex*
Vanilla extract	**Lotions:** *Barrier Cream, Skin Enhancer, Tender Care*
Vegetable protein extract	**Deodorants:** *Subdue*
Vitamin A	**Lotions:** *Tender Care*
Vitamin E (Tocopherol)	**Beauty Aids:** *Endau Progesterone Cream* **Lotions:** *Skin Enhancer, Tender Care* **Soaps:** *TLC* **Suncare:** *Body Bronze, Great Tan, Lipceutical, Sunbrero*
Vitamin E (D-alpha Tocopheryl acetate)	**Suncare:** *Neways Tanning Oil*
Water, purified	**Beauty Aids:** *Bio-Mist Activator, Endau Progesterone Cream, Imperfection Lotion, Lash Enhancer, Lightning Drops, Retention Plus, Snap Back, Wrinkle Drops* **Bubble Baths:** *Indulge* **Conditioners:** *2nd Chance, Exuberance* **Lotions:** *Barrier Cream, NightScience, Skin Enhancer, Tender Care* **Mouthwashes:** *Eliminator* **Shampoos:** *2nd Chance, Silken, Ultimate* **Shaving:** *Close Shaving Gel* **Soaps:** *1st Impression, Extra Gentle, Milky Cleanser, Refresh, TLC* **Styling Aids:** *Finishing Touch, Free Flex, Replenishing Mist, Sassy, Sculpting Gel, Super Booster* **Suncare:** *Body Bronze, Great Tan, Rebound, Sunbrero, Tanacity* **Toothpastes:** *Radiance, Ultrashine Radiance*
Watercress extract	**Shampoos:** *Silken*
Wheat amino acids	**Shampoos:** *Silken*
Wheat starch (modified)	**Lotions:** *NightScience*
Wild cherry extract	**Shampoos:** *Ultimate*
Wild yam extract	**Beauty Aids:** *Endau Progesterone Cream*
Willowbark extract	**Beauty Aids:** *Imperfection Lotion*
Wintergreen flavor	**Dental Aids:** *NDK Gum*
Witch hazel distillate	**Beauty Aids:** *Bio-Mist Activator, Imperfection Lotion* **Deodorants:** *Subdue*
Xanthan gum	**Suncare:** *Body Bronze, Sunbrero*
Xylitol	**Toothpastes:** *Ultrashine Radiance*
Yarrow extract	**Shampoos:** *2nd Chance*
Yarrow flowers extract	**Soaps:** *1st Impression* **Suncare:** *Rebound, Tanacity*
Yeast cell derivatives	**Beauty Aids:** *Wrinkle Drops*
Yeast extract	**Lotions:** *NightScience, Skin Enhancer* **Suncare:** *Rebound*

Ylang Ylang extract	**Conditioners:** *2nd Chance* **Shampoos:** *2nd Chance, Silken* **Shaving:** *Close Shaving Gel*
Zinc gluconate	**Conditioners:** *2nd Chance* **Styling Aids:** *Super Booster*
Zinc oxide	**Suncare:** *Sunbrero*

Total Ingredients: 264

Designations

[ ] -- Brackets connote that the enclosed ingredient is in the process of being phased out.

 * -- Asterisk identifies fragrances that composed of ten or fewer ingredients, primarily of floral or herbal origin.

Table 6.3: INGREDIENTS IN NEWAYS COSMETIC PRODUCTS

Ingredient	Products
Acetylated lanolin	**Foundations:** *Almond, Dark Bronze, Dark Mocha, Honey, Peach, Porcelain*
Acrylated oligomer photosynthesizers	**Nail Care:** *Ultra High Gloss/White Tip Gel*
Acrylated urethane	**Nail Care:** *Nail Gels, Ultra High Gloss/White Tip Gel*
Aliphatic urethane acrylate	**Nail Care:** *Nail Whitener*
Alkyl acrylate copolymer	**Nail Enamels:** *Barely Bronze, Raspberry, Ruby Red, Soft Shell Pink, Vegas Pink, Watermelon, Carmel, Cinnamon, Fuchsia, Heather, Inca Bronze, Mad About Mauve, Magenta, Neways Red*
Allantoin	**Eye Pencils:** *Autumn* **Lip Pencils:** *Wild Cherry* **Nail Care:** *Nail Enhancer*
Avocado oil unsaponifiables	**Blushes:** *Autumn Glow, Carnation, Rose Pink, Warm Peach, Tawny, Terracotta* **Eye Shadows:** *Brown, Brown Suede, Charcoal, Chocolate, Chocolate Mousse, Cinnamon Spray, Dark Tan, Grey Stone, Light Russet, Misty Grey, Ochre, Plum Crazy, Russet, Sand, Soft Brown, Natural, Rich Sand, Soft Pink, White Essence* **Lipsticks:** *Carmel, Cinnamon, Barely Bronze, Fuchsia, Heather, Inca Bronze, Mad About Mauve, Magenta, Neways Red, Raspberry, Ruby Red, Soft Shell Pink, Vegas Pink, Watermelon*
Beeswax	**Mascaras:** *Charcoal, Jet Black* **Eye Pencils:** *Autumn, Silver Fox* **Lip Pencil:** *Wild Cherry*
Benzil dimethyl ketal	**Nail Care:** *Nail Gels*
Betaglucan	**Blushes:** *Autumn Glow, Carnation, Rose Pink, Warm Peach, Tawny, Terracotta* **Eye Shadows:** *Brown, Brown Suede, Charcoal, Chocolate, Chocolate Mousse, Cinnamon Spray, Dark Tan, Grey Stone, Light Russet, Misty Grey, Natural Pink, Ochre, Plum Crazy, Russet, Sand, Soft Brown, Natural, Rich Sand, Soft Pink, White Essence* **Facial Powders:** *Honeytone, Translucent*
Bismuth oxychloride	**Nail Enamels:** *Barely Bronze, Heather, Inca Bronze, Mad About Mauve, Magenta, Raspberry, Vegas Pink*
Black iron oxide	**Eye Pencils:** *Autumn, Dark Sable, Midnight Ebony, Silver Fox*
Boron nitride	**Blushes:** *Autumn Glow, Carnation, Rose Pink, Warm Peach, Tawny, Terracotta* **Eye Shadows:** *Brown, Brown Suede, Charcoal, Chocolate, Chocolate Mousse, Cinnamon Spray, Dark Tan, Grey Stone, Light Russet, Misty Grey, Natural Pink, Ochre, Plum Crazy, Russet, Sand, Soft Brown, Natural, Rich Sand, Soft Pink, White Essence*
Calcium pantothenate	**Nail Enamels:** *Carmel, Cinnamon, Barely Bronze, Fuchsia, Heather, Inca Bronze, Mad About Mauve, Magenta, Neways Red, Raspberry, Ruby Red, Soft Shell Pink, Vegas Pink, Watermelon*
Camphor	**Nail Enamels:** *Carmel, Cinnamon, Barely Bronze, Fuchsia, Heather, Inca Bronze, Mad About Mauve, Magenta, Neways Red, Raspberry, Ruby Red, Soft Shell Pink, Vegas Pink, Watermelon, Top and Base Coat*
Candelilla cera (candelilla wax)	**Nail Care:** *Nail Gels*
Carnauba wax	**Lipsticks:** *Carmel, Cinnamon, Barely Bronze, Fuchsia, Heather, Inca Bronze, Mad About Mauve, Magenta, Neways Red, Raspberry, Ruby Red, Soft Shell Pink, Vegas Pink, Watermelon* **Mascaras:** *Charcoal, Jet Black*
Cera alba (beeswax)	**Lipsticks:** *Carmel, Cinnamon, Barely Bronze, Fuchsia, Heather, Inca Bronze, Mad About Mauve, Magenta, Neways Red, Raspberry, Ruby Red, Soft Shell Pink, Vegas Pink, Watermelon*
Cetearyl alcohol	**Foundations:** *Almond, Dark Bronze, Dark Mocha, Honey, Peach, Porcelain* **Lipsticks:** *Carmel, Cinnamon, Barely Bronze, Fuchsia, Heather, Inca Bronze, Mad About Mauve, Magenta, Neways Red, Raspberry, Ruby Red, Soft Shell Pink, Vegas Pink, Watermelon*
Cetearyl glucoside	**Lipsticks:** *Barely Bronze, Carmel, Cinnamon, Fuchsia, Heather, Inca Bronze, Mad About Mauve, Magenta, Neways Red, Raspberry, Ruby Red, Soft Shell Pink, Vegas Pink, Watermelon*
Cetyl alcohol	**Foundations:** *Almond, Dark Bronze, Dark Mocha, Honey, Peach, Porcelain*
Cetyl dimethicone	**Foundations:** *Almond, Dark Bronze, Dark Mocha, Honey, Peach, Porcelain* **Lipsticks:** *Carmel, Cinnamon, Barely Bronze, Fuchsia, Heather, Inca Bronze, Mad About Mauve, Magenta, Neways Red, Raspberry, Ruby Red, Soft Shell Pink, Vegas Pink, Watermelon* **Mascaras:** *Charcoal, Jet Black*
Cetyl ester	**Foundations:** *Almond, Dark Bronze, Dark Mocha, Honey, Peach, Porcelain*
Cetyl laurate	**Lip Pencil:** *Wild Cherry* **Eye Pencils:** *Autumn, Silver Fox*
Chamomile oil	**Lip Pencil:** *Soft Cinnamon* **Eye Pencils:** *Dark Sable, Midnight Ebony, Silver Fox*
Chloroxylenol	**Nail Care:** *Nail Enhancer*
Chocolate flavour	**Lipsticks:** *Barely Bronze, Carmel, Cinnamon, Inca Bronze*

Cross linked elastin	**Blushes**: *Autumn Glow, Carnation, Rose Pink, Warm Peach, Tawny, Terracotta* **Eye Shadows**: *Brown, Brown Suede, Charcoal, Chocolate, Chocolate Mousse, Cinnamon Spray, Dark Tan, Grey Stone, Light Russet, Misty Grey, Natural Pink, Ochre, Plum Crazy, Russet, Sand, Soft Brown, Natural, Rich Sand, Soft Pink, White Essence* **Facial Powders**: *Honeytone, Translucent*
Cyanoacrylate ester	**Nail Care**: *Nail Glue*
[D&C Red #30 lake]	**Blushes**: *Peach, Rose Pink* **Eye Shadows**: *Natural, Natural Pink, Soft Pink, White Essence* **Lipsticks**: *Barely Bronze, Cinnamon, Fuchsia, Inca Bronze, Magenta, Raspberry, Ruby Red, Soft Shell Pink, Vegas Pink, Watermelon*
[D&C Red #33 Al lake]	**Lipsticks**: *Barely Bronze, Inca Bronze, Raspberry, Vegas Pink*
[D&C Red #34 Ca lake]	**Nail Enamels**: *Barely Bronze, Carmel, Cinnamon, Fuchsia, Heather, Mad About Mauve, Raspberry, Soft Shell Pink, Watermelon*
[D&C Red #6 Ba lake]	**Lipstick**: *Mad About Mauve* **Nail Enamels**: *Fuchsia, Neways Red, Raspberry, Ruby Red, Vegas Pink*
[D&C Red #7 Ca lake]	**Eye Shadows**: *Plum Crazy* **Nail Enamels**: *Fuchsia*
[D&C Red #7 Ba lake]	**Nail Enamel**: *Vegas Pink*
[D&C Red #7 Ca lake]	**Blushes**: *Carnation, Peach, Rose Pink, Terracotta* **Eye Shadows**: *Plum Crazy, Soft Pink* **Lipsticks**: *Barely Bronze , Carmel, Fuchsia, Heather, Mad About Mauve, Neways Red, Raspberry, Ruby Red, Soft Shell Pink, Vegas Pink, Watermelon* **Nail Enamels**: *Fuchsia, Inca Bronze, Magenta, Neways Red, Raspberry, Ruby Red, Soft Shell Pink, Watermelon*
[D&C Red #7 lake]	**Eye Shadows**: *Natural* **Lip Pencils**: *Wild Cherry*
[D&C Yellow #5 Al lake]	**Lipsticks**: *Barely Bronze, Carmel, Fuchsia, Inca Bronze, Soft Shell Pink, Vegas Pink, Watermelon*
Deionised cold water	**Foundations**: *Almond, Dark Bronze, Dark Mocha, Honey, Peach, Porcelain* **Mascaras**: *Charcoal, Jet Black*
[Dibutyl pthalate]	**Nail Enamels**: *Barely Bronze, Carmel, Cinnamon, Fuchsia, Heather, Inca Bronze, Mad About Mauve, Magenta, Neways Red, Raspberry, Ruby Red, Soft Shell Pink, Vegas Pink, Watermelon, Top and Base Coat*
Diisopropyl adipate	**Blushes**: *Autumn Glow, Carnation, Peach, Rose Pink, Tawny, Terracotta* **Eye Shadows**: *Brown, Brown Suede, Charcoal, Chocolate, Chocolate Mousse, Cinnamon Spray, Dark Tan, Grey Stone, Light Russet, Misty Grey, Natural, Natural Pink, Ochre, Plum Crazy, Rich Sand, Russet, Sand, Soft Brown, Soft Pink, White Essence* **Lipsticks**: *Barely Bronze, Carmel, Cinnamon, Fuchsia, Heather, Inca Bronze, Mad About Mauve, Magenta, Neways Red, Raspberry, Ruby Red, Soft Shell Pink, Vegas*
Dimethicone copolyol (beeswax)	**Foundations**: *Almond, Dark Bronze, Dark Mocha, Honey, Peach, Porcelain* **Lipsticks**: *Barely Bronze, Carmel, Cinnamon, Fuchsia, Heather, Inca Bronze, Mad About Mauve, Magenta, Neways Red, Raspberry, Ruby Red, Soft Shell Pink, Vegas Pink, Watermelon*
Ethyl acetate	**Nail Enamels**: *Barely Bronze, Carmel, Cinnamon, Fuchsia, Heather, Inca Bronze, Mad About Mauve, Magenta, Neways Red, Raspberry, Ruby Red, Soft Shell Pink, Vegas Pink, Watermelon, Top and Base Coat* **Nail System**: *Cleansing Solution*
Ethyl alcohol	**Nail Enamels**: *Barely Bronze, Carmel, Cinnamon, Fuchsia, Heather, Inca Bronze, Mad About Mauve, Magenta, Neways Red, Raspberry, Ruby Red, Soft Shell Pink, Vegas Pink, Watermelon*
[FD&C Yellow #5 Al lake]	**Blushes**: *Carnation, Peach, Rose Pink* **Eye Shadows**: *Cinnamon Spray, Natural, Soft Pink* **Nail Enamels**: *Barely Bronze, Cinnamon, Fuchsia, Inca Bronze, Magenta, Neways Red, Raspberry, Ruby Red, Soft Shell Pink, Vegas Pink, Watermelon*
Ferric ferrocyanide	**Eye Pencils**: *Midnight Ebony*
Ginkgo biloba extract	**Nail Care**: *Nail Enhancer*
Glucose/glucose oxidase/lactoperoxidase	**Foundations**: *Almond, Dark Bronze, Dark Mocha, Honey, Peach, Porcelain* **Mascaras**: *Charcoal, Jet Black*
Glyceryl abietate	**Eye Pencils**: *Dark Sable, Midnight Ebony* **Lip Pencils**: *Soft Cinnamon, Wild Cherry*
Glyceryl caprate	**Foundations**: *Almond, Dark Bronze, Dark Mocha, Honey, Peach, Porcelain*
Glyceryl caprate (coconut extract)	**Mascaras**: *Charcoal, Jet Black*
Grapefruit powder	**Blushes**: *Autumn Glow, Carnation, Rose Pink, Warm Peach, Tawny, Terracotta* **Eye Shadows**: *Brown, Brown Suede, Charcoal, Chocolate, Chocolate Mousse, Cinnamon Spray, Dark Tan, Grey Stone, Light Russet, Misty Grey, Natural Pink, Ochre, Plum Crazy, Russet, Sand, Soft Brown, Natural, Rich Sand, Soft Pink, White Essence* **Facial Powders**: *Honeytone, Translucent*
Hydrogenated castor oil	**Eye Pencils**: *Dark Sable, Midnight Ebony* **Lip Pencils**: *Soft Cinnamon*
Hydrogenated coco-glycerides	**Eye Pencils**: *Autumn, Dark Sable, Midnight Ebony, Silver Fox* **Lip Pencils**: *Soft Cinnamon, Wild Cherry*
Hydrogenated palm oil	**Eye Pencils**: *Autumn, Silver Fox* **Lip Pencils**: *Wild Cherry*
Hydrogenated rice bran wax	**Eye Pencils**: *Dark Sable, Midnight Ebony* **Lip Pencils**: *Soft Cinnamon*
Hydrolyzed mucopolysaccharides	**Nail Care**: *Nail Enhancer*
Hydroxyethycellulose	**Foundations**: *Almond, Dark Bronze, Dark Mocha, Honey, Peach, Porcelain* **Mascaras**: *Charcoal, Jet Black*

Hydroxy-2-methyl-1-phenyl-1-propanone	**Nail Care:** *Nail Gels*
Iron oxide	**Blushes:** *Autumn Glow, Peach, Terracotta* **Eye Shadows:** *Brown, Brown Suede, Charcoal, Chocolate, Chocolate Mousse, Cinnamon Spray, Dark Tan, Grey Stone, Light Russet, Misty Grey, Natural, Natural Pink, Ochre, Plum Crazy, Rich Sand, Russet, Sand, Soft Brown, Soft Pink, White Essence* **Facial Powders:** *Honeytone, Translucent* **Foundations:** *Almond, Dark Bronze, Dark Mocha, Honey, Peach, Porcelain* **Lipsticks:** *Barely Bronze, Carmel, Cinnamon, Heather, Inca Bronze, Mad About Mauve, Soft Shell Pink, Watermelon* **Mascaras:** *Charcoal, Jet Black* **Nail Enamels:** *Barely Bronze, Carmel, Cinnamon, Fuchsia, Heather, Inca Bronze, Mad About Mauve, Raspberry, Soft Shell Pink, Watermelon*
Isopropyl palmitate	**Lip Pencils:** *Wild Cherry*
Isostearyl neopentanoate	**Blushes:** *Autumn Glow, Carnation, Rose Pink, Warm Peach, Tawny, Terracotta* **Eye Shadows:** *Brown, Brown Suede, Charcoal, Chocolate, Chocolate Mousse, Cinnamon Spray, Dark Tan, Grey Stone, Light Russet, Misty Grey, Natural Pink, Russet, Sand, Soft Brown, Natural, Rich Sand, Soft Pink, White Essence*
Jojoba esters	**Blushes:** *Autumn Glow, Carnation, Peach, Rose Pink, Tawny, Terracotta* **Eye Shadows:** *Brown, Brown Suede, Charcoal, Chocolate, Chocolate Mousse, Cinnamon Spray, Dark Tan, Grey Stone, Light Russet, Misty Grey, Natural, Natural Pink, Ochre, Plum Crazy, Rich Sand, Russet, Sand, Soft Brown, Soft Pink, White Essence* **Lipsticks:** *Barely Bronze, Carmel, Cinnamon, Fuchsia, Heather, Inca Bronze, Mad About Mauve, Magenta, Neways Red, Raspberry, Ruby Red, Soft Shell Pink, Vegas*
Lanolin	**Lip Pencils:** *Wild Cherry*
Lauroyl lysine	**Facial Powders:** *Honeytone, Translucent*
Lauryl palmitate	**Eye Pencils:** *Dark Sable, Midnight Ebony* **Lip Pencils:** *Soft Cinnamon*
Lysine PCA	**Foundations:** *Almond, Dark Bronze, Dark Mocha, Honey, Peach, Porcelain*
Magnesium carbonate	**Blushes:** *Autumn Glow, Carnation, Rose Pink, Warm Peach, Tawny, Terracotta* **Eye Shadows:** *Brown, Brown Suede, Charcoal, Chocolate, Chocolate Mousse, Cinnamon Spray, Dark Tan, Grey Stone, Light Russet, Misty Grey, Natural Pink, Ochre, Plum Crazy, Russet, Sand, Soft Brown, Natural, Rich Sand, Soft Pink, White Essence*
Magnesium silicate	**Mascaras:** *Charcoal, Jet Black*
Magnesium stearate	**Blushes:** *Autumn Glow, Carnation, Rose Pink, Warm Peach, Tawny, Terracotta* **Eye Shadows:** *Brown, Brown Suede, Charcoal, Chocolate, Chocolate Mousse, Cinnamon Spray, Dark Tan, Grey Stone, Light Russet, Misty Grey, Natural Pink, Ochre, Plum Crazy, Russet, Sand, Soft Brown, Natural, Rich Sand, Soft Pink, White Essence*
Mandarin flavour	**Lipsticks:** *Fuchsia, Mad About Mauve, Magenta, Neways Red, Raspberry, Ruby Red, Soft Shell Pink, Vegas Pink, Watermelon*
Mandarin oil	**Lipsticks:** *Fuchsia, Mad About Mauve, Magenta, Neways Red, Raspberry, Ruby Red, Soft Shell Pink, Vegas Pink, Watermelon*
Methylsilanol hydroxyproline	**Blushes:** *Autumn Glow, Carnation, Peach, Rose Pink, Tawny, Terracotta* **Eye Shadows:** *Brown, Brown Suede, Charcoal, Chocolate, Chocolate Mousse, Cinnamon Spray, Dark Tan, Grey Stone, Light Russet Misty Grey, Natural, Natural Pink, Ochre, Plum Crazy, Rich Sand, Russet, Sand Soft Brown, Soft Pink, White Essence*
Mica	**Blushes:** *Terracotta* **Facial Powders:** *Honeytone, Translucent* **Nail Enamels:** *Raspberry, Ruby Red, Soft Shell Pink, Watermelon*
Mica/iron oxide	**Lipsticks:** *Barely Bronze, Carmel, Heather, Inca Bronze, Magenta* **Nail Enamel:** *Barely Bronze, Heather*
Mica/iron oxide/titanium	**Nail Enamel:** *Magenta*
Mica/lauroyl lysine	**Blushes:** *Autumn Glow, Carnation, Peach, Rose Pink, Tawny, Terracotta* **Eye Shadows:** *Brown, Brown Suede, Charcoal, Chocolate, Chocolate Mousse, Dark Tan, Grey Stone, Light Russet, Misty Grey, Natural, Natural Pink, Ochre, Plum Crazy, Rich Sand, Russet, Sand, Soft Brown, Soft Pink, White Essence* **Foundations:** *Almond, Dark Bronze, Dark Mocha, Honey, Peach, Porcelain* **Lipsticks:** *Raspberry* **Nail Enamels:** *Cinnamon, Fuchsia, Inca Bronze, Neways Red*
Myristyl lactate	**Mascaras:** *Charcoal, Jet Black*
Myrrh extract	**Nail Care:** *Nail Enhancer*
N-butyl acetate	**Nail Enamels:** *Barely Bronze, Carmel, Cinnamon, Fuchsia, Heather, Inca Bronze, Mad About Mauve, Magenta, Neways Red, Raspberry, Ruby Red, Soft Shell Pink, Vegas Pink, Watermelon, Top and Base Coat*
Neem seed oil	**Foundations:** *Almond, Dark Bronze, Dark Mocha, Honey, Peach, Porcelain* **Lipsticks:** *Barely Bronze, Carmel, Cinnamon, Fuchsia, Heather, Inca Bronze, Mad About Mauve, Magenta, Neways Red, Raspberry, Ruby Red, Soft Shell Pink, Vegas Pink, Watermelon* **Mascaras:** *Charcoal, Jet Black*
Niacinamide	**Nail Care:** *Nail Enhancer*
Nitrocellulose	**Nail Enamels:** *Barely Bronze, Carmel, Cinnamon, Fuchsia, Heather, Inca Bronze, Mad About Mauve, Magenta, Neways Red, Raspberry, Ruby Red, Soft Shell Pink, Vegas Pink, Watermelon, Top and Base Coat*
Nylon	**Blushes:** *Autumn Glow, Carnation, Peach, Rose Pink, Tawny, Terracotta* **Eye Shadows:** *Brown, Brown Suede, Charcoal, Chocolate, Chocolate Mousse, Cinnamon Spray, Dark Tan, Grey Stone, Light Russet Misty Grey, Natural, Natural Pink, Ochre, Plum Crazy, Rich Sand, Russet, Sand Soft Brown, Soft Pink, White Essence*
Oat flour	**Blushes:** *Autumn Glow, Carnation, Rose Pink, Warm Peach, Tawny, Terracotta* **Eye Shadows:** *Brown, Brown Suede, Charcoal, Chocolate, Chocolate Mousse, Cinnamon Spray, Dark Tan, Grey Stone, Light Russet, Misty Grey, Natural Pink, Ochre, Plum Crazy, Russet, Sand, Soft Brown, Natural, Rich Sand, Soft Pink, White Essence* **Facial Powders:** *Honeytone, Translucent*

Ingredient	Products
Octyl methoxycinnamate	**Blushes:** *Autumn Glow, Carnation, Peach, Rose Pink, Tawny, Terracotta* **Eye Shadows:** *Brown, Brown Suede, Charcoal, Chocolate, Chocolate Mousse, Cinnamon Spray, Dark Tan, Grey Stone, Light Russet, Misty Grey, Natural, Natural Pink, Ochre, Plum Crazy, Rich Sand, Russet, Sand, Soft Brown, Soft Pink, White Essence* **Foundations:** *Almond, Dark Bronze, Dark Mocha, Honey, Peach, Porcelain* **Lipsticks:** *Barely Bronze, Carmel, Cinnamon, Fuchsia, Heather, Inca Bronze, Mad About Mauve, Magenta, Neways Red, Raspberry, Ruby Red, Soft Shell Pink, Vegas Pink, Watermelon*
Octyldodecanol	**Lipsticks:** *Barely Bronze, Carmel, Cinnamon, Fuchsia, Heather, Inca Bronze, Mad About Mauve, Magenta, Neways Red, Raspberry, Ruby Red, Soft Shell Pink, Vegas Pink, Watermelon*
Oleyl alcohol	**Lipsticks:** *Barely Bronze, Carmel, Cinnamon, Fuchsia, Heather, Inca Bronze, Mad About Mauve, Magenta, Neways Red, Raspberry, Ruby Red, Soft Shell Pink, Vegas Pink, Watermelon*
Panthenol	**Blushes:** *Autumn Glow, Carnation, Rose Pink, Warm Peach, Tawny, Terracotta* **Eye Shadows:** *Brown, Brown Suede, Charcoal, Chocolate, Chocolate Mousse, Cinnamon Spray, Dark Tan, Grey Stone, Light Russet, Misty Grey, Natural Pink, Ochre, Plum Crazy, Russet, Sand, Soft Brown, Natural, Rich Sand, Soft Pink, White Essence* **Facial Powders:** *Honeytone, Translucent* **Mascaras:** *Charcoal, Jet Black*
Perfluoropolymethylisopropyl ether	**Blushes:** *Autumn Glow, Carnation, Peach, Rose Pink, Tawny, Terracotta* **Eye Shadows:** *Brown, Brown Suede, Charcoal, Chocolate, Chocolate Mousse, Cinnamon Spray, Dark Tan, Grey Stone, Light Russet, Misty Grey, Natural, Natural Pink, Ochre, Plum Crazy, Rich Sand, Russet, Sand, Soft Brown, Soft Pink, White Essence* **Lipsticks:** *Barely Bronze, Carmel, Cinnamon, Fuchsia, Heather, Inca Bronze, Mad About Mauve, Magenta, Neways Red, Raspberry, Ruby Red, Soft Shell Pink, Vegas*
Phenoxyethanol	**Nail Care:** *Nail Enhancer*
Polyester acrylate oligomer	**Nail Care:** *Nail Gels*
Polyester acrylates	**Nail Care:** *Ultra High Gloss/White Tip Gel*
Propylene carbonate	**Lip Pencils:** *Wild Cherry Lip Pencil*
PVP	**Mascaras:** *Charcoal, Jet Black*
PVP/eicosene copolymer	**Mascaras:** *Charcoal, Jet Black*
PVP/hexadecene copolymer	**Blushes:** *Autumn Glow, Carnation, Peach, Rose Pink, Tawny, Terracotta* **Eye Shadows:** *Brown, Brown Suede, Charcoal, Chocolate, Chocolate Mousse, Cinnamon Spray, Dark Tan, Grey Stone, Light Russet Misty Grey, Natural, Natural Pink, Ochre, Plum Crazy, Rich Sand, Russet, Sand Soft Brown, Soft Pink, White Essence*
Reactive polyester diacrylate	**Nail Care:** *Nail Gels*
Red iron oxide	**Blushes:** *Tawny* **Eye Pencils:** *Autumn, Dark Sable, Silver Fox* **Lip Pencils:** *Soft Cinnamon, Wild Cherry* **Nail Enamels:** *Cinnamon*
Rose hip oil	**Blushes:** *Autumn Glow, Carnation, Peach, Rose Pink, Tawny, Terracotta* **Eye Shadows:** *Brown, Brown Suede, Charcoal, Chocolate, Chocolate Mousse, Cinnamon Spray, Dark Tan, Grey Stone, Light Russet Misty Grey, Natural, Natural Pink, Ochre, Plum Crazy, Rich Sand, Russet, Sand Soft Brown, Soft Pink, White Essence*
SD Alcohol 40B	**Nail Care:** *Cleansing Solution*
Silica	**Eye Pencils:** *Dark Sable, Midnight Ebony* **Lip Pencils:** *Soft Cinnamon*
Silk amino acids	**Blushes:** *Autumn Glow, Carnation, Rose Pink, Warm Peach, Tawny, Terracotta* **Eye Shadows:** *Brown, Brown Suede, Charcoal, Chocolate, Chocolate Mousse, Cinnamon Spray, Dark Tan, Grey Stone, Light Russet, Misty Grey, Natural Pink, Ochre, Plum Crazy, Russet, Sand, Soft Brown, Natural, Rich Sand, Soft Pink, White Essence* **Foundations:** *Almond, Dark Bronze, Dark Mocha, Honey, Peach, Porcelain* **Facial Powders:** *Honeytone, Translucent* **Mascaras:** *Charcoal, Jet Black*
Sodium PCA	**Foundations:** *Almond, Dark Bronze, Dark Mocha, Honey, Peach, Porcelain*
Stearalkonium hectorite	**Nail Enamels:** *Barely Bronze, Carmel, Cinnamon, Fuchsia, Heather, Inca Bronze, Mad About Mauve, Magenta, Neways Red, Raspberry, Ruby Red, Soft Shell Pink, Vegas Pink, Watermelon*
Stearyl heptanoate	**Eye Pencils:** *Dark Sable, Midnight Ebony* **Lip Pencils:** *Soft Cinnamon*
Sunflower seed oil (Helianthus annus)	**Foundations:** *Almond, Dark Bronze, Dark Mocha, Honey, Peach, Porcelain* **Lipsticks:** *Barely Bronze, Carmel, Cinnamon, Fuchsia, Heather, Inca Bronze, Mad About Mauve, Magenta, Neways Red, Raspberry, Ruby Red, Soft Shell Pink, Vegas Pink, Watermelon*
Talc	**Lip Pencils:** *Soft Cinnamon, Wild Cherry*
Titanium dioxide	**Eye Pencils:** *Autumn, Silver Fox* **Lip Pencils:** *Soft Cinnamon*
Tocopheryl acetate	**Eye Pencils:** *Autumn, Dark Sable, Midnight Ebony, Silver Fox* **Lip Pencils:** *Soft Cinnamon, Wild Cherry* **Lipsticks:** *Barely Bronze, Carmel, Cinnamon, Fuchsia, Heather, Inca Bronze, Mad About Mauve, Magenta, Neways Red, Raspberry, Ruby Red, Soft Shell Pink, Vegas Pink, Watermelon* **Mascaras:** *Charcoal, Jet Black* **Nail Enamels:** *Barely Bronze, Carmel, Cinnamon, Fuchsia, Heather, Inca Bronze, Mad About Mauve, Magenta, Neways Red, Raspberry, Ruby Red, Soft Shell Pink, Vegas*
Toluene	**Nail Care:** *Nail Whitener*
Tricontanyl PVP	**Lipsticks:** *Barely Bronze, Carmel, Cinnamon, Fuchsia, Heather, Inca Bronze, Mad About Mauve, Magenta, Neways Red, Raspberry, Ruby Red, Soft Shell Pink, Vegas Pink, Watermelon*

Tridecyl neopentanoate	**Foundations:** *Almond, Dark Bronze, Dark Mocha, Honey, Peach, Porcelain*
Tripropylene glycol diacrylate	**Nail Care:** *Nail Whitener*
Ultramarine	**Blushes:** *Peach, Rose Pink* **Eye Shadows:** *Charcoal, Grey Stone, Light Russet, Natural, Plum Crazy, Russet*
Umber 7065	**Blushes:** *Tawny*
Vanilla	**Lipsticks:** *Heather*
Water (purified)	**Nail Care:** *Cleansing Solution, Nail Enhancer*
Yellow iron oxide	**Eye Pencils:** *Autumn, Dark Sable, Silver Fox*
Zinc dimethicone	**Facial Powders:** *Honeytone, Translucent* **Lipsticks:** *Barely Bronze, Carmel, Cinnamon, Fuchsia, Heather, Inca Bronze, Mad About Mauve, Magenta, Neways Red, Raspberry, Ruby Red, Soft Shell Pink, Vegas Pink, Watermelon*
Zinc oxide	**Blushes**: *Autumn Glow, Carnation, Rose Pink, Warm Peach, Tawny, Terracotta* **Eye Shadows**: *Brown, Brown Suede, Charcoal, Chocolate, Chocolate Mousse, Cinnamon Spray, Dark Tan, Grey Stone, Light Russet, Misty Grey, Natural Pink, Ochre, Plum Crazy, Russet, Sand, Soft Brown, Natural, Rich Sand, Soft Pink, White Essence* **Foundations**: *Almond, Dark Bronze, Dark Mocha, Honey, Peach, Porcelain* **Facial Powders**: *Honeytone, Translucent* **Mascaras**: *Charcoal, Jet Black*

Total Ingredients: 121

Designations

[ ] -- Brackets connote that the enclosed ingredient is in the process of being phased out.

Table 6.4: INGREDIENTS COMMON TO NEWAYS PERSONAL CARE AND COSMETIC PRODUCTS

Allantoin
Betaglucan
Calcium pantothenate
Candelilla cera (candelilla wax)
Carnauba wax
Cetearyl alcohol
Cetearyl glucoside
Cetyl alcohol
Chloroxylenol
Dimethicone copolyol (beeswax)
Ginkgo biloba extract
Hydrolyzed mucopolysaccharides
Hydroxyethycellulose
Isostearyl neopentanoate
Myrrh extract
Niacinamide
Panthenol
Perfluoropolymethylisopropyl ether
Phenoxyethanol
PVP
PVP/hexadecene copolymer
Rose hip oil
SD Alcohol 40B
Silk amino acids
Sodium PCA
Titanium dioxide
Water (purified)
Zinc oxide

Total Common Ingredients: 28

Table 6.5: INDEX OF NEWAYS COSMETICS and PERSONAL CARE CATEGORIES,
CLASSIFIED BY PRODUCTS, INGREDIENTS, USAGE AND COUNTRY OF AVAILABILITY

COSMETICS (*Leslie DeeAnn*)

Category	Product	Ingredient

A. Blushes
Product used by:
  W
	1. Autumn Glow
	Product unavailable in:
	  KR
		Magnesium stearate
		Iron oxide
		Nylon
		Mica/lauroyl lysine
		Magnesium carbonate
		Octyl methoxycinnamate
		Oat flour
		Diisopropyl adipate
		Grapefruit powder
		Isostearyl neopentanoate
		Cross linked elastin
		Avocado oil unsaponifiables
		Silk amino acids
		Perfluoropolymethylisopropyl ether
		Jojoba esters
		Boron nitride
		Rose hip oil
		PVP/hexadecene copolymer
		Zinc oxide
		Methylsilanol hydroxyproline
		Betaglucan
		Panthenol

	2. Carnation *Product unavailable in:* KR	Magnesium stearate Zinc oxide Nylon Mica/lauroyl lysine Magnesium carbonate Octyl methoxycinnamate Oat flour Diisopropyl adipate Isostearyl neopentanoate Grapefruit powder Cross linked elastin [FD&C Yellow #5 Al lake] Avocado oil unsaponifiables Silk amino acids Perfluoropolymethylisopropyl ether Jojoba esters Boron nitride Rose hip oil PVP/hexadecene copolymer [D&C Red #7 Ca lake] Methylsilanol hydroxyproline Betaglucan Panthenol
	3. Peach *Product unavailable in:* KR	Magnesium stearate Zinc oxide Nylon Mica/lauroyl lysine Magnesium carbonate [FD&C Yellow #5 Al lake] [D&C Red #7 Ca lake] Octyl methoxycinnamate Oat flour Diisopropyl adipate Isostearyl neopentanoate Grapefruit powder Cross linked elastin Avocado oil unsaponifiables Iron oxide Silk amino acids Perfluoropolymethylisopropyl ether Ultramarine [D&C Red #30 lake] Jojoba esters Boron nitride

Category	Product	Ingredient
		Rose hip oil
		PVP/hexadecene copolymer
		Methylsilanol hydroxyproline
		Betaglucan
		Panthenol
	4. Rose Pink *Product unavailable in:* KR	Magnesium stearate
		Zinc oxide
		Nylon
		Mica/lauroyl lysine
		Magnesium carbonate
		[FD&C Yellow #5 Al lake]
		Octyl methoxycinnamate
		Oat flour
		Diisopropyl adipate
		Isostearyl neopentanoate
		Grapefruit powder
		Cross linked elastin
		Avocado oil unsaponifiables
		Silk amino acids
		Perfluoropolymethylisopropyl ether
		[D&C Red #7 Ca lake]
		[D&C Red #30 lake]
		Jojoba esters
		Boron nitride
		Rose hip oil
		Ultramarine
		PVP/hexadecene copolymer
		Methylsilanol hydroxyproline
		Betaglucan
		Panthenol
	5. Tawny *Product unavailable in:* KR, ML	Magnesium stearate
		Zinc oxide
		Nylon
		Mica/lauroyl lysine
		Red Iron Oxide
		Magnesium carbonate
		Octyl methoxycinnamate
		Umber 7065
		Oat flour
		Grapefruit powder
		Diisopropyl adipate
		Isostearyl neopentanoate
		Cross linked elastin
		Avocado oil unsaponifiables
		Silk amino acids
		Perfluoropolymethylisopropyl ether
		Jojoba esters
		Rose hip oil
		Boron nitride
		PVP/hexadecene copolymer
		Methylsilanol hydroxyproline
		Betaglucan
		Panthenol
	6. Terracotta *Product unavailable in:* KR, ML	Magnesium stearate
		Iron oxide
		Mica
		Zinc oxide
		Nylon
		Mica/lauroyl lysine
		Octyl methoxycinnamate
		Magnesium carbonate
		[D&C Red #7 Ca lake]
		Grapefruit powder
		Diisopropyl adipate
		Isostearyl neopentanoate
		Oat flour
		Avocado oil unsaponifiables
		Silk amino acids

Category	Product	Ingredient
		Cross linked elastin
		Perfluoropolymethylisopropyl ether
		Jojoba esters
		Rose hip oil
		PVP/hexadecene copolymer
		Boron nitride
		Methylsilanol hydroxyproline
		Betaglucan
		Panthenol

B. Foundations
Product used by:
   W, M
	1. Almond
	Product unavailable in:
	   KR
		Deionized cold water

		Tridecyl neopentanoate
		Zinc oxide
		Acetylated lanolin
		Sunflower seed oil
		Cetyl dimethicone
		Glyceryl caprate
		Octyl methoxycinnamate
		Iron oxide
		Sodium PCA
		Glucose/glucose oxidase/lactoperoxidase
		Mica/lauroyl lysine
		Dimethicone copolyol (beeswax)
		Lysine PCA
		Neem seed oil
		Silk amino acids
		Cetyl alcohol
		Cetearyl alcohol
		Cetyl esters
		Hydroxyethylcellulose
	2. Dark Bronze *Product unavailable in:* KR	Deionized cold water
		Tridecyl neopentanoate
		Zinc oxide
		Acetylated lanolin
		Sunflower seed oil
		Cetyl dimethicone
		Iron oxide
		Octyl methoxycinnamate
		Dimethicone copolyol (beeswax)
		Glucose/glucose oxidase/lactoperoxidase
		Glyceryl caprate
		Mica/lauroyl lysine
		Sodium PCA
		Lysine PCA
		Neem seed oil
		Silk amino acids
		Cetyl alcohol
		Cetearyl alcohol
		Cetyl ester
		Hydroxyethylcellulose
	3. Dark Mocha *Product unavailable in:* KR	Deionized cold water
		Iron oxide
		Tridecyl neopentanoate
		Acetylated lanolin
		Zinc oxide
		Sunflower seed oil
		Cetyl dimethicone
		Octyl methoxycinnamate
		Dimethicone copolyol (beeswax)
		Glucose/glucose oxidase/lactoperoxidase
		Mica/lauroyl lysine
		Sodium PCA
		Lysine PCA
		Neem seed oil
		Silk amino acids
		Cetyl alcohol
		Cetearyl alcohol
		Cetyl ester
		Hydroxyethylcellulose

Category	Product	Ingredient
	4. Honey *Product unavailable in:* KR	Deionized cold water
		Sunflower seed oil
		Tridecyl neopentanoate
		Zinc oxide
		Acetylated lanolin
		Cetyl dimethicone
		Iron oxide
		Octyl methoxycinnamate
		Dimethicone copolyol (beeswax)
		Glucose/glucose oxidase/lactoperoxidase
		Glyceryl caprate
		Mica/lauroyl lysine
		Sodium PCA
		Lysine PCA
		Neem seed oil
		Silk amino acids
		Cetyl alcohol
		Cetearyl alcohol
		Cetyl esters
		Hydroxyethylcellulose
	5. Peach *Product unavailable in:* KR	Deionized cold water
		Tridecyl neopentanoate
		Zinc oxide
		Acetylated lanolin
		Sunflower seed oil
		Cetyl dimethicone
		Octyl methoxycinnamate
		Dimethicone copolyol (beeswax)
		Glucose/glucose oxidase/lactoperoxidase
		Glyceryl caprate
		Mica/lauroyl lysine
		Sodium PCA
		Iron oxide
		Lysine PCA
		Neem seed oil
		Silk amino acids
		Cetyl alcohol
		Cetyl ester
		Cetearyl alcohol
		Hydroxyethylcellulose
	6. Porcelain *Product unavailable in:* KR	Deionized cold water
		Tridecyl neopentanoate
		Zinc oxide
		Acetylated lanolin
		Sunflower seed oil
		Cetyl dimethicone
		Mica/lauroyl lysine
		Octyl methoxycinnamate
		Glucose/glucose oxidase/lactoperoxidase
		Glyceryl caprate
		Sodium PCA
		Iron oxide
		Lysine PCA
		Neem seed oil
		Silk amino acids
		Cetyl alcohol
		Cetearyl alcohol
		Cetyl esters
		Dimethicone copolyol (beeswax)
		Hydroxyethylcellulose
C. Facial Powders *Product used by:* W	1. Honeytone *Product unavailable in:* KR	Mica
		Oat flour
		Magnesium stearate
		Iron oxide
		Grapefruit powder
		Panthenol
		Zinc dimethicone
		Silk amino acids

Category	Product	Ingredient
		Lauroyl lysine
		Betaglucan
		Cross linked elastin
	2. Translucent *Product unavailable in:* KR	Mica
		Oat flour
		Magnesium stearate
		Iron oxide
		Grapefruit powder
		Silk amino acids
		Zinc dimethicone
		Lauroyl lysine
		Betaglucan
		Panthenol
		Cross linked elastin
D. Mascara *Product used by:* W	1. Charcoal *Product unavailable in:* KR	Deionised cold water
		PVP/eicosene copolymer
		Iron oxide
		Beeswax
		PVP
		Carnauba wax
		Cetyl dimethicone
		Glyceryl caprate (coconut extract)
		Myristyl lactate
		Zinc oxide
		Glucose/glucose oxidase/lactoperoxidase
		Hydroxyethylcellulose
		Tocopheryl acetate
		Neem seed oil
		Magnesium silicate
		Panthenol
		Silk amino acids
	2. Jet Black *Product unavailable in:* KR	Deionised cold water
		PVP/eicosene copolymer
		Beeswax
		Iron oxide
		PVP
		Carnauba wax
		Cetyl dimethicone
		Glyceryl caprate (coconut extract)
		Myristyl lactate
		Glucose/glucose oxidase/lactoperoxidase
		Hydroxyethycellulose
		Tocopheryl acetate
		Neem seed oil
		Magnesium silicate
		Panthenol
		Zinc oxide
		Silk amino acids
E. Eye Shadows, Highlighters and Eyeliner Pencils *Product used by:* W	1. Brown *Product unavailable in:* KR, UK	Magnesium stearate
		Iron oxide
		Mica/lauroyl lysine
		Nylon
		Zinc oxide
		Magnesium carbonate
		Octyl methoxycinnamate
		Oat flour
		Grapefruit powder
		Diisopropyl adipate
		Isostearyl neopentanoate
		Cross linked elastin
		Avocado oil unsaponifiables
		Silk amino acids
		Perfluoropolymethylisopropyl ether
		Jojoba esters
		Boron nitride
		Rose hip oil

Category	Product	Ingredient
		PVP/hexadecene copolymer
		Methylsilanol hydroxyproline
		Betaglucan
		Panthenol
	2. Brown Suede *Product unavailable in:* KR, UK	Iron oxide
		Magnesium stearate
		Nylon
		Mica/lauroyl lysine
		Zinc oxide
		Magnesium carbonate
		Octyl Methoxycinnamate
		Oat flour
		Grapefruit powder
		Diisopropyl adipate
		Isostearyl neopentanoate
		Cross linked elastin
		Silk amino acids
		Perfluoropolymethylisopropyl ether
		Avocado oil unsaponifiables
		Boron nitride
		Jojoba esters
		Rose hip oil
		PVP/hexadecene copolymer
		Methylsilanol hydroxyproline
		Betaglucan
		Panthenol
	3. Charcoal *Product unavailable in:* KR, UK	Magnesium stearate
		Iron oxide
		Mica/lauroyl lysine
		Nylon
		Magnesium carbonate
		Octyl Methoxycinnamate
		Oat flour
		Grapefruit powder
		Ultramarine
		Zinc oxide
		Diisopropyl adipate
		Isostearyl neopentanoate
		Cross linked elastin
		Avocado oil unsaponifiables
		Silk amino acids
		Perfluoropolymethylisopropyl ether
		Jojoba esters
		Boron nitride
		Rose hip oil
		PVP/hexadecene copolymer
		Methylsilanol hydroxyproline
		Betaglucan
		Panthenol
	4. Chocolate *Product unavailable in:* KR	Magnesium stearate
		Mica/lauroyl lysine
		Iron oxide
		Nylon
		Zinc oxide
		Magnesium carbonate
		Octyl methoxycinnamate
		Oat flour
		Grapefruit powder
		Diisopropyl adipate
		Isostearyl neopentanoate
		Cross linked elastin
		Avocado oil unsaponifiables
		Silk amino acids
		Perfluoropolymethylisopropyl ether
		Boron nitride
		Jojoba esters
		Rose hip oil
		PVP/hexadecene copolymer

Category	Product	Ingredient
		Methylsilanol hydroxyproline
		Betaglucan
		Panthenol
	5. Chocolate Mousse *Product unavailable in:* KR, UK	Magnesium stearate
		Iron oxide
		Nylon
		Mica/lauroyl lysine
		Zinc oxide
		Magnesium carbonate
		Oat flour
		Grapefruit powder
		Octyl methoxycinnamate
		Cross linked elastin
		Diisopropyl adipate
		Isostearyl neopentanoate
		Avocado oil unsaponifiables
		Silk amino acids
		Perfluoropolymethylisopropyl ether
		Boron nitride
		Jojoba esters
		Rose hip oil
		PVP/hexadecene copolymer
		Methylsilanol hydroxyproline
		Betaglucan
		Panthenol
	6. Cinnamon Spray *Product unavailable in:* KR, UK	Magnesium stearate
		Zinc oxide
		Nylon
		Magnesium carbonate
		Iron oxide
		Oat flour
		[FD&C Yellow #5 Al lake]
		Octyl Methoxycinnamate
		Grapefruit powder
		Cross linked elastin
		Diisopropyl adipate
		Isostearyl neopentanoate
		Avocado oil unsaponifiables
		Silk amino acids
		Perfluoropolymethylisopropyl ether
		Boron nitride
		Jojoba esters
		Rose hip oil
		PVP/hexadecene copolymer
		Methylsilanol hydroxyproline
		Betaglucan
		Panthenol
	7. Dark Tan *Product unavailable in:* KR, UK	Magnesium stearate
		Zinc oxide
		Mica/lauroyl lysine
		Nylon
		Iron oxide
		Magnesium carbonate
		Octyl Methoxycinnamate
		Oat flour
		Grapefruit powder
		Diisopropyl adipate
		Isostearyl neopentanoate
		Cross linked elastin
		Avocado oil unsaponifiables
		Silk amino acids
		Perfluoropolymethylisopropyl ether
		Jojoba esters
		Boron nitride
		Rose hip oil
		PVP/hexadecene copolymer
		Methylsilanol hydroxyproline
		Betaglucan

Category	Product	Ingredient
		Panthenol
	8. Grey Stone *Product unavailable in:* KR, UK	Magnesium stearate
		Iron oxide
		Nylon
		Mica/lauroyl lysine
		Oat flour
		Octyl methoxycinnamate
		Grapefruit powder
		Ultramarine
		Zinc oxide
		Cross linked elastin
		Diisopropyl adipate
		Isostearyl neopentanoate
		Avocado oil unsaponifiables
		Silk amino acids
		Perfluoropolymethylisopropyl ether
		Boron nitride
		Jojoba esters
		Rose hip oil
		PVP/hexadecene copolymer
		Methylsilanol hydroxyproline
		Betaglucan
		Panthenol
	9. Light Russet *Product unavailable in:* KR, UK	Magnesium stearate
		Iron oxide
		Nylon
		Mica/lauroyl lysine
		Ultramarine
		Zinc oxide
		Magnesium carbonate
		Oat flour
		Octyl methoxycinnamate
		Grapefruit powder
		Cross linked elastin
		Diisopropyl adipate
		Isostearyl neopentanoate
		Avocado oil unsaponifiables
		Silk amino acids
		Perfluoropolymethylisopropyl ether
		Boron nitride
		Jojoba esters
		Rose hip oil
		PVP/hexadecene copolymer
		Methylsilanol hydroxyproline
		Betaglucan
		Panthenol
	10. Misty Grey *Product unavailable in:* KR, UK	Magnesium stearate
		Nylon
		Mica/lauroyl lysine
		Magnesium carbonate
		Iron oxide
		Oat flour
		Octyl methoxycinnamate
		Grapefruit powder
		Cross linked elastin
		Diisopropyl adipate
		Isostearyl neopentanoate
		Avocado oil unsaponifiables
		Silk amino acids
		Perfluoropolymethylisopropyl ether
		Boron nitride
		Jojoba esters
		Rose hip oil
		PVP/hexadecene copolymer
		Methylsilanol hydroxyproline
		Betaglucan
		Panthenol
	11. Natural Pink	Magnesium stearate

Category	Product	Ingredient
	Product unavailable in: KR, UK	Iron oxide Mica/lauroyl lysine Nylon [D&C Red #30 lake] Magnesium carbonate Octyl methoxycinnamate Oat flour Grapefruit powder Diisopropyl adipate Isostearyl neopentanoate Iron oxide Cross linked elastin Avocado oil unsaponifiables Silk amino acids Perfluoropolymethylisopropyl ether Jojoba esters Boron nitride Rose hip oil PVP/hexadecene copolymer Methylsilanol hydroxyproline Betaglucan Panthenol
	12. Ochre *Product unavailable in:* KR	Magnesium stearate Iron oxide Mica/lauroyl lysine Nylon Zinc oxide Magnesium carbonate Octyl methoxycinnamate Oat flour Grapefruit powder Diisopropyl adipate Isostearyl neopentanoate Cross linked elastin Avocado oil unsaponifiables Silk amino acids Perfluoropolymethylisopropyl ether Boron nitride Jojoba esters Rose hip oil PVP/hexadecene copolymer Methylsilanol hydroxyproline Betaglucan Panthenol
	13. Plum Crazy *Product unavailable in:* KR, UK	Magnesium stearate Nylon Mica/lauroyl lysine Iron oxide Magnesium carbonate Oat flour Zinc oxide Octyl methoxycinnamate Grapefruit powder Cross linked elastin Diisopropyl adipate Isostearyl neopentanoate Avocado oil unsaponifiables Silk amino acids Perfluoropolymethylisopropyl ether [D&C Red # 7 Ca lake] Boron nitride Jojoba esters Rose hip oil PVP/hexadecene copolymer Ultramarine Methylsilanol hydroxyproline Betaglucan Panthenol

Category	Product	Ingredient
	14. Russet *Product unavailable in:* KR	Magnesium stearate Iron oxide Mica/lauroyl lysine Nylon Zinc oxide Ultramarine Magnesium carbonate Octyl methoxycinnamate Grapefruit powder Oat flour Diisopropyl adipate Isostearyl neopentanoate Cross linked elastin Avocado oil unsaponifiables Silk amino acids Perfluoropolymethylisopropyl ether Jojoba esters Rose hip oil Boron nitride PVP/hexadecene copolymer Methylsilanol hydroxyproline Betaglucan Panthenol
	15. Sand *Product unavailable in:* KR	Magnesium stearate Zinc oxide Mica/lauroyl lysine Iron oxide Nylon Magnesium carbonate Octyl methoxycinnamate Oat flour Grapefruit powder Diisopropyl adipate Isostearyl neopentanoate Cross linked elastin Avocado oil unsaponifiables Silk amino acids Perfluoropolymethylisopropyl ether Jojoba esters Boron nitride Rose hip oil PVP/hexadecene copolymer Methylsilanol hydroxyproline Betaglucan Panthenol
	16. Soft Brown *Product unavailable in:* KR, UK	Magnesium stearate Zinc oxide Nylon Mica/lauroyl lysine Iron oxide Magnesium carbonate Oat flour Octyl methoxycinnamate Grapefruit powder Cross linked elastin Diisopropyl adipate Isostearyl neopentanoate Avocado oil unsaponifiables Silk amino acids Perfluoropolymethylisopropyl ether Boron nitride Jojoba esters Rose hip oil PVP/hexadecene copolymer Methylsilanol hydroxyproline Betaglucan Panthenol
Highlighters	17. Natural	Magnesium stearate

Category	Product	Ingredient
	Product unavailable in: KR	Zinc oxide Nylon Mica/lauroyl lysine Magnesium carbonate [FD&C Yellow #5 Al lake] Octyl methoxycinnamate Oat flour Grapefruit powder Diisopropyl adipate Isostearyl neopentanoate [D&C Red # 30 lake] Cross linked elastin Avocado oil unsaponifiables Iron oxide Silk amino acids Perfluoropolymethylisopropyl ether Ultramarine Jojoba esters Boron nitride Rose hip oil PVP/hexadecene copolymer Methylsilanol hydroxyproline Betaglucan Panthenol [D&C Red #7 lake]
	18. Rich Sand *Product unavailable in:* KR	Magnesium stearate Zinc oxide Iron oxide Nylon Mica/lauroyl lysine Magnesium carbonate Oat flour Grapefruit powder Octyl methoxycinnamate Cross linked elastin Diisopropyl adipate Isostearyl neopentanoate Avocado oil unsaponifiables Silk amino acids Perfluoropolymethylisopropyl ether Boron nitride Jojoba esters Rose hip oil PVP/hexadecene copolymer Methylsilanol hydroxyproline Betaglucan Panthenol
	19. Soft Pink *Product unavailable in:* KR	Magnesium stearate Nylon Mica/lauroyl lysine Magnesium carbonate Octyl methoxycinnamate Oat flour [D&C Red #30 lake] Grapefruit powder Diisopropyl adipate Cross linked elastin Isostearyl neopentanoate [FD&C Yellow #5 Al lake] Avocado oil unsaponifiables Iron oxide Silk amino acids Perfluoropolymethylisopropyl ether Zinc oxide [D&C Red #7 Ca lake] Boron nitride Jojoba esters Rose hip oil

Category	Product	Ingredient
		PVP/hexadecene copolymer
		Methylsilanol hydroxyproline
		Betaglucan
		Panthenol
	20. White Essence *Product unavailable in:* KR	Zinc oxide
		Magnesium stearate
		Nylon
		Mica/lauroyl lysine
		Magnesium carbonate
		Oat flour
		Grapefruit powder
		Octyl methoxycinnamate
		Cross linked elastin
		Diisopropyl adipate
		Isostearyl neopentanoate
		Iron oxide
		Avocado oil unsaponifiables
		Silk amino acids
		Perfluoropolymethylisopropyl ether
		Boron nitride
		Jojoba esters
		Rose hip oil
		[D&C Red #30 lake]
		PVP/hexadecene copolymer
		Methylsilanol hydroxyproline
		Betaglucan
		Panthenol
Eyeliner Pencils	21. Autumn *Product unavailable in:* KR	Red iron oxide
		Hydrogenated palm oil
		Hydrogenated coco-glycerides
		Cetyl laurate
		Titanium dioxide
		Yellow iron oxide
		Beeswax
		Black iron oxide
		Tocopheryl acetate
		Allantoin
	22. Dark Sable *Product unavailable in:* KR	Lauryl palmitate
		Black iron oxide
		Red iron oxide
		Hydrogenated castor oil
		Hydrogenated coco-glycerides
		Hydrogenated rice bran wax
		Glyceryl abietate
		Stearyl heptanoate
		Silica
		Yellow iron oxide
		Chamomile oil
		Tocopheryl acetate
	23. Midnight Ebony *Product unavailable in:* KR	Black iron oxide
		Lauryl palmitate
		Hydrogenated castor oil
		Hydrogenated coco-glycerides
		Hydrogenated rice bran wax
		Glyceryl abietate
		Stearyl heptanoate
		Silica
		Ferric ferrocyanide
		Chamomile oil
		Tocopheryl acetate
	24. Silver Fox *Product unavailable in:* KR	Titanium dioxide
		Hydrogenated palm oil
		Hydrogenated coco-glycerides
		Black iron oxide
		Cetyl laurate
		Yellow iron oxide
		Beeswax
		Red iron oxide

Category	Product	Ingredient
		Chamomile oil
		Tocopheryl acetate
F. Lipsticks and Lip Pencils *Product used by:* W	1. Barely Bronze *Product unavailable in:* KR	Sunflower seed oil (Helianthus annus)
		Octyldodecanol
		Mica/iron oxide
		Cera alba (beeswax)
		Zinc dimethicone
		Octyl methoxcinnamate
		Oleyl alcohol
		[D&C Red #7 Ca lake]
		Cetyl dimethicone
		Dimethicone copolyol (beeswax)
		Carnuaba wax
		Candelilla cera (candelilla wax)
		Diisopropyl adipate
		[D&C Yellow #5 Al lake]
		Iron oxide
		Jojoba esters
		Avocado oil unsaponifiables
		Cetearyl alcohol
		Chocolate flavour
		Cetearyl glucoside
		Neem seed oil
		Tricontanyl PVP
		Tocopheryl acetate
		[D&C Red #30 lake]
		[D&C Red #33 Al lake]
		Perfluoropolymethylisopropyl ether
	2. Carmel *Product unavailable in:* KR, UK, ML, AU	Octyldodecanol
		Sunflower seed oil (Helianthus annus)
		Cera alba (beeswax)
		Octyl methoxcinnamate
		Oleyl alcohol
		Cetyl dimethicone
		Dimethicone copolyol (beeswax)
		Carnuaba wax
		Candelilla cera (candelilla wax)
		Diisopropyl adipate
		Avocado oil unsaponifiables
		Jojoba esters
		Cetearyl alcohol
		Zinc dimethicone
		Cetearyl glucoside
		Neem seed oil
		Chocolate flavour
		Tricontanyl PVP
		Tocopheryl acetate
		Mica/iron oxide
		[D&C Red #7 Ca lake]
		Perfluoropolymethylisopropyl ether
		[D&C Yellow #5 Al lake]
		Iron oxide
	3. Cinnamon *Product unavailable in:* KR	Sunflower seed oil (Helianthus annus)
		Octyldodecanol
		Cera alba (beeswax)
		Zinc dimethicone
		Octyl methoxcinnamate
		Iron oxide
		Oleyl alcohol
		Cetyl dimethicone
		Dimethicone copolyol (beeswax)
		Carnuaba wax
		Candelilla cera (candelilla wax)
		Diisopropyl adipate
		Avocado oil unsaponifiables
		Jojoba esters
		Cetearyl alcohol
		Cetearyl glucoside

Category	Product	Ingredient
		Chocolate flavour
		Neem seed oil
		Tricontanyl PVP
		Tocopheryl acetate
		[D&C Red #30 lake]
		Perfluoropolymethylisopropyl ether
	4. Fuchsia *Product unavailable in:* KR	Sunflower seed oil (Helianthus annus)
		Octyldodecanol
		Cera alba (beeswax)
		Octyl methoxycinnamate
		Oleyl alcohol
		Zinc dimethicone
		[D&C Red #7 Ca lake]
		Cetyl dimethicone
		Dimethicone copolyol (beeswax)
		Carnuaba wax
		Candelilla cera (candelilla wax)
		Diisopropyl adipate
		[D&C Red #30 lake]
		[D&C Yellow #5 Al lake]
		Avocado oil unsaponifiables
		Jojoba esters
		Cetearyl alcohol
		Mandrain oil
		Cetearyl glucoside
		Neem seed oil
		Tricontanyl PVP
		Tocopheryl acetate
		Madrain flavour
		Perfluoropolymethylisopropyl ether
	5. Heather *Product unavailable in:* KR, UK, ML	Octyldodecanol
		Sunflower seed oil (Helianthus annus)
		Zinc dimethicone
		[D&C Red #7 Ca lake]
		Mica/iron oxide
		Cera alba (beeswax)
		Octyl methoxycinnamate
		Iron oxide
		Oleyl alcohol
		Cetyl dimethicone
		Dimethicone copolyol (beeswax)
		Carnuaba wax
		Candelilla cera (candelilla wax)
		Diisopropyl adipate
		Avocado oil unsaponifiables
		Jojoba esters
		Vanilla
		Cetearyl alcohol
		Cetearyl glucoside
		Neem seed oil
		Tricontanyl PVP
		Tocopheryl acetate
		Perfluoropolymethylisopropyl ether
	6. Inca Bronze *Product unavailable in:* KR	Sunflower seed oil (Helianthus annus)
		Mica/iron oxide
		Octyldodecanol
		Cera alba (beeswax)
		Octyl methoxycinnamate
		Zinc dimethicone
		Oleyl alcohol
		Iron oxide
		Cetyl dimethicone
		Dimethicone copolyol (beeswax)
		Carnuaba wax
		Candelilla cera (candelilla wax)
		Diisopropyl adipate
		Avocado oil unsaponifiables
		Jojoba esters

Category	Product	Ingredient
		Chocolate flavour
		Cetearyl alcohol
		Cetearyl glucoside
		[D&C Red #30 lake]
		[D&C Red #33 Al lake]
		Neem seed oil
		Tricontanyl PVP
		Tocopheryl acetate
		[D&C Yellow #5 Al lake]
		Perfluoropolymethylisopropyl ether
	7. Mad About Mauve *Product unavailable in:* KR, UK, ML	Octyldodecanol
		Zinc dimethicone
		[D&C Red #6 Ba lake]
		[D&C Red #7 Ca lake]
		Sunflower seed oil (Helianthus annus)
		Cera alba (beeswax)
		Octyl methoxycinnamate
		Oleyl alcohol
		Cetyl dimethicone
		Dimethicone copolyol (beeswax)
		Iron oxide
		Carnuaba wax
		Candelilla cera (candelilla wax)
		Diisopropyl adipate
		Avocado oil unsaponifiables
		Jojoba esters
		Cetearyl alcohol
		Cetearyl glucoside
		Mandarin oil
		Neem seed oil
		Tricontanyl PVP
		Tocopheryl acetate
		Mandarin flavour
		Perfluoropolymethylisopropyl ether
	8. Magenta *Product unavailable in:* KR	Sunflower seed oil (Helianthus annus)
		Octyldodecanol
		Cera alba (beeswax)
		Mica/iron oxide
		Octyl methoxycinnamate
		Oleyl alcohol
		Zinc dimethicone
		Cetyl dimethicone
		Dimethicone copolyol (beeswax)
		Carnuaba wax
		Candelilla cera (candelilla wax)
		Diisopropyl adipate
		Avocado oil unsaponifiables
		Jojoba esters
		[D&C Red #30 lake]
		Cetearyl alcohol
		[D&C Red #7 Ca lake]
		Cetearyl glucoside
		Mandarin oil
		Neem seed oil
		Tricontanyl PVP
		Tocopheryl acetate
		Perfluoropolymethylisopropyl ether
		Mandarin flavour
	9. Neways Red *Product unavailable in:* KR	Sunflower seed oil (Helianthus annus)
		Octyldodecanol
		Cera alba (beeswax)
		Octyl methoxycinnamate
		Oleyl alcohol
		Cetyl dimethicone
		Dimethicone copolyol (beeswax)
		[D&C Red #7 Ca lake]
		Zinc dimethicone
		Carnuaba wax

Category	Product	Ingredient
		Candelilla cera (candelilla wax)
		Diisopropyl adipate
		Avocado oil unsaponifiables
		Jojoba esters
		Cetearyl alcohol
		Cetearyl glucoside
		Mandarin oil
		Neem seed oil
		Tricontanyl PVP
		Tocopheryl acetate
		Mandarin flavour
		Perfluoropolymethylisopropyl ether
	10. Raspberry *Product unavailable in:* KR	Sunflower seed oil (Helianthus annus)
		Octyldodecanol
		Cera alba (beeswax)
		[D&C Red# 7 Ca lake]
		Octyl methoxycinnamate
		Oleyl alcohol
		Mica/lauroyl lysine
		[D&C Red #30 lake]
		Cetyl dimethicone
		Dimethicone copolyol (beeswax)
		Carnuaba wax
		Candelilla cera (candelilla wax)
		Diisopropyl adipate
		Avocado oil unsaponifiables
		Jojoba esters
		Zinc dimethicone
		Mandarin oil
		Cetearyl alcohol
		Cetearyl glucoside
		[D&C Red #33 Al lake]
		Neem seed oil
		Tricontanyl PVP
		Tocopheryl acetate
		Mandarin flavour
		Perfluoropolymethylisopropyl ether
	11. Ruby Red *Product unavailable in:* KR	Sunflower seed oil (Helianthus annus)
		Octyldodecanol
		Cera alba (beeswax)
		Octyl methoxycinnamate
		Oleyl alcohol
		Cetyl dimethicone
		Dimethicone copolyol (beeswax)
		Carnuaba wax
		Candelilla cera (candelilla wax)
		Diisopropyl adipate
		Avocado oil unsaponifiables
		Jojoba esters
		[D&C Red #30 lake]
		Cetearyl alcohol
		Zinc dimethicone
		Mandarin oil
		Cetearyl glucoside
		[D&C Red #7 Ca lake]
		Neem seed oil
		Tricontanyl PVP
		Tocopheryl acetate
		Mandarin flavour
		Perfluoropolymethylisopropyl ether
	12. Soft Shell Pink *Product unavailable in:* KR, ML	Sunflower seed oil (Helianthus annus)
		Octyldodecanol
		Zinc dimethicone
		Cera alba (beeswax)
		[D&C Red #30 lake]
		Oleyl alcohol
		Octyl methoxycinnamate
		Cetyl dimethicone

Category	Product	Ingredient
		Dimethicone copolyol (beeswax)
		Carnuaba wax
		Candelilla cera (candelilla wax)
		Diisopropyl adipate
		Avocado oil unsaponifiables
		Jojoba esters
		Cetearyl alcohol
		Cetearyl glucoside
		Mandarin oil
		Neem seed oil
		Tricontanyl PVP
		Iron oxide
		[D&C Yellow #5 Al lake]
		Tocopheryl acetate
		[D&C Red #7 Ca lake]
		Mandarin flavour
		Perfluoropolymethylisopropyl ether
	13. Vegas Pink *Product unavailable in:* KR	Sunflower seed oil (Helianthus annus)
		Octyldodecanol
		Cera alba (beeswax)
		Octyl methoxycinnamate
		Zinc dimethicone
		Oleyl alcohol
		Cetyl dimethicone
		Dimethicone copolyol (beeswax)
		Carnuaba wax
		Candelilla cera (candelilla wax)
		Diisopropyl adipate
		[D&C Red #30 lake]
		Avocado oil unsaponifiables
		Jojoba esters
		[D&C Red #7 Ca lake]
		[D&C Yellow #5 Al lake]
		Cetearyl alcohol
		Mandarin oil
		Cetearyl glucoside
		Neem seed oil
		[D&C Red #33 Al lake]
		Tricontanyl PVP
		Tocopheryl acetate
		Mandarin flavour
		Perfluoropolymethylisopropyl ether
	14. Watermelon *Product unavailable in:* KR	Sunflower seed oil (Helianthus annus)
		Octyldodecanol
		Cera alba (beeswax)
		Octyl methoxycinnamate
		Oleyl alcohol
		Zinc dimethicone
		Cetyl dimethicone
		Dimethicone copolyol (beeswax)
		[D&C Yellow #5 Al lake]
		Carnuaba wax
		Candelilla cera (candelilla wax)
		Diisopropyl adipate
		[D&C Red #30 lake]
		Avocado oil unsaponifiables
		Jojoba esters
		Iron oxide
		Cetearyl alcohol
		Mandarin oil
		Cetearyl glucoside
		Neem seed oil
		[D&C Red #7 Ca lake]
		Tricontanyl PVP
		Tocopheryl acetate
		Mandarin flavour
		Perfluoropolymethylisopropyl ether
Lip Pencils	15. Soft Cinnamon	Red iron oxide

Category	Product	Ingredient
	Product unavailable in: KR	Lauryl palmitate
		Hydrogenated castor oil
		Hydrogenated coco-glycerides
		Titanium dioxide
		Hydrogenated rice bran wax
		Glyceryl abietate
		Stearyl heptanoate
		Silica
		Talc
		Chamomille oil
		Tocopheryl acetate
	16. Wild Cherry *Product unavailable in:* KR	Hydrogenated palm oil
		[D&C Red # 7 lake]
		Hydrogenated coco-glycerides
		Talc
		Cetyl laurate
		Red iron oxide
		Beeswax
		Glyceryl abietate
		Lanolin
		Tocopheryl acetate
		Isopropyl palmitate
		Allantoin
		Stearalkonium hectorite
		Propylene carbonate
G. Nail Polishes *Product used by:* W	1. Barely Bronze *Product unavailable in:* KR	N-butyl acetate
		Ethyl alcohol
		Bismuth oxychloride
		Ethyl acetate
		Alkyl acrylate copolymer
		Nitrocellulose
		Iron oxide
		Stearalkonium hectorite
		Calcium pantothenate
		Camphor
		Dibutyl pthalate
		Tocopheryl acetate
		Mica/iron oxide
		[D&C Red #34 Ca lake]
		[FD&C Yellow #5 Al lake]
	2. Carmel *Product unavailable in:* KR, UK, ML, AU	N-butyl acetate
		Ethyl alcohol
		Ethyl acetate
		Alkyl acrylate copolymer
		Nitrocellulose
		Iron oxide
		Stearalkonium hectorite
		Calcium pantothenate
		Camphor
		Dibutyl pthalate
		Tocopheryl acetate
		[D&C Red #34 Ca lake]
	3. Cinnamon *Product unavailable in:* KR	N-butyl acetate
		Ethyl alcohol
		Ethyl acetate
		Alkyl acrylate copolymer
		Nitrocellulose
		Red iron oxide
		Mica/lauroyl lysine
		Stearalkonium hectorite
		[FD&C Yellow #5 Al lake]
		Calcium pantothenate
		Camphor
		Dibutyl pthalate
		Tocopheryl acetate
		[D&C Red #34 Ca lake]
		Iron oxide
	4. Fuchsia	N-butyl acetate

Category	Product	Ingredient
	Product unavailable in: KR	Ethyl acetate Ethyl alcohol Alkyl acrylate copolymer Nitrocellulose [D&C Red # 7 Ca lake] Mica/lauroyl lysine Stearalkonium hectorite Calcium pantothenate Camphor Dibutyl pthalate Tocopheryl acetate [FD&C Yellow #5 Al lake] [D&C Red #34 Ca lake] [D&C Red #6 Ba lake] Iron oxide
	5. Heather *Product unavailable in:* KR, UK, ML	N-butyl acetate Bismuth oxychloride [D&C Red #34 Ca lake] Ethyl alcohol Ethyl acetate Alkyl acrylate copolymer Iron oxide Nitrocellulose Mica/iron oxide Stearalkonium hectorite Calcium pantothenate Camphor Dibutyl pthalate Tocopheryl acetate
	6. Inca Bronze *Product unavailable in:* KR	N-butyl acetate Ethyl alcohol Ethyl acetate Alkyl acrylate copolymer Nitrocellulose Iron oxide Mica/lauroyl lysine Stearalkonium hectorite Calcium pantothenate [FD&C Yellow #5 Al lake] Camphor Dibutyl pthalate Tocopheryl acetate Bismuth oxychloride [D&C Red #7 Ca lake]
	7. Mad About Mauve *Product unavailable in:* KR, UK, ML	N-butyl acetate Ethyl alcohol Bismuth oxychloride Ethyl acetate Iron oxide Alkyl acrylate copolymer Nitrocellulose Stearalkonium hectorite [D&C Red #34 Ca lake] Calcium pantothenate Camphor Dibutyl pthalate Tocopheryl acetate
	8. Magenta *Product unavailable in:* KR	N-butyl acetate Ethyl alcohol Bismuth oxychloride Ethyl acetate Mica/iron oxide/titanium Alkyl acrylate copolymer Nitrocellulose Stearalkonium hectorite [D&C Red #7 Ca lake] Calcium pantothenate Camphor

Category	Product	Ingredient
		Dibutyl pthalate
		Tocopheryl acetate
		[FD&C Yellow #5 Al lake]
	9. Neways Red *Product unavailable in:* KR	N-butyl acetate
		Ethyl alcohol
		Ethyl acetate
		Alkyl acrylate copolymer
		[D&C Red #7 Ca lake]
		Nitrocellulose
		[FD&C Yellow #5 Al lake]
		Stearalkonium hectorite
		Calcium pantothenate
		Camphor
		Dibutyl pthalate
		Tocopheryl acetate
		[D&C Red #6 Ba lake]
		Mica/lauroyl lysine
	10. Raspberry *Product unavailable in:* KR	N-butyl acetate
		Ethyl acetate
		Ethyl alcohol
		Alkyl acrylate copolymer
		Nitrocellulose
		Bismuth oxychloride
		Stearalkonium hectorite
		Calcium pantothenate
		Camphor
		Dibutyl pthalate
		Tocopheryl acetate
		[D&C Red #7 Ca lake]
		[D&C Red #6 Ba lake]
		[FD&C Yellow #5 Al lake]
		[D&C Red #34 Ca lake]
		Mica
		Iron oxide
	11. Ruby Red *Product unavailable in:* KR	N-butyl acetate
		Ethyl alcohol
		Ethyl acetate
		[D&C Red #7 Ca lake]
		Alkyl acrylate copolymer
		Nitrocellulose
		Stearalkonium hectorite
		Calcium pantothenate
		Mica
		Camphor
		Dibutyl pthalate
		Tocopheryl acetate
		[D&C Red #6 Ba lake]
		[FD&C Yellow #5 Al lake]
	12. Soft Shell Pink *Product unavailable in:* KR, UK, ML	N-butyl acetate
		Mica
		Ethyl alcohol
		Ethyl acetate
		Alkyl acrylate copolymer
		Nitrocellulose
		Stearalkonium hectorite
		Calcium pantothenate
		Camphor
		Dibutyl pthalate
		Tocopheryl acetate
		[D&C Red #7 Ca lake]
		[FD&C Yellow #5 Al lake]
		[D&C Red #34 Ca lake]
		Iron oxide
	13. Vegas Pink *Product unavailable in:* KR	N-butyl acetate
		Ethyl alcohol
		Ethyl acetate
		Alkyl acrylate copolymer
		Nitrocellulose

Category	Product	Ingredient
		Bismuth oxychloride
		[D&C Red #6 Ba lake]
		Stearalkonium hectorite
		Calcium pantothenate
		Camphor
		Dibutyl pthalate
		Tocopheryl acetate
		[FD&C Yellow #5 Al lake]
		[D&C Red #7 Ba lake]
	14. Watermelon *Product unavailable in:* KR	N-butyl acetate
		Ethyl acetate
		Ethyl alcohol
		Alkyl acrylate copolymer
		Nitrocellulose
		Mica
		[FD&C Yellow #5 Al lake]
		Stearalkonium hectorite
		Calcium pantothenate
		[D&C Red #7 Ca lake]
		Camphor
		Dibutyl pthalate
		Tocopheryl acetate
		[D&C Red #7 Ca lake (dark)]
		Iron oxide
		[D&C Red #34 Ca lake]
	15. Top and Base Coat *Product unavailable in:* KR, UK, ML, AU	N-butyl acetate
		Nitrocellulose
		Ethyl acetate
		Dibutyl pthalate
		Camphor
H. Nail Care System *Product used by:* W	1. Cleansing Solution *Product unavailable in:* KR, UK, ML, AU	SD Alcohol 40B
		Ethyl acetate
		Purified water
	2. Nail Enhancer *Product unavailable in:* KR, UK, ML, AU	Purified water
		Myrrh extract
		Panthenol
		Ginkgo biloba extract
		Hydrolyzed mucopolysaccharides
		Allantoin
		Niacinamide
		Phenoxyethanol
		Chloroxylenol
	3. Nail Whitener *Product unavailable in:* KR, UK, ML, AU	Aliphatic urethane acrylate
		Tripropylene glycol diacrylate
		Toluene
	4. Nail Gels *Product unavailable in:* KR, UK, ML, AU	Acrylated urethanes
		Benzil dimethyl ketal
		2-Hydroxy-2-methyl-1-phenyl-1-propanone
		Polyester acrylate oligomer
		Reactive polyester diacrylate
	5. Nail Glue KR, UK, ML, AU	Cyanoacrylate ester
	6. Ultra High Gloss/White Tip Gel *Product unavailable in:* KR, UK, ML, AU	Acrylated urethane
		Polyester acrylates
		Acrylated oligomer photosynthesizers

PERSONAL CARE

CATEGORY	PRODUCT	INGREDIENTS
A. Hair Conditioner *Product used by:* W, M, C	1. 2nd Chance	Purified water
		Polysorbate 60 (dioxane free)
		Polysorbate 80 (dioxane free)
		Ginseng extract
		Arginine
		Acetyl tyrosine
		Burdock extract
		Hydrolyzed soy protein

Category	Product	Ingredient
		Polyquaternium-11 (dioxane free)
		Dimethicone copolyol
		Calcium pantothenate
		Zinc gluconate
		Niacinamide
		Ornithine
		Citrulline
		Glucosamine HCL
		Biotin
		dL-Panthenol
		Orange extract
		Bergamot extract
		Tangerine extract
		Lavender extract
		Ylang Ylang extract
		Geranium extract
		Retinyl palmiate
		Hydrolyzed mucopolysaccharides
		Phenoxyethanol
		Methylparaben
		Propylparaben
	2. Exuberance	Purified water
		Dicetyldimonium chloride
		Myristyl alcohol
		Cetrimonium chloride
		Hair keratin amino acids
		Stearalkonium chloride
		Hydroxyethylcellulose
		Cetyl alcohol
		Panthenol
		Phenoxyethanol
		[Aromatic fragrance*]
B. Shampoos *Product used by:* W, M, C, I	1. 2nd Chance	Purified water
		Sodium C14-16 olefin sulfonate
		Ammonium lauryl sulfate
		Ammonium cocoyl isethionate
		Cocamidopropyl hydoxysultaine
		Sodium isostearoyl lactylate
		Matricaria extract
		Sage extract
		Nettle extract
		Rosemary extract
		Yarrow extract
		Kiwi extract
		Aloe barbadensis extract
		Orange extract
		Bergamot extract
		Tangerine extract
		Lavender extract
		Ylang Ylang extract
		Geranium extract
		dL-Panthenol
		Ammonium chloride
		Methylchloroisothiazolinone
		Methylisothiazolinone
	2. Silken Shampoo	Purified water
		Sodium C14-16 olefin sulfonate
		Cocamidopropyl hydroxysultaine
		Decyl polyglucose
		Sodium C12-15 pareth-15 sulfonate (dioxane free)
		Ammonium cocoyl isethionate
		Caprylyl pyrrolidone
		Nettle extract
		Arnica extract
		Watercress extract
		Rosemary extract
		Sage extract
		Wheat amino acids

Category	Product	Ingredient
		Lemon extract
		Orange extract
		Bergamot extract
		Tangerine extract
		Lavender extract
		Ylang Ylang extract
		Geranium extract
		Ammonium chloride
		Methylchloroisothiazolinone
		Methylisothiazolinone
	3. Ultimate	Purified water
		Sodium C14-16 olefin sulfonate
		Cocamidopropyl hydroxysultaine
		Decyl polyglucose
		Disodium cocoamphodiacetate
		Wild cherry extract
		Henna extract
		Hops extract
		Calendula extract
		Horsetail extract
		Matricaria extract
		Quillaja extract
		Curcuma longa (Curcuminoids)
		Basil extract
		Tangelo extract (orange oil)
		Ammonium chloride
		Methylchloroisothiazolinone
		Methylisothiazolinone
C. Hair Sprays and Styling Preparations *Product used by:* W, M, C	1. Finishing Touch *Product unavailable in:* KR	Purified water Acrylates copolymer Triethyl citrate dL-Panthenol Silk amino acids Octyl methoxycinnamate Dioctyl sodium sulfosuccinate [Aromatic fragrance*]
	2. Free Flex *Product unavailable in:* KR	SD Alcohol 40 Ethyl ester of PVM/MA copolymer Purified water VA/butyl maleate/isobornyl/acrylate copolymer Caprylyl pyrrolidone dL-Panthenol Triethyl citrate Aloe vera Octyl methoxycinnamate Dimethicone copolyol [Aromatic fragrance*]
	3. Replenishing Mist *Product unavailable in:* KR	Purified water Hair keratin amino acids Panthenol Hydrolyzed mucopolysaccharides Cetrimonium chloride Sandlewood extract Sage extract Geranium extract Rosemary extract Lavender extract Phenoxyethanol Methylparaben Propylparaben
	4. Sassy	SD Alcohol 40 Ethyl ester of PVM/MA copolymer Purified water Silk amino acids Hair keratin amino acids Dimethicone copolyol [Aromatic fragrance*]

Category	Product	Ingredient
	5. Sculpting Gel *Product unavailable in:* KR	Purified water Polyquaternium-11 (dioxane free) PVP Polyquaternium-10 (dioxane free) Dimethicone copolyol Hydoxyethylcellulose Phenoxyethanol Methylparaben Propylparaben [Aromatic fragrance*]
	6. Super Booster *Product unavailable in:* KR	Purified water Ginseng extract Arginine Acetyl tyrosine Burdock extract Hydrolyzed soy protein Polyquaternium-11 (dioxane free) Dimethicone copolyol Calcium pantothenate Zinc gluconate Niacinamide Ornithine Citrulline Glucosamine HCl Biotin Nettle extract *Ginko biloba extract* Retinyl palmitate Panthenol Phenoxyethanol Methylparaben Propylparaben
D. Mouthwashes *Product used by:* W, M, C	1. Eliminator *Product unavailable in:* KR, JP	Purified water Stabilized chlorine dioxide Flavor
E. Toothpastes and Dental Aids *Product used by:* W, M, C, I	1. NDK Gum *Product unavailable in:* KR, JP	Sorbitol powder Sorbitol liquid Nova-T gum base Casein hydrolysate Lycasin 85% (hydrogenated starch hydrolysate) Magna-T gum base Tutti-frutti flavor Glycerine Citric acid Titanium dioxide Natural vanilla flavor Wintergreen flavor Stevia powder Acesulfame potassium Lecithin Tween-60 (polysorbate 60--dioxane free)
	2. Radiance *Product unavailable in:* KR, JP	Sorbitol Glycerine Hydrated silica Purified water Sodium lauroyl sarcosinate Stabilized chlorine dioxide Cellulose gum Flavor
	3. Ultrashine Radiance *Product unavailable in:* KR, JP, AU, UK, MX	Sorbitol Hydrated silica Purified water Sodium coco sulfate Xylitol Peppermint oil Calcium glycerophosphate

Category	Product	Ingredient
		Micellar casein
		Stabilized chlorine dioxide
		Cellulose gum
		Sucralose
		Chlorophyllin-copper complex
	4. Whiten	Glycerine
	Product unavailable in:	Urea peroxide
	KR, JP	Carbomer
F. Antiperspirants and Deodorants *Product used by:* W, M	**1. Subdue Deodorant** *Product unavailable in:* KR	Methylpropanediol Myrrh extract Sage extract Eucalyptus extract Coriander extract Witch hazel distillate Aloe vera Vegetable protein extract Odor destroying fragrance*
G. Bubble Baths, Mineral Baths and Bath Oils *Product used by:* W, M, C, I	**1. Indulge Bubble Bath**	Purified water Sodium C14-16 olefin sulfonate Cocamidopropyl hydroxysultaine Sodium isostearoyl lactylate Sodium C12-15 pareth-15 sulfonate (dioxane-free) Spirea extract Hops extract Matricaria extract Laurel extract Ammonium chloride Phenoxyethanol Methylparaben Propylparaben [Aromatic fragrance*]
H. Shaving Creams *Product used by:* W, M	**1. Close Shaving Gel**	Purified water Sodium C14-16 olefin sulfonate Decyl glucoside Cocamidopropyl betaine Sorbitol Sodium isostearoyl lactylate Cetyl triethylammonium dimethicone copolyol phthalate Glycol distearate Honeysuckle extract Hydroxypropyl guar Aloe vera Allantoin Cocophosphatidyl PG-dimonium chloride Orange extract Bergamot extract Tangerine extract Lavender extract Ylang Ylang extract Geranium extract
I. Skin Lotions *Product used by:* W, M, C, I	**1. Barrier Cream** *Product unavailable in:* UK	Purified water Sweet almond oil Dimethiconol fluoroalcohol dilinoleate Sodium stearoyl lactylate Cetearyl alcohol Stearic acid Methylpropanediol PVP/hexadecene copolymer Polyalkylmethicone Octyldodecyl neopentanoate Dimethicone Honeysuckle extract Perfluoropolymethylisopropyl ether Vanilla extract Cetyl hydroxyethylcellulose

Category	Product	Ingredient
	2. NightScience *Product unavailable in:* JP, UK, ML, AU, MX	Purified water Cyclomethicone Dimethicone/vinyl dimethicone crosspolymer Rice peptides Oriental mushroom extract Wheat starch (modified) Sodium behenoyl lactylate Saccharide isomerate Cetyl alcohol Stearic acid Retinol Lecithin *Micrococcus lysate* Betaglucan Aloe vera extract Ergothioneine Spiriulina extract Rose hips oil Methylpropanediol Yeast extract Sorbitol Dipotassium glycyrrhizate Pyridoxine dicaprylate Lavender extract Chamomile extract Phenoxyethanol Methylparaben Propylparaben
	3. Skin Enhancer *Product unavailable in:* KR, UK	Purified water Sodium behenoyl lactylate Cetyl alcohol Stearic acid Saccharide isomerate Rose hip oil Sunflower seed extract Octyl palmitate *Anacystis nidulans extract* Menthyl anthranilate Oat extract Betaglucan Soybean (glycine soja) protein Oxido reductases Ergothioneine Spirulina extract Aloe vera Rosacea extract Magnoliaceae extract Algae extract Sorbitol Yeast extract Dipotassium glycyrrhizate Pyridoxine dicaprylate *Curcuma longa extract* Tetrahexydecyl ascorbate (vitamin C) Vitamin E Dimethicone Cetyl hydroxyethylcellulose Vanilla extract Phenoxyethanol Methylparaben Propylparaben
	4. Tender Care *Product unavailable in:* KR, UK	Purified water Sweet almond oil Methylsulfonylmethane (MSM) Sodium behenoyl lactylate Cetyl alcohol Stearic Acid Octyl Palmitate

Category	Product	Ingredient
		Sorbitol
		Rose Hip oil
		Sodium PCA
		Vitamin E
		Vitamin A
		Dimethicone
		Vanilla extract
		Phenoxyethanol
		Methylparaben
		Propylparaben
J. Soaps *Product used by:* W, M, C, I	1. 1st Impression *Product unavailable in:* KR, JP	Purified water
		Sodium C14-16 olefin sulfonate
		Ammonium cocoyl isethionate
		Disodium cocoamphodiacetate
		Sodium C12-15 pareth-15 sulfonate (dioxane-free)
		Decyl polyglucose
		Cocamidopropyl hydroxysultaine
		Grapefruit extract
		Hibiscus extract
		Honeysuckle extract
		Papaya extract
		Yarrow flowers extract
		dL-Panthenol
		Niacinamide
		Ammonium chloride
		Methylchloroisothiazolinone
		Methylisothiazolinone
	2. Extra Gentle	Purified water
		Decyl polyglucose
		Ammonium cocoyl isethionate
		Sodium C12-15 pareth-15 sulfonate (dioxane-free)
		Hydroxypropyl methylcellulose
		Orange blossom extract
		Mango extract
		Apricot extract
		Quillaja extract
		Basil extract
		Tangelo extract (orange oil)
		Methylchloroisothiazolinone
		Methylisothizolinone
	3. Milky Cleanser	Purified water
		Sweet almond oil
		Sorbitol
		Polyacrylamide
		Decyl polyglucose
		Silk amino acids
		Sodium PCA
		Aloe vera
		Allantoin
		C13-14 Isoparaffin
		Laureth-7 (dioxane-free)
		Sodium borate
		Phenoxyethanol
		Methylparaben
		Propylparaben
	4. Refresh	Purified water
		Sodium C14-16 olefin sulfonate
		Cocamidopropyl hydroxysultaine
		Sodium methyl cocoyl taurate
		Sodium isostearoyl lactylate
		Rosemary extract
		Sambucus extract
		Ginseng extract
		Horsetail extract
		Sage extract
		Basil extract
		Tangelo extract (Orange oil)
		Aloe vera

Category	Product	Ingredient
		Ammonium chloride
		Methylchloroisothiazolinone
		Methylisothiazolinone
	5. TLC	Purified water
	Product unavailable in:	Shea butter
	AU	Polyacrylamide
		Aloe vera
		Linoleic acid
		Silk amino acids
		Sodium PCA
		Myrrh extract
		C13-14 Isoparaffin
		Vitamin E
		Laureth-7 (dioxane-free)
		Phenoxyethanol
		Methylparaben
Soap, cont.	*TLC, cont.*	Propylparaben
K. Beauty Aids	1. Bio-Mist Activator	Purified water
Product used by:		Red raspberry leaf extract
W		Witch hazel distillate
		Hydrolyzed mucopolysaccharides
		Sodium PCA
		Hydrolyzed milk protein
		Allantoin
		Decyl glucoside
		Tangerine extract
		Phenoxyethanol
	2. Endau Progesterone Cream	Purified water
	Product unavailable in:	Sweet almond oil
	KR, JP, UK	Dimethyl isosorbide
		Sodium behenoyl lactylate
		Cetyl alcohol
		Stearic acid
		Sorbitol
		Octyl palmitate
		Progesterone
		Lecithin
		Wild yam extract
		Aloe vera
		Vitamin E
		Chamomile extract
		Dimethicone
		Phenoxyethanol
		Methlparaben
		Propylparaben
	3. Imperfection Lotion	Purified water
		Willowbark extract
		Farnesyl acetate
		Farnesol
		Panthenyl triacetate
		Polyacrylamide
		Cetearyl glucoside
		Myrrh extract
		Lappa extract
		Plantain extract
		Thyme extract
		Retinyl palmitate
		Dipotassium glycyrrhizate
		Witch hazel distillate
		C13-14 Isoparaffin
		Laureth-7 (dioxane-free)
		Phenoxyethanol
		Methylparaben
		Propylparaben
	4. Lash Enhancer	Purified water
	Product unavailable in:	Myrrh extract
	KR	Ginko biloba extract

Category	Product	Ingredient
		Panthenol
		Niacinamide
		Phenoxyethanol
		Chloroxylenol
	5. Lightning Drops *Product unavailable in:* KR	Purified water
		Methylpropanediol
		Sodium citrate
		Lemon extract
		Cucumber extract
		Sugar Cane extract
		Citrus extract
		Apple extract
		Green Tea extract
		Mulberry Root extract
		Licorice extract
		Magnesium ascorbyl phosphate (vitamin C)
		Tocopheryl acetate (vitamin E)
		Lecithin
		Decyl polyglucose
		Phenoxyethanol
		Methylparaben
		Propylparaben
	6. Retention Plus *Product unavailable in:* KR, UK	Purified water
		Rose hip oil
		Sodium behenoyl lactylate
		Cetyl alcohol
		Stearic acid
		Ahnfeltia concinna extract
		Tetrahexydecyl ascorbate (Vitamin C)
		Ceramide 6 (dioxane free)
		Phytosphingosine
		Cross-linked elastin
		Grape seed extract
		Ergotheoneine
		Stearyl glycyrrhetinate
		Retinyl palmitate (vitamin A)
		Aloe vera
		Dimethicone
		[Fragrance*]
		Phenoxyethanol
		Methylparaben
		Propylparaben
	7. Wrinkle Drops *Product unavailable in:* KR	Purified water
		Polysorbate 80 (dioxane free)
		Cross-linked elastin
		Glycolic acid
		Yeast cell derivatives
		Phospholipids
		Phenoxyethanol
		Methylparaben
		Propylparaben
		[Aromatic fragrance*]
	8. Wrinkle Garde *Product unavailable in:* UK	Rose hip oil
		Hydrogenated polyisobutene
		Tocopherol acetate
		Retinyl palmitate
		Cholecalciferol
		Corn oil
	9. Snap Back *Product unavailable in:* KR	Purified water
		Methylsilanol hydroxyproline aspartate
		Sorbitol
		Centella asiatica phytosome
		Polyacrylamide
		Ginko biloba dimeric flavonoid phytosomes
		Palm oil
		Dimethicone
		Arnica extract
		C13-14 Isoparaffin

Category	Product	Ingredient
		Laureth-7 (dioxane-free)
		Phenoxyethanol
		Methylparaben
		Propylparaben
L. Suncare *Product used by:* W, M, C, I	1. Body Bronze *Product unavailable in:* KR, JP, CN, UK, ML, AU, MX	Octyl methoxycinnamate
		Octyl salicylate
		Purified water
		Dihydroxyacetone
		Cetearyl alcohol
		Cetearyl glucoside
		Sweet almond oil
		Octyl palmitate
		Methylpropane diol
		Erythrulose
		Dimethicone
		Xanthan gum
		Methylsilanol carboxymethyl theophyline alginate
		Vitamin E
		Mango extract
		Phenoxyethanol
		Methylparaben
		Propylparaben
	2. Great Tan *Product unavailable in:* KR, JP	Octyl methoxycinnamate
		Octyl salicylate
		Purified water
		Dihydroxyacetone
		Erythrulose
		Polyacrylamide
		Palm oil
		Copper acetyl tyrosinate methylsilanol
		Dimethicone
		C13-14 Isoparaffin
		Vitamin E
		Laureth-7 (dioxane-free)
		Phenoxyethanol
		Methylparaben
		Propylparaben
	3. Lipceutical *Product unavailable in:* KR, JP, AU, CN	Octyl methoxycinnamate
		Octyl salicylate
		Isostearyl alcohol
		Stearic acid
		Candellila wax
		Diisostearoyl trimethylolpropane siloxy silicate
		Caranauba wax
		Cetyl alcohol
		Palm oil
		Octyldodacanol
		Trilaurin
		Sunflower seed extract
		Safflower oil
		Aloe extract
		Acrylates/octylacrylamide copolymer
		Vitamin E
		Propylparaben
	4. Rebound *Product unavailable in:* JP, MX	Purified water
		Saccharide isomerate
		Cetearyl gucoside
		Cassia betaglucan
		Polyacrylamide
		Micrococcus lysate
		Lecithin
		Ergothioneine
		Spirulina extract
		Palmitoyl hydrolized wheat protein
		Rose hip oil
		Aloe vera
		Dimethicone
		Sorbitol

Category	Product	Ingredient
		Yeast extract
		Sodium carboxymethyl betaglucan
		Dipotassium glycyrrhizate
		Yarrow flowers extract
		Calendula extract
		Rosemary extract
		Pyroxidine dicaprylate
		C 13-14 Isoparaffin
		Laureth-7 (dioxane-free)
		Phenoxyethanol
		Methylparaben
		Propylparaben
	5. Sunbrero *Product unavailable in:* JP, CN	Octocrylene
		Octyl methoxycinnamate
		Zinc oxide
		Purified water
		Octodecyl neopentanoate
		Dimethicone
		PVP/hexadecene copolymer
		Cetearyl alcohol
		Cyclomethicone
		Polyacrylamide
		Allantoin
		Aloe vera
		Ascorbyl methylsilanol pectinate
		Xanthan gum
		C13-14 Isoparaffin
		Vitamin E
		Laureth-7 (dioxane-free)
		Phenoxyethanol
		Methylparaben
		Propylparaben
	6. Tanacity *Product unavailable in:* KR, JP, MX	Purified water
		Rose hip oil
		Macadamia nut oil
		Polyacrylamide
		Micrococcus lysate
		Lecithin
		Dimethicone
		Aloe vera extract
		Yarrow flowers extract
		Calendula extract
		Rosemary extract
		C13-14 Isoparaffin
		Laureth-7 (dioxane-free)
		Phenoxyethanol
		Methylparaben
		Propylparaben
	7. Neways Tanning Oil *Product unavailable in:* KR, JP, UK, ML, AU, CN, MX	Octocrylene
		Homosalate
		Octyl methoxycinnamate
		Octyl salicylate
		Methyl anthranilate
		Hydrogenated polyisobutene
		Isodecyl neopentanoate
		Diisopropyl sebacate
		Lauryl lactate
		Cyclomethicone
		Aloe vera
		Tetrahexydecyl ascorbate (stabilized vitamin C)
		Retinyl palmitate (vitamin A)
		Vitamin E (D-alpha-Tocopheryl acetate)
		Guava extract
		Coconut extract
		Phenoxyethanol
		Methylparaben
		Propylparaben

Country	Country Abbreviation
Australia	AU
Canada	CN
Japan	JP
Korea	KR
Malasyia	ML
Mexico	MX
United Kingdom	UK

All products are available in the United States.

Users	Usage Abbreviations
Men	M
Women	W
Children	C
Infants	I

Other Designations

[ ] -- Brackets connote that the enclosed ingredient is in the process of being phased out.

* -- Asterisk identifies fragrances that composed of ten or fewer ingredients, primarily of floral or herbal origin.

EPILOGUE

More than 20 years ago, Dr. Donald Kennedy, the activist and scholarly FDA Commissioner from 1977 to 1979 (9), stressed "information strategy", particularly the labeling of consumer products with explicit warnings of health risks, as an integral function of regulation (18):

"It is by now clear to almost everyone that personal health behavior is an absolutely critical determinant of health outcomes. That requirement fits well with what I think of as the idealized role of regulation. Regulation, after all, arises as a consequence of the generation of public costs by private activity. **The best regulation is a clear signal that identifies these costs and allows members of the public to avoid them voluntarily**. Sometimes the regulator has to do more, as when the costs are impossibly cryptic or public understanding is inadequate. **In most cases, the regulator's task is to provide information. This role puts the Food and Drug Administration in the middle of the health education business.**"

Kennedy's position is a vigorous statement on the "responsibility of government to intervene actively, if only with information, to protect the public from health risks which are not sufficiently warded off by the forces of the market" (21). However, the U.S. government still denies the citizens' right-to-know of health risks from common consumer products—food, household, cosmetics and personal care. In diametric contrast, since the classic 1964 U.S. Surgeon General's Advisory Committee on Smoking and Health, over ten governmental agencies, including the FDA, have collaborated to warn citizens of the cancer risks of cigarettes, and other tobacco consumer products.

Evidence on the carcinogenicity of cigarette smoke is based on its content of a wide range of carcinogens as determined by rodent tests, and on epidemiological studies comparing lung and other cancer rates in non-smokers and smokers. While the chemistry of cigarette smoke (15) and of cosmetics and personal care products (Tables 2.2-2.4) is very different, several of the same carcinogens, including formaldehyde, nitrosodiethanolamine, arsenic, DDT and endrin, are found in both tobacco and personal care products.

The strong epidemiological evidence on the risks of smoking is based on comparisons of cancer rates in large population groups that smoke different amounts of cigarettes daily over different periods of time, and those in groups that have never smoked. In contrast, no such comparisons are feasible for cosmetics and personal care products as their use is virtually universal in most industrialized nations. However, there are two notable exceptions where it has been possible to define exposed and non-exposed population groups. In these cases, epidemiological studies have demonstrated major excess risks of ovarian cancer in women frequently dusting their genital area with talc (Chapter 2; Appendix 3A), and of multiple myeloma, non-Hodgkin's disease, Hodgkin's disease, leukemia and breast cancer in women regularly using permanent or semi-permanent black or dark brown hair dyes (Chapter Two; Appendix 4).

While fully recognizing that smoking tobacco is in itself the single most important cause of cancer, it should again be emphasized that non-smoking causes of cancer account for about 75% of the increased incidence of cancer in the U.S. and other major industrialized nations since the 1950's (Chapter One). In this context, it should be emphasized that there are striking and revealing differences between risks of smoking and those of cosmetics and personal care products (Table 1).

TABLE 1: CANCER RISKS OF SMOKING TOBACCO PRODUCTS COMPARED TO MAINSTREAM INDUSTRY COSMETICS AND PERSONAL CARE PRODUCTS

CANCER RISK	SMOKING TOBACCO PRODUCTS	USE OF COSMETICS AND PERSONAL CARE PRODUCTS
INDUSTRY KNOWLEDGE	Well documented	Well documented
REGULATORY KNOWLEDGE	Well documented	Well documented
CONSUMER KNOWLEDGE	Well documented	Virtually none
REGULATION	Limited	Virtually none
WARNING LABELS	Explicit in most nations	None
EXPOSURE	Voluntary	Involuntary
ONSET EXPOSURE	Usually in adolescence	Infancy
ROUTE EXPOSURE	Inhalation	Skin and inhalation
POPULATIONS EXPOSED	Largely lower socioeconomic (except in some Asiatic nations)	Virtually universal
RESPONSIBLE CARCINOGENS	Multiple	Multiple

Smoking in the U.S. and most major industrialized nations, other than the Asiatic, is increasingly restricted to lower socioeconomic groups, while the use of cosmetics and personal care products is population-wide. Moreover, smoking is uncommon prior to adolescence, while direct exposure to personal care products commences in infancy when sensitivity to carcinogens is maximal. Furthermore, it should be recognized that prior to addiction, especially in adolescents, smoking is a voluntary act with an inherent assumption of risk. This risk is emphasized by explicit cigarette warning labels, while there is no such warning and assumption of risk by the multimillion worldwide users of cosmetics and personal care products. So for all these reasons, it must be emphasized that cosmetics and personal care products are one of the most important, if not the single most important, causes of avoidable and involuntary lifelong exposure to multiple carcinogens (Chapter 2).

That the incidence of cancer in the U.S., Canada, U.K., Japan and other major industrialized nations has escalated to epidemic proportions over recent decades is unarguable. That consumers are unknowingly exposed to carcinogenic ingredients and contaminants in mainstream industry cosmetics, personal care products, food and household products, is unarguable. That cosmetics and personal care products are in varying degrees contaminated with dozens of carcinogens, and are usually applied daily to large areas of skin virtually from birth to death is also unarguable. This point becomes much more critical as such carcinogens are readily absorbed through the skin, with absorption facilitated by common detergent ingredients.

Equally unarguable, regardless of these life threatening but avoidable exposures, is the reckless indifference of: the multibillion dollar mainstream CPCP industries and their powerful global trade associations backed by indentured scientists; the U.S. Food and Drug Administration and other regulatory agencies worldwide; and governmental and "charitable" cancer institutions, such as the National Cancer Institute, and American Cancer Society, respectively, and similar cancer establishments worldwide. These institutions and industries have recklessly failed to warn congresses, parliaments and the public of well-documented scientific evidence of the lifelong risks of avoidable exposures to multiple carcinogens in mainstream industry cosmetic and personal care products. Compounding the abysmal policies and practices of the powerful industry/regulation/cancer establishment complex, is the surprising silence or ignorance of nearly all activist, consumer, and public interest groups.

This gaping chasm between cancer risks and those directly or indirectly responsible for preventing such risks leaves the market place as the final and only mechanism for assuring the safety of consumer products. Once health-conscious citizens are provided with information on the hazards of mainstream consumer products and the safety of alternative non-mainstream products, they will boycott the former, and instead purchase the latter. Thus by default, the market place is becoming the last refuge and mechanism for achieving non-regulatory reform of consumer products.

While a relatively small MLM company, compared to giant global mainstream industries, Neways has emerged as one of the very few successful marketers of safe cosmetics and personal care products and as a leading proponent of product safety; Aveda is another such exception. Not only is Neways future success assured but, as importantly, mainstream industries will eventually be forced to play catch-up.

APPENDICES

CANCER PREVENTION COALITION STATEMENT OF PURPOSE

The Cancer Prevention Coalition, Inc. (CPC), which opened its national office in Chicago in July 1994, is a unique nationwide coalition of leading independent experts in cancer prevention and public health, together with citizen activists and representatives of organized labor, public interest, environmental and women's health groups. Our goal is to reduce cancer rates through a comprehensive strategy of outreach, public education, advocacy and public policy initiatives to establish prevention as the nation's foremost cancer policy.

An overemphasis on the diagnosis and treatment of cancer and relative neglect of its prevention, coupled with ineffective regulation of carcinogens in air, water, food, consumer products, and the workplace, have contributed to escalating cancer rates and an annual death toll of over 500,000. The National Cancer Institute (NC1) and American Cancer Society (ACS)--which should be the chief advocates of cancer prevention--instead mislead the public and policy makers into believing that we are winning the war against cancer, and trivialize the role of avoidable exposures to industrial carcinogens.

The Coalition's activities are dual and complementary. The first is directed to cancer prevention on the personal level by informing consumers of their avoidable risks from undisclosed carcinogenic ingredients and contaminants in a wide range of foods and consumer products, such as cosmetics and home and garden pesticides. With this information, consumers will be empowered to demand safer alternatives and explicit food and product labeling. A major objective of our educational programs is to generate a critical mass of support for establishing prevention as a top priority in cancer and public health policies.

Our second activity is directed to advocating reform of national cancer policies, and the priorities of the NCI and ACS, to produce major emphasis on cancer prevention, particularly the elimination of avoidable exposures to environmental and occupational carcinogens. To this end, CPC advocates phasing out the manufacture, use and disposal of industrial carcinogens and their replacement with non-carcinogenic alternatives. In this regard we will seek out and work with socially responsible industries.

The ultimate and longer term objective of CPC is to truly advance the war against cancer by reducing modern epidemic cancer rates to their relatively low pre-1940 levels.

THE AMERICAN CANCER SOCIETY IS THREATENING THE NATIONAL CANCER PROGRAM WARNS SAMUEL S. EPSTEIN, M.D. AND QUENTIN D. YOUNG, M.D.

CHICAGO, June 12, 2001

The following was released by Samuel S. Epstein, M.D., Chairman of the Cancer Prevention Coalition and Quentin Young, M.D., Chairman of the Health and Medicine Policy Research Group and past President of the American Public Health Association.

Operating behind closed doors and with powerful political connections, Dr. Samuel Epstein, charges the American Cancer Society (ACS) with forging a questionably legal alliance with the federal Centers for Disease Control and Prevention (CDC) in attempts to hijack the National Cancer Program. The ACS is also charged with virtual neglect of cancer prevention.

Dr. Quentin Young, warns: "The ACS political agenda reveals a pattern of self interest, conflicts of interest, lack of accountability and non-transparency to all of which the media have responded with deafening silence".

Among their concerns:

- The National Cancer Act, the cornerstone of the National Cancer Institute's (NCI) war on cancer, is under powerful attack by the ACS, the world's largest non-religious "charity". The plan was hatched in September 1998 when, meeting behind closed doors, the ACS created a "National Dialogue on Cancer" (NDC), co-chaired by former President Bush and Barbara Bush, with representatives from the CDC, the giant cancer drug industry, and Collaborating Partners from survivor advocacy groups. The NDC leadership then unilaterally spun off a National Cancer Legislative Committee, co-chaired by Dr. John Seffrin, CEO of the ACS and Dr. Vincent DeVita, Director of the Yale Cancer Center and former NCI Director, to advise Congress on re-writing the National Cancer Act.

- The relationships between the ACS, NDC and its Legislative Committee raise questions on conflicts of interest. John Durant, former executive president of the American Society for Clinical Oncology, charged: "It has always seemed to me that this was an issue of control by the ACS over the cancer agenda--. They are protecting their own fundraising capacity" from competition by survivor groups. The leading U.S. charity watchdog, The Chronicle of Philanthropy, further concluded, "The ACS is more interested in accumulating wealth than saving lives".

• The ACS-CDC relationship is focused on diverting political emphasis and funds away from NCI's peer-reviewed scientific research to CDC's community programs, which center on community screening, behavioral intervention, and tobacco cessation rather than prevention.

• There are major concerns on interlocking ACS-CDC interests. CDC has improperly funded ACS with a $3 million sole source four-year cooperative agreement. In turn, ACS has made strong efforts to upgrade CDC's role in the National Cancer Program, increase appropriations for CDC's non-peer reviewed programs, and facilitate its access to tobacco litigation money.

• The ACS priority for tobacco cessation programs is inconsistent with its strong ties to the industry. Shandwick International, representing R.J. Reynolds, and Edelman, representing Brown & Williamson Tobacco Company, have been major PR firms for the NDC and its Legislative Committee.

• ACS has made questionably legal contributions to Democratic and Republican Governors' Associations. "We wanted to look like players and be players", ACS explained.

• DeVita, the Legislative Committee co-chair, is also chairman of the Medical Advisory Board of CancerSource.com, a website launched by Jones & Bartlett which publishes the ACS Consumer's Guide to Cancer Drugs; three other members of the Committee also serve on the board. DeVita thus appears to be developing his business interests in a publicly-funded forum.

• The ACS has a longstanding track record of indifference and even hostility to cancer prevention. This is particularly disturbing in view of the escalating incidence of cancer now striking one in two men and one in three women in their lifetimes. Recent examples include issuing a joint statement with the Chlorine Institute justifying the continued global use of persistent organochlorine pesticides, and also supporting the industry in trivializing dietary pesticide residues as avoidable risks of childhood cancer.

ACS policies are further exemplified by allocating under 0.1 percent of its $700 million annual budget to environmental and occupational causes of cancer.

These considerations clearly disqualify the ACS from any leadership role in the National Cancer Program. The public should be encouraged to redirect funding away from the ACS to cancer prevention advocacy groups. ACS conduct, particularly its political lobbying and relationship to CDC, should be investigated by Congressional Appropriations and Oversight committees. These committees should also recommend that the National Cancer Program direct the highest priority to cancer prevention.

U.K. CANCER CHARITIES INDICTED FOR LOSING THE WINNABLE WAR AGAINST CANCER

CHICAGO, Sept. 13, 1999

The major U.K. cancer "charities" are comprised by the Imperial Cancer Research Fund (ICRF) and the Cancer Research Campaign (CRC), under the umbrella organization of the Coordinating Committee on Cancer Research.

For decades, the policies and priorities of these charities have remained narrowly fixated on damage control—diagnosis and treatment—and closely related genetic research. As emphasized by Sir Richard Doll, the leading spokesman for these charities, their function is research and not prevention or education. This myopic mindset is compounded by interlocking conflicts of interest with the multimillion pound cancer drug, besides other, industries. This mindset is further exemplified by a long track record of indifference or hostility to cancer prevention, and to the evaluation of alternative or complementary cancer therapy and use of those for which there is evidence of efficacy.

A. Conflicts of Interest

The major charities have close interlocking interests with the cancer drug, chemotherapy and gene therapy, industries. These charities receive substantial funding from the drug industries and operate as multimillion pound corporations fronting for these industries. Additionally, these charities barely disguise their strong commercial structure and interests. Both ICRF and CRC have spun off wholly owned subsidiaries, ICRF Trading Ltd. and ICRF Technology Ltd., and CRC Technology Co., respectively. CRC Technology has funded research on the breast cancer gene BRCA2, defects of which are strongly associated with increased breast cancer risks, and subsequently applied for its patent rights.

These conflicts of interest are more striking with regard to Doll who has been the dominant figure and spokesman for the cancer charities and a determining influence on national, besides international, policies. Since 1978, when Doll was appointed Warden and Director of the Industry financed Green College, Oxford, which was established as a "special point of entry for industrial interests wishing to collaborate with University departments in research," his research and public positions have closely reflected industry interests and his indentured status to the disregard of fundamental public health and cancer prevention considerations. His extensive industry support, largely funneled through cancer charities, has included General Motors, British Nuclear Fuels and the National Radiation Protection Board. Not surprisingly, Doll has given a clean bill of health to leaded petroleum, low level radiation from nuclear processing plants such as Sellafield, atom bomb test radiation, and dioxin and Agent Orange. Also, not surprisingly has been Doll's trivializing or explaining away the escalating incidence of cancer, and the major causal role of involuntary and avoidable exposures to industrial carcinogens for much modern cancer. It should however be noted that Doll's more recent track record is in striking contrast to his activism and distinguished research on smoking, asbestos, gas production and radioactivity from the 1950's to the mid 1970's.

A current flagrant conflict of interest is exemplified by Dr. Karol Sikora, recently resigned from the WHO's cancer campaign, and who now holds the dual positions of Professor of Cancer Medicine at the Hammersmith Hospital and Vice President of Oncology at Pharmacia and UpJohn. Sikora has recently become closely associated with the cancer charities.

B. Invalid Claims for Major Advancements in Treatment

Based on a recent report on cancer survival trends from 1970-1990 by the Office of National Statistics, the London School of Hygiene and Tropical Medicine and the CRC, its Director General Dr. Gordon McVie has claimed improvements in treatment and survival rates, some quite dramatic, for 46 out of all 47 cancer studied. However, analysis of the underlying data reveals that the claimed improvements are not statistically significant for about half of the cancers. Furthermore, as emphasized in an April 24, 1999 editorial in The Lancet, for those 5 cancers (lung, pleura, esophagus, pancreas and liver) which account for 32% of all cancers in males and 17% in women, survival trends have been "uniformly poor." Moreover, the report provides no basis for determining whether any improved survival rates were due to improved access to health care and earlier diagnosis, rather than to any advances in treatment. Furthermore, the report failed to consider whether the claimed improved survival rates for prostate and breast cancers reflect recent diagnostic overkill, especially for pre-invasive forms of these cancers.

 C. Misrepresentation to the Prime Minister

On May 20, 1999, Prime Minister Blair announced a 10 year national crusade against cancer aimed at saving 60,000 of the 160,000 annual cancer deaths. At the same time, Blair invited 10 cancer experts to a meeting at 10 Downing Street to discuss his initiative. These experts included oncologists funded by CRC and ICRF, McVie and Sikora.

In an unsuccessful effort to pressure Blair to provide substantial governmental funding for cancer treatment, statements attributed to McVie and Sikora warned that Britain was "at the bottom of the table" with regard to treatment compared with the rest of Europe. This claim, however, misrepresented the findings of the EU funded 1999 EUROCARE study on which it was based. As reported in The Lancet on April 24, the study specifically warned that interpreting national differences as due to differences in diagnostic and treatment services is "fraught with difficulty", as the EUROCARE team conceded. Further invalidating such national comparisons was the absence of any information on the stage of diagnosis and treatment, differences of which could substantially influence survival rates in different European nations.

It is of further interest to note that the striking discrepancy between the cancer experts' doom and gloom presentation to Blair and the CRC's highly upbeat claims of major improvements in survival rates in its April 1999 report "CRC Cancer Stats: Survival, England and Wales 1971-1995". The report stated: "Cancer survival rates are improving over time. It is probable that survival for patients diagnosed in the late 1990's will be higher than those reported here." McVie has gone even further with his unfounded claims of improved survival rates for virtually all cancers.

Noteworthy also is that, by all accounts of the 10 Downing Street meeting, no reference was made to the overdue critical need for much less costly and more cost-effective large scale cancer prevention research programs, including providing the public with available information on avoidable and involuntary carcinogenic exposures.

D. Monopolistic Practices and Unaccountability

The major cancer charities have virtually demanded an exclusive monopoly on cancer funding and research, and have attempted to stifle initiatives by smaller non-mainstream charities with particular reference to alternative or complementary treatment. Illustrative is a July 1998 speech by McVie warning against public support of the smaller charities as these have difficulties in "obtaining high quality advice from external experts."

On May 15, 1998, Lord Baldwin of Bewdley wrote to the Times, calling for "accountability" from scientists and doctors working on cancer research and for an evaluation of alternative cancer therapy. McVie responded defensively by insisting that the major cancer charities were totally accountable, and that CRC had just funded trials on aromatherapy and controlled relaxation, without any reference to alternative drugs and nutritional therapy.

E. Trivializing the Cancer Epidemic and its Avoidable Causes

Over recent decades, the incidence of cancer has escalated to epidemic proportions, with lifetime risks now approaching one in two for men and one in three for women. As the lead front man for the charities, Doll has attempted to deny the reality of the cancer epidemic, apart from misrepresenting its causes. He has trivialized escalating incidence rates by emphasizing the relatively static incidence rates of most cancers in people under the age of 60, conveniently ignoring dramatic increases in childhood cancer and testicular cancer in young men, to the exclusion of much higher rates in people over the age of 60. It should be emphasized that such increases cannot be explained away by increasing longevity, as both incidence and mortality rates are statistically adjusted (age standardized) to reflect such trends. Doll has gone even further in trying to explain away any increases in cancer incidence on the basis of "blame-the-victim" distortions. With a series of unfounded guesstimates and with the unqualified backing of the cancer charities and the Ministry of Health, Doll stills asserts that smoking, fatty diet, alcohol and sexual behavior accounts for about 75% of cancers, while industrial pollution and occupation only account for 3% and 4% respectively. These assertions are scientific travesties and contrary to extensive scientific documentation.

While smoking is clearly the most important single cause of cancer, the incidence and mortality of lung cancer in men, but not women, is declining due to reduction in smoking. Meanwhile, the incidence of a wide range of non-smoking cancers, such as non-Hodgkin's lymphoma, multiple myeloma, prostate, testis, breast, colon, brain and childhood cancers, has increased steeply, in some instances by up to 200%. Nor can the role of high fat diets per se, be incriminated as significant causes of cancer. Not only are breast cancer rates lower in Mediterranean women despite diets with up 40% olive oil fat, but also epidemiological studies over the last few decades have consistently failed to find any causal relation between breast and colon cancers and the fat consumption.

Not surprisingly, in view of their preoccupation with "blame-the-victim" distortions of cancer causation and industrial conflicts of interest, the cancer charities have trivialized or ignored the strong body of scientific evidence incriminating the role of run-away industrial technologies, particularly the petrochemical and nuclear. The explosive growth of these industries since the 1950's has resulted in pervasive contamination of the total environment with a wide range of often persistent industrial carcinogens. As a consequence, the public has been and continues to be unknowingly exposed to avoidable carcinogens in air, water, consumer products—food, cosmetics and toiletries and household products—from conception to death. The failure of the cancer charities to have informed Parliament, regulatory authorities and the public with such information, which is relatively inaccessible in the scientific literature or which remains buried in government and industry files, has prevented the development of corrective legislative and regulatory action, and has denied the public its basic democratic right-to-know and the opportunity to take individual action to reduce avoidable risks of cancer. This dereliction of public health responsibility is compounded by the failure of the charities to have undertaken scientific research on avoidable causes of cancer, other than a recent study on future risks of asbestos in Western Europe and a literature survey on the causes of testicular cancer, with particular regard to involuntary and avoidable carcinogenic exposures.

F. Needed Reforms

Drastic reforms of the policies and priorities of the cancer charities are urgently and belatedly needed. These include:

Development of research and public outreach programs directed to avoidable causes of cancer, particularly those whose incidence has dramatically increased over recent decades and those involving unknowing and involuntary carcinogenic exposures. These programs should be phased in over a maximum period of five years, by when their funding should achieve parity with that of all other programs combined.

Clinical trials should be initiated on those alternative and complementary therapies for which there is substantial or reasonable preliminary evidence of efficacy. In the first instance, priority should be given to those therapies identified in the 200 promising studies identified by the U.S. Congressional Office of Technology Assessment in September 1990. Criteria for assessing the efficacy of these therapies should be no more stringent than those for conventional toxic chemotherapy and gene therapy.

Problems of conflicts of interest should be fully recognized and appropriate corrective action should be taken. All executive and advisory committees should be restructured to ensure parity of membership with scientific and lay representatives of public interest and citizen prevention and alternative therapy advocacy groups.

There is little likelihood that such reforms will be freely undertaken in the absence of well organized grass roots pressures and publicity. Failure to undertake such reforms would clearly merit a national economic boycott of the major charities with diversion of public funds to non-mainstream charities dedicated to prevention and investigation of alternative therapies, and use of those for which there is evidence of efficacy.

For further details, see:

Epstein, S.S. "The Politics of Cancer, Revisited," 1998. East Ridge Press, Fremont Center, NY 12741.

Walker, M. "Sir Richard Doll: A questionable Pillar of the Cancer Establishment." The Ecologist 28(2): 82-92, 1998

CANCER GROUP AND RALPH NADER RELEASE "DIRTY DOZEN" CONSUMER PRODUCT LIST

WASHINGTON, D.C., Sept. 20, 1995

The Cancer Prevention Coalition (CPC) and Ralph Nader will release tomorrow a "Dirty Dozen" list of consumer products used in most American homes, and manufactured by giant U.S. corporations. Brand named "Dirty Dozen" products include: Ajax Cleanser®, Clairol® Nice n'Easy Haircolor and Lysol® Disinfectant.

The "Dirty Dozen" products contain a wide-range of carcinogenic and other toxic ingredients and contaminants to which most of us are exposed daily.

CPC Chairperson Samuel Epstein, M.D., and investigative journalist, David Steinman, compiled the "Dirty Dozen" from data on over 3,500 consumer products analyzed and ranked in their recently published The Safe Shopper's Bible. The good news is that safer alternatives are available for all the "Dirty Dozen".

Nader and CPC urged the manufacturers of the "Dirty Dozen" to reformulate their products with non-toxic alternatives. "Ironically, some "Dirty Dozen" manufacturers also market safer alternatives", said Dr. Epstein.

"What is particularly galling about the "Dirty Dozen", emphasized Ralph Nader, "is that these toxic chemicals don't have to be there. Yet these corporations continue to expose people to health hazards unnecessarily".

Current product labeling provides no warning for cancer and other chronic health risks. Food is labeled for cholesterol, but not for carcinogens. Cosmetics are labeled for major ingredients, but not for those that form carcinogens or contain carcinogenic contaminants. Except for pesticides, household products contain no information on their ingredients.

Cancer rates are skyrocketing. Currently, more than one-third of all of us will develop cancer in our lifetime, and one-fourth will die from the disease. Many cancers are due to avoidable exposures to industrial carcinogens in the food we eat, and the cosmetics and household products we use.

"Americans have a fundamental right-to-know about hazardous chemicals in all consumer products they buy, and the cancer and other risks of those chemicals—information that remains hidden in government and industry files," concluded Dr. Epstein. "With this knowledge, consumers can protect themselves by voting with their shopping dollars and buying safer alternatives".

"TRADE SECRETS": THE LATEST IN A LONG LINE OF INDUSTRY CONSPIRACIES

CHICAGO, March 23, 2001

Bill Moyers is to be warmly commended for his March 26 program "Trade Secrets". This PBS Special will document the chemical industry's conspiracy in denying information on the grave cancer risks to hundreds of thousands of workers manufacturing the potent carcinogen vinyl chloride (VC) and its polyvinyl chloride (PVC) product.

As newsworthy is the fact that there is a decades-long track record of numerous such conspiracies involving a wide range of industries and chemicals, besides VC. These conspiracies have resulted in an escalation in the incidence and mortality of cancer, and chronic disease, among workers and the general public unknowingly exposed to toxics and carcinogens in the workplace, air, water and consumer products—food, household products, and cosmetics and toiletries.

This misconduct involves negligence, manipulation, suppression, distortion and destruction of health and environmental data by mainstream industries, their consultants and trade associations, notably the Chemical Manufacturers Association (CMA). These practices are so frequent as to preclude dismissal as exceptional aberrations and, in many instances, arguably rise to the level of criminality as illustrated below:

- Suppression of evidence from the early 1960's on the toxicity of VC by Dow Chemical, and on its carcinogenicity from 1970 by the VC/PVC industry and CMA. Based on these findings, a blue ribbon committee of the American Association for the Advancement of Science charged in 1976 that: "Because of the suppression of these data (by the CMA), tens of thousands of workers were exposed without warning—to toxic concentrations of VC".

- Suppression of evidence since the 1930's on the hazards of asbestos, asbestosis and lung cancer, by Johns-Manville and Raybestos-Manhattan, besides the Metropolitan Life Insurance Company. This information was detailed in industry documents dubbed the "Asbestos Pentagon Papers", released at 1978 Congressional Hearings.

- Suppression by Rohm and Haas of information, known since 1962 but not released until 1971, on the potent carcinogenicity of the resin bischloromethylether. This resulted in deaths from lung cancer of some 50 men, many non-smokers and under the age of 50.

- Suppression of carcinogenicity data on organochlorine pesticides: Aldrin/Dieldrin, by Shell Chemical Company since 1962; Chlordane/Heptachlor, by Velsicol Chemical Company since 1959; and Kepone, by Allied Chemical Company since the early 1960's.

- Falsification in the early 1970's of test data on the drug Aldactone and artificial sweetener Aspartame by Hazleton Laboratories under contract to G.D. Searle Company.

- Falsification and manipulation by Monsanto since the 1960's of data on dioxin, and its contamination of products including the herbicide Agent Orange, designed to block occupational exposure claims and tightening of federal regulations. This evidence was detailed in 1990 by Environmental Protection Agency's Office of Criminal Investigation which charged Monsanto with a "long pattern of fraud" and with reporting "false information" to the Agency.

- Fraudulent claims by Monsanto since 1985 that genetically engineered (rBGH) milk is indistinguishable from natural milk. These claims persist despite contrary evidence.

- Monsanto's reckless marketing in 1976 of plastic Coke bottles made from acrylonitrile, a chemical closely related to VC, prior to its testing for carcinogenicity and migration into the Coke. The bottles were subsequently banned after acrylonitrile was found to be a potent carcinogen contaminating the Coke.

- Destruction of epidemiological data on ethyleneimine and other chemicals by Dow and DuPont. This was admitted at 1973 Department of Labor Advisory Committee meetings in response to challenges to produce data on whose basis industry had falsely claimed that these chemicals were not carcinogens.

- Destruction of test data on drugs, food additives, and pesticides as admitted in 1977 by Industrial Biotest Laboratories, under contract to major chemical industries.

- Failure of the mainstream cosmetics and toiletry industries to warn of the wide range of avoidable carcinogenic ingredients, contaminants and precursors in their products used by the great majority of the U.S. population over virtually their lifetimes.

(For supporting documentation of the above charges, see the author's: Testimony on White Collar Crime, H.R. 4973, before the Subcommittee on Crime of the House Judiciary Committee, 12/13/79; The Politics of Cancer, 1979; and The Politics of Cancer, Revisited, 1998.)

Hopefully, the public and the media will be outraged by this longstanding evidence of recklessness and conspiracies, graphically reinforced by Moyers' program. The public and the media should finally hold industry accountable, and demand urgent investigation and radical reform of current industry practices besides governmental unresponsiveness. The Moyers' program has already galvanized formation of a coalition of grassroots citizen groups, "Coming Clean", to demand more responsible and open industry practices, including phasing out the use and manufacture of toxic chemicals.

Criticism should also be directed to the multibillion dollar cancer establishment—the National Cancer Institute and American Cancer Society—for their failure to warn Congress, regulatory agencies and the general public of the scientific evidence on the permeation of the totality of the environment with often persistent industrial carcinogens thus precluding corrective legislation and regulation, besides denying workers and the public of their inalienable right-to-know.

DUSTING WITH CANCER: COALITION URGES CHICAGO DRUG STORES TO LABEL TALC

CHICAGO, Nov. 17, 1994

According to the Cancer Prevention Coalition, the regular use of talc increases the risk of ovarian cancer.   The Cancer Prevention Coalition (CPC) will announce its plans for a talcum powder labeling initiative here in Chicago at a Thursday, November 17, 1994 press briefing.

Speakers at the press briefing will include CPC Chair Dr. Samuel Epstein, CPC Board members Dr. Quentin Young and Dr. Peter Orris, and an ovarian cancer survivor. The speakers will explain why a labeling initiative is important to residents of Chicago, and will also answer questions from the press.

Recently, CPC sent letters to the Chicago corporate offices of Osco and Walgreen drug stores urging that they provide customers with information on the dangers associated with the use of talc. Additionally, CPC is filing a petition with the FDA requesting that talc products be explicitly labeled.

The use of talc poses a serious risk of ovarian cancer. Estimates are that up to 17% of American women regularly use talc in the genital area. Women have been compelled through advertisements of the cosmetic industry, to dust themselves to mask odors. Talcum powder has historically been a symbol of freshness, cleanliness and purity. Talc is even more commonly used on infants.

Ovarian cancer is a silent killer. It causes 38 deaths daily among American women—totalling 14,000 deaths annually. It is the fourth highest women's cancer death rate in the U.S. Over 60% of ovarian cancer victims die within five years of diagnosis.

"Studies seem to indicate that talc poses an increased risk factor for ovarian cancer, thus I would support a warning label to alert women to this possible risk," stated Diane Farrell, a Chicago resident who has been fighting ovarian cancer for the last two years.

According to Dr. Samuel Epstein, of the Cancer Prevention Coalition, "A wide range of scientific studies over the last three decades have clearly linked regular talc use by women and ovarian cancer."

The talc labeling project is the first phase of a "Consumer Labeling Initiative" that will inform citizens of the presence of undisclosed carcinogenic ingredients and contaminants in cosmetics, other consumer products, and food and how to avoid them.

RESULTS FROM AN INFORMAL SURVEY OF TALC PRODUCTS IN CHICAGO DRUG STORES

BABY POWDERS

Johnson & Johnson Baby Powder (Johnson & Johnson, Skillman, NJ)
    Contains: TALC, fragrance

Osco Brand Baby Powder (Osco Drug, Oak Brook, IL)
    Contains: TALC, fragrance

Body Powders

Jean Nate Perfumed Talc (Revlon, New York, NY)
    Contains: TALC, kaolin, magnesium carbonate, fragrance

Shower to Shower (Johnson & Johnson, Skillman, NJ)
    Contains: TALC, cornstarch, sodium bicarbonate, fragrance, polysaccarides

Osco Brand Body Powder (Osco Drug, Oak Brook, IL)
    Contains: TALC, cornstarch, sodium bicarbonate, fragrance, polysaccarides

Ammens Medicated Powder (Bristol-Myers Squibb, New York, NY)
    Contains: Zinc oxide, cornstarch, fragrance, isostearic acid, PPG-20, methyl glucose ether, TALC

Cashmere Bouquet Perfumed Powder (Colgate, New York, NY)
    Contains: TALC, magnesium carbonate, zinc stearate, fragrance

Gold Bond Medicated Powder (Martin Himmel, Hypoluxo, FL)
    Contains: Menthol, zinc oxide, boric acid, eucalyptol, methyl salicylate, salicylic acid, TALC, thymol, zinc stearate

FEMININE PRODUCTS

Vagisil Feminine Powder (COMBE, Inc., White Plains, NY)
Contains: Cornstarch, aloe, mineral oil, magnesium stearate, silica, benzethonium chloride, fragrance

Vaginex Feminine Powder (Schmid Laboratories, Sarasota, FL)
Contains: Zinc oxide, cornstarch, fragrance, 6-hydroxyquinoline, 8-hydroxyquinoline, sulfate, isostearic acid, PPG-20, methyl glucose, ether, TALC

Summer's Eve Feminine Powder (CB Fleet Co., Lynchburg, VA)
Contains: Cornstarch, tricalcium phosphate, oxoxynol-9, benzethonium chloride, fragrance

FDS Feminine Deodorant Spray (Alberto Culver, Melrose Park, IL)
Contains: isobutene, isopropyl myristate, cornstarch, mineral oil, fragrance, lanolin, alcohol, hydrated silica, magnesium stearate, benzyl alcohol

THEY MAKE YOU SMELL, FEEL, AND LOOK GOOD BUT CAN COSMETICS INCREASE YOUR RISK OF CANCER? CANCER COALITION CALLS FOR TOUGH COSMETIC STANDARDS

CHICAGO, Oct. 22, 1996

In a petition to the Food and Drug Administration (FDA) released today, the Cancer Prevention Coalition (CPC) urged the labeling or phasing out of DEA in cosmetic products. DEA is a precursor of nitrosodiethanolamine (NDEA), a proven carcinogen as recognized by four Federal agencies and institutions and the World Health Organization. The proposed label would read, "Caution - This product may contain N-nitrosodiethanolamine, a known cancer-causing agent."

DEA-based detergents are widely used in shampoos, lotions and creams. Since 1976, worker exposed to NDEA in metal working fluids, at levels similar to those in cosmetics, have been warned of cancer risks and steps are taken to protect them.

Aubrey Hampton, founder of Aubrey Organics, noted that DEA is not an essential ingredient in hair and skin care products. There are natural, safe and effective alternatives to DEA that pose no financial hardship for the manufacturer or the consumer"

In 1979, the FDA urged the cosmetics industry to take "immediate action to eliminate" NDEA in cosmetics. However, the FDA has taken no subsequent action while industry remains unresponsive. In striking contrast, the EEC has sharply reduced permissible uses of DEA. German cosmetic industry has also resolved this problem by phasing out DEA detergents, thereby preventing the formation of NDEA.

"We feel confident that responsible companies will take prompt action to protect American consumers", stressed Mary Haight, a CPC representative.

Dr. William Lijinksy, leading international nitrosamine researcher, emphasized, "The continued use of DEA is unacceptable especially in view of the overwhelming scientific evidence of its cancer risks and the availability of safe alternatives."

Samuel S. Epstein, M.D., professor of environmental and occupational medicine at the University of Illinois School of Public Health and chairman of the Cancer Prevention Coalition said that, "Faced with escalating cancer rates, the FDA and other health agencies should take overdue action to reduce avoidable exposures to carcinogens. NDEA in cosmetics, used by many million consumers for many decades, is a prime example of such an avoidable carcinogen".

MAJOR COSMETIC AND TOILETRY INGREDIENT POSES AVOIDABLE CANCER RISK

CHICAGO, Feb. 22, 1998

As reported on CBS Morning News today, the National Toxicology Program (NTP) recently found that repeated skin application to mouse skin of diethanolamine (DEA), or its fatty acid derivative cocamide-DEA, induced liver and kidney cancer. Besides this "clear evidence of carcinogenicity," NTP also emphasized that DEA is readily absorbed through the skin and accumulates in organs, such as the brain, where it induces chronic toxic effects.

High concentrations of DEA-based detergents are commonly used in a wide range of cosmetics and toiletries, including shampoos, hair dyes and conditioners, lotions, creams and bubble baths, besides liquid dishwashing and laundry soaps. Lifelong use of these products thus clearly poses major avoidable cancer risks to the great majority of U.S. consumers, particularly infants and young children.

Further increasing these cancer risks is longstanding evidence that DEA readily interacts with nitrite preservatives or contaminants in cosmetics or toiletries to form nitrosodiethanolamine (NDELA), another carcinogen as well recognized by Federal agencies and institutions and the World Health Organization, which, like DEA, is also rapidly absorbed through the skin. In 1979, FDA warned that over 40% of all cosmetic products were contaminated with NDELA and called for industry "to take immediate action to eliminate this carcinogen from cosmetic products." In two 1991 surveys, 27 out of 29 products were found to be contaminated with high concentrations of this carcinogen, results which were subsequently confirmed by the FDA. Based on this information, the European Union and European industry have both taken strong action to reduce or eliminate DEA and NDELA from cosmetics and toiletries. In sharp contrast, the FDA has taken no such action, nor has it responded to a 1996 petition from the Cancer Prevention Coalition to phase out the use of DEA or to label DEA-containing products with an explicit cancer warning. The mainstream U.S. industry has been similarly unresponsive, even to the extent of ignoring an explicit warning by the Cosmetics, Toiletries and Fragrance Association to discontinue uses of DEA. Such reckless intransigence is in strong contrast to the responsiveness of the growing safe cosmetic industry.

Tom Mower, CEO of Neways Inc., a major distributor of carcinogen-free cosmetics, emphasizes: "I see no reason at all to use DEA, as there are safe and cost-effective alternatives which we have been using in a wide range of our cosmetics and toiletries for the last decade."

Faced with escalating cancer rates, now striking more than one in three Americans, FDA should take immediate action to prevent further exposure to the avoidable carcinogens DEA and NDELA in cosmetics, toiletries and liquid soaps. Safe and effective alternatives to DEA are readily available.

PERFUME: CUPID'S ARROW OR POISON DART

CHICAGO, Feb. 7, 2000/PR Newswire*

Lovers looking for the perfect Valentine's gift should think twice before giving a bottle of toxic chemicals to their sweethearts. Recent analysis of Calvin Klein's "Eternity Eau de Parfum" (Eternity) by an industry laboratory specializing in fragrance chemistry revealed 41 ingredients. These include some known to be toxic to the skin, respiratory tract, nervous, and reproductive systems, and others known to be carcinogens; no toxicity data are available on several ingredients, while data on most are inadequate. Additionally, some ingredients are volatile and a source of indoor air pollution. Since 1995, several consumers have complained to the Food and Drug Administration (FDA) of neurological and respiratory problems due to Eternity.

The analysis was recently commissioned by the Environmental Health Network (EHN) as many members had complained of asthma, migraine, sensitization, or multiple chemical sensitivity when exposed to Eternity. Based on this analysis, EHN filed a Citizen Petition with the FDA on May 11, 1999, which was subsequently endorsed by the Cancer Prevention Coalition. The petition requests that the FDA take administrative action and declare Eternity "misbranded" or "adulterated" since it does not carry a warning label as required by the terms of the Food, Drug, and Cosmetic Act and the Fair Packaging and Labeling Act. Grounds for requesting the warning label include FDA regulation 21CFR Sec. 740/10: "Each ingredient used in a cosmetic product and each finished cosmetic product shall be adequately substantiated for safety prior to marketing. Any such ingredient or product whose safety is not adequately substantiated prior to marketing is misbranded unless it contains the following conspicuous statement on the principal display panel: Warning: the safety of this product has not been determined."

Since May, over 700 consumers with health problems from exposure to various mainstream fragrances have written to the FDA supporting EHN's petition. The FDA responded on November 30 to the effect that they had been unable to reach a decision on the grounds of "other priorities and the limited availability of resources." The petition is thus still open for further public complaints and endorsements.

A wide range of mainstream fragrances and perfumes, predominantly based on synthetic ingredients, are used in numerous cosmetics and toiletries, and also soaps and other household products. Currently, the fragrance industry is virtually unregulated. Its recklessness is abetted and compounded by FDA's complicity. The FDA has refused to require the industry to disclose ingredients due to trade secrecy considerations, and still takes the position that "consumers are not adversely affected — and should not be deprived of the enjoyment" of these products. The Cancer Prevention Coalition and EHN take the unequivocal position that the FDA should implement its own regulations and act belatedly to protect consumer health and safety.

Valentine sweethearts should switch to organically grown (pesticide-free) roses or other flowers as safe alternatives to mainstream perfumes.

---

*Joint Press Release with the Environmental Health Network, California

APPENDIX 21:

UNDISCLOSED CARCINOGENS IN COSMETICS AND PERSONAL CARE PRODUCTS POSE AVOIDABLE RISKS OF CANCER

CHICAGO, Jan. 15, 2001

Government scientists recently identified a group of toxic chemicals known as phthalates in urine of adults, with highest levels in premenopausal women, resulting from inhalation and skin exposure to volatile parent ingredients used extensively as solvents and plasticizers in personal care and cosmetic (PCC) products. These include perfumes, shampoos, hair sprays and nail polishes. These findings raise major concerns in view of documented evidence, dating back to 1985, that these phthalates induce birth defects, low sperm counts, and other reproductive toxicity in experimental animals. The Food and Drug Administration (FDA), authorized by the 1938 Food, Drug and Cosmetics Act to ban unsafe PCC products, responded that it will now consider this longstanding information. While obviously important, the phthalate findings merely reflect the tip of an iceberg of more fundamental problems which have received minimal, if any, attention, from Congress, the media and the public.

The FDA's relaxed response reflects reckless regulatory abdication matched by unresponsiveness of mainstream industries. A 1990 report by the U.S. General Accounting Office charging that the FDA commits no resources for assessing PCC safety had no impact on the agency's policies. The agency's sole requirement is restricted to ingredient labeling of PCC products, with the exception of fragrances and perfumes. With rare exceptions, such as children's bubble baths, the FDA has never required industry to label PCC products with any warning of well-documented toxic or cancer risks, nor has it banned the sale of unsafe products to an unsuspecting public.

- Black and dark brown permanent hair dyes contain numerous ingredients, such as diaminoanisole and FD&C Red 33, recognized as carcinogens in experimental animals. This evidence is supported by studies establishing that regular use of these dyes poses major risks of relatively rare cancers—non-Hodgkin's lymphoma, Hodgkin's disease and multiple myeloma.

- Cosmetic grade talc is carcinogenic in experimental animals. Also, frequent genital dusting with talc, routinely practiced by some 17% of women, increases risks of ovarian cancer.

- A group of widely used preservatives, such as quaternium15 and bronopol, widely used in baby products, though not carcinogenic themselves, break down to release formaldehyde, a potent irritant and carcinogen.

- Lanolin, widely used on babies' skin and nipples of nursing mothers, is commonly contaminated with DDT and other carcinogenic pesticides.

- Commonly used PCC detergents and foaming agents, such as polysorbates and PEG, are usually contaminated with the volatile carcinogen dioxane, although this could be easily removed by vacuum stripping during manufacture.

- DEA, another widely used chemical detergent, has been known since 1975 to combine with nitrite preservatives or contaminants in PCC products to form a highly carcinogenic nitrosamine. Furthermore, recent government studies showed that DEA itself is also carcinogenic following application to mouse skin.

Citizen petitions to the FDA by the Cancer Prevention Coalition in 1994 and 1996 detailing evidence on the cancer risks of talc and DEA-containing products, respectively, and "Seeking Carcinogenic Labeling " on these products, met with no substantive response.

Concerns on cancer risks from PCC products are emphasized by: lifelong use of multiple products by the majority of the U.S. population; the ready skin absorption of carcinogenic ingredients, further increased by detergents, especially when left on the skin for prolonged periods; and by decades-long suppression of information by the FDA and industry, abetted by a roll-over media, in flagrant denial of consumers' right-to-know.

Mainstream industry products thus pose major risks of avoidable cancer. Their role in the escalating incidence of cancer, now striking one in two men and one in three women in their lifetimes, remains largely unrecognized by our apparently health conscious society. Armed with such information, consumers should protect themselves by shopping for safe alternative products available from the growing non-mainstream industry.

CITIZEN PETITION SEEKING CARCINOGENIC LABELING ON ALL COSMETIC TALC PRODUCTS

November 17, 1994

David A. Kessler, M.D.
Commissioner
Food and Drug Administration, Room 1-23
12420 Parklawn Drive
Rockville, MD 20857

The undersigned submits on behalf of the Cancer Prevention Coalition, Inc. (CPC), Samuel S. Epstein, M.D., Chair and National Advisor of the Ovarian Cancer Early Detection and Prevention Foundation (OCEDPF), Nancy Nehls Nelson, member of the Ovarian Cancer Early Detection and Prevention Foundation, Peter Orris, M.D. and Quentin Young, M.D. This citizen petition is based on scientific papers dating back to the 1960s which warn of increased cancer rates resulting from frequent exposure to cosmetic grade talc.

The undersigned submits this petition under 21 U.S.C. 321 (n), 361, 362, and 371 (a); and 21 CFR 740.1, 740.2 of 21 CFR 10.30 of the Federal Food, Drug, and Cosmetic Act to request the Commissioner of Food and Drugs to require that all cosmetic talc products bear labels with a warning such as "Talcum powder causes cancer in laboratory animals. Frequent talc application in the female genital area increases risk of ovarian cancer."

A. AGENCY ACTION REQUESTED

This petition requests that FDA take the following action:

(1) Immediately require cosmetic talcum powder products to bear labels with a warning such as "Talcum powder causes cancer in laboratory animals. Frequent talc application in the female genital area increases the risk of ovarian cancer."

(2) Pursuant to 21 CFR 10.30 (h) (2), a hearing at which time we can present our scientific evidence.

B. STATEMENT OF GROUNDS

Ovarian cancer is the fourth deadliest women's cancer in the U.S., striking approximately 23,000 and killing approximately 14,000 women this year. Ovarian cancer is very difficult to detect at the early stages of the disease, making the survival rate very low. Only three percent of ovarian cancer cases can be attributed to family history.[1] One of the avoidable risk factors for ovarian cancer is the daily use of talcum powder in the genital area.[2]

Research done as early as 1961 has shown that particles, similar to talc and asbestos particles, can translocate from the exterior genital area to the ovaries in women.[3,4,5] These findings provide support to the unexpected high rate of mortality from ovarian cancer in female asbestos workers.[6,7,8] Minute particles, such as talc are able to translocate through the female reproductive tract and cause foreign body reactions in the ovary.

There is a large body of scientific evidence, dating back thirty years, on the toxicity and mineralogy of cosmetic talc products. As early as 1968, Cralley et al. concluded:

> All of the 22 talcum products analyzed have a ... fiber content ... averaging 19%. The fibrous material was predominantly talc but probably contained minor amounts of tremolite, anthophyllite, and chrysotile [asbestos-like fibers] as these are often present in fibrous talc mineral deposits... Unknown significant amounts of such materials in products that may be used without precautions may create an unsuspected problem.[9]

As a follow-up to previous findings, Rohl, et al., examined 21 samples of consumer talcums and powders, including baby powders, body powders, facial powders and pharmaceutical powders between 1971-1975. The study concluded:

"...cosmetic grade talc was not used exclusively. The presence in these products of asbestiform anthophyllite and tremolite, chrysotile, and quartz indicates the need for a regulatory standard for cosmetic talc ... We also recommend that evaluation be made to determine the possible health hazards associated with the use of these products."[10]

Talc is a carcinogen, with or without the presence of asbestos-like fibers. In 1993, the National Toxicology Program published a study on the toxicity of non-asbestiform talc and found *clear evidence of carcinogenic activity.*[11]

Recent cancer research in the United States has found conclusively that frequent talcum powder application in the genital area increases a woman's risk of developing ovarian cancer.[12,13,14,15] Cramer, et al, suggested that talc application directly to the genital area around the time of ovulation might lead to talc particles becoming deeply imbedded in the substance of the ovary and perhaps causing foreign body reaction (granulomas) capable of causing growth of epithelial ovarian tissue.[16,17]

Harlow, et al, found that frequent talc use directly on the genital area during ovulation increased a woman's risk threefold. That study also found:

> "The most frequent method of talc exposure was use as a dusting powder directly to the perineum [genitals] ... Brand or generic "baby powder" was used most frequently and was the category associated with a statistically significant risk for ovarian cancer."

In Harlow's report, arguably the most comprehensive study of talc use and ovarian cancer to date, 235 ovarian cancer cases were identified and compared to 239 controls, women with no sign of ovarian cancer or related health problems. Through personal interviews, Harlow, et al, found that 16.7% of the control group reported frequent talc application to the perineum.[18] This percentage is useful in estimating the number of women in the general population exposed to cosmetic talc in the genital area on a regular basis. Harlow, et al, concludes:

> ". . . given the poor prognosis for ovarian cancer, any potentially harmful exposures should be avoided, particularly those with limited benefits. For this reason, we discourage the use of talc in genital hygiene, particularly as a daily habit."

Clearly, large numbers of women—an estimated 17%—are using cosmetic talc in the genital area and may not be adequately warned of the risk of ovarian cancer from daily use.

C. CLAIM FOR CATEGORICAL EXCLUSION

A claim for categorical exclusion is asserted pursuant to 21 CFR 25.24 (a) (11).

D. CERTIFICATION

The undersigned certifies, that, to the best knowledge and belief of the undersigned, this petition includes all information and views on which the petition relies, and that is includes representative data and information known to the petitioner which are unfavorable to the petition.

This petition is submitted by:

Samuel S. Epstein, M.D.
Cancer Prevention Coalition
520 North Michigan Avenue, Suite 410
Chicago, Illinois 60611
312-467-0600 phone
312-467-0599 fax

Samuel S. Epstein, M.D.   November 17, 1994

Council to the Cancer Prevention Coalition
Center for Constitutional Rights
Michael E. Deutsch, Legal Director
666 Broadway
New York, NY 10012
212-614-6427

CITATIONS

1. SEER Cancer Statistics, 1973-1990.

2. Harlow BL, Cramer DW, Bell DA, Welch WR. "Perineal exposure to talc and ovarian cancer risk" Obstet Gynecol, 80:19-26, 1992.

3. Egli GE, Newton M. "The transport of carbon particles in the human female reproductive tract" Fertility Sterility, 12:151-155, 1961.

4. Venter FF, Iturralde M. "Migration of particulate radioactive tracer from the vagina to the peritoneal cavity and ovaries" S African Med J, 55:917-919, 1979.

5. Henderson WJ, Hamilton TC, Baylis MS, Pierrepoint CG, Griffiths K. "The demonstration of migration of talc from the vagina and posterior uterus to the ovary in the rat" Environ Research, 40:247-250, 1986.

6. Newhouse ML, Berry G, Wagner JC, Turok ME. "A study of the mortality of female asbestos workers" Brit J Indust Med, 29:134-141, 1972.

7. Wignall BK, Fox AJ. "Mortality of female gas mask assemblers" Brit J Indust Med, 39:24-38, 1982.

8. Acheson ED, Gardner MJ, Pippard E, Grime LP. "Mortality of two groups of women who manufactured gas masks from chrysotile and crocidolite asbestos: a 40-year follow-up" Brit J Indust Med, 39:344-348, 1982.

9. Cralley LJ, Key MM, Groch DK, Lainhart WS, Ligo RM. "Fibrous and mineral content of cosmetic talcum products" Am Industrial Hygiene Assoc J, 29:350-354, 1968.

10. Rohl AN, Langer AM, Selifoff LJ, Tordini A, Klimentidis R, Bowes DR, Skinner DL. "Consumer talcums and powders: mineral and chemical characterization" J Toxicol Environ Health, 2:255-284, 1976.

11. National Toxicology Program. "Toxicology and carcinogenesis studies of talc (CAS No 14807-96-6) in F344/N rats and B6C3F, mice (Inhalation studies)". Technical Report Series No 421, September 1993.

12. Hartge P, Hoover R, Lasher LP, McGowan L. "Talc and ovarian cancer" Letter. JAMA, 250:1844, 1983.

13. Rosenblatt KA, Szklo M, Rosenshein NE. "Mineral fiber exposure and the development of ovarian cancer" Gynecol Oncol, 45:20-25, 1992.

14. Whittemore AS, Wu ML, Paffenbarger RS, Sarles DL, Kampert JB, Grosser S, Jung DL, Ballon S, Hendrickson M. "Personal and environmental characteristics related to epithelial ovarian cancer. II. Exposures to talcum powder, tobacco, alcohol and coffee" Am J Epidemiol, 1128:1228-1240, 1988.

15. Harlow, 1992.

16. Ibid.

17. Cramer DW, Welch WR, Scully RE, Wojciechowski CA. "Ovarian cancer and talc: a case study" Cancer, 50:372-376, 1982.

<u>FDA RESPONSE (July 11, 1995)</u>

FDA has not been able to reach a decision "because of the limited availability of resources and other agency priorities".

CITIZEN PETITION SEEKING CANCER WARNING ON COSMETICS
CONTAINING DEA

October 22, 1996

David A. Kessler, M.D.
Commissioner
Food and Drug Administration, Room #14-71
Rockville, MD 20857

The undersigned submits on behalf of the Cancer Prevention Coalition, Inc., and its Chairman, Samuel S. Epstein, M.D., and on behalf of the Center for Constitutional Rights, Michael Deutsch, Esquire. This petition is based on scientific evidence of increased cancer risks from exposure to nitrosamines in cosmetics.

The undersigned submits this petition under 21 U.S.C. 321 (n), 361, 362 and 371 (a); and 21 CFR 740.1, 740.2 of 21 CFR 10.30 of the Federal Food, Drug, and Cosmetic Act to the Commissioner of Food and Drugs requiring that all cosmetic products containing diethanolamine (DEA) bear labels with a warning: "Caution — This product may contain N-nitrosodiethanolamine, a known cancer -causing agent."

A. AGENCY ACTION REQUESTED

This petition requests that FDA takes the following action:

(1) Issue a regulation under the Federal Food, Drug and Cosmetic Act, Section 601(a), stating that "All cosmetics containing diethanolamine (DEA), a constituent of diethanolamide soaps that may react with nitrosating agents to form N-nitrosodiethanolamine (NDEA), bear a label as an adulterated product containing poisonous and deleterious substances which may render it injurious to users under the conditions of use prescribed in the labeling thereof, or under such conditions of use as are customary or usual: that which contains DEA also bears the following legend conspicuously displayed thereon: 'Caution — This product may contain N-nitrosodi-ethanolamine, a known cancer-causing agent.'"

(2) For purposes of enforcement of this act, the Secretary should conduct examinations and investigations of products which may be contaminated with NDEA through regular and

routine analytical testing by officers and employees of the Department or through any health, food, or drug officer or employee of any State, Territory or political subdivision thereof, duly commissioned by the Secretary of the Department. Such examinations should result in removal of products from the shelves if products do not comply with labeling regulations.

(3) Pursuant to 21 CFR 10.30 (h) (2), a hearing at which time we can present our scientific evidence.

B. STATEMENT OF GROUNDS

Widespread Contamination of Cosmetics with DEA and NDEA

Diethanolamine (DEA) is a high production chemical used in a wide range of cosmetic products, including shampoos, lotions and creams. In the presence of long-chain fatty acids DEA reacts to form neutral ethanolamide soaps, which are used as wetting agents in cosmetics. These soaps contain unreacted DEA. Triethanolamine (TEA), also used widely in cosmetics, may also be contaminated with DEA.[1] According to the Cosmetics, Toiletries and Fragrance Association,

Cocamide DEA, Lauramide DEA, Linoleamide DEA and Oleamide DEA are fatty acid diethanolamides which may contain 4 to 33 percent diethanolamine. These ingredients are used in cosmetics at concentrations of <0.1 percent to 50 percent, with most products containing 1 percent to 25 percent diethanolamide.[2]

As of 1980, FDA reported that approximately 42 percent of all cosmetic products were contaminated with NDEA at the following concentrations: facial cosmetics from .042 to 49 mg/kg, lotions from less than .010 to .140 mg/kg, shampoos from less than 10 to 160 mg/kg.[3] In two surveys of cosmetics, 27 out of 29 American products contained up to 48 mg/kg NDEA.[4] A more recent FDA analysis (1991-1992) found that NDEA is present in some products at mg/kg concentrations.[5]

DEA IS A PRECURSOR OF NDEA

N-nitrosodiethanolamine (NDEA), is readily formed in cosmetic by nitrosation of DEA. Even small amounts of DEA in cosmetics can react with nitrosating agents to form nitrosamines. According to the Cosmetics, Toiletries and Fragrance Association: Nitrosamine contamination of diethanolamine and fatty acid diethanolamides, and nitrosamine formation are potential problems in using these diethanolamides. The diethanolamides used in cosmetic products should be free of nitrosamines, and the finished product should not contain nitrosating agents as ingredients.[6]

Nitrosating agents are added to cosmetics in one of three ways: (a) Nitrites are added directly as anti-corrosive agents; (b) Nitrites are released by the degradation of 2-nitro-1,3-propanediol (BNDP); and (c) Nitrites are contaminants in the raw materials or resulting from the exposure of cosmetics to air. Secondary amines, such as DEA, are rapidly nitrosated by nitrogen oxides. Nitrosamines formation from nitrite and amines is accelerated under specific conditions by formaldehyde, paraformaldehyde, thiocyanate, nitrophenols and certain metal salts (e.g. ZnI_2, CuCl, $AgNO_3$, $SnCl_2$ and $HgCl_2$).[7,8,9,10,11]

Cosmetics remain on store shelves and in cabinets of consumers for long periods of time, allowing nitrosamines to form. If DEA is present, nitrosamines can continue to form throughout storage, especially at elevated temperatures.[12]

Acidic pH is an optimal reaction condition for nitrosamine formation. Although cosmetics generally have neutral pH,[13] N-nitrosamines can be formed at neutral or alkaline pH by the reaction of a nitrosating agent with an amine in the presence of carbonyl compounds such as formaldehyde.[14,15] Formaldehyde is present in cosmetics either from in situ formaldehyde-releasing agents, such as BNDP, or from its use as a preservative.[16]

DERMAL ABSORPTION OF NDEA
There is substantial evidence of the dermal absorption of NDEA in both rodents and humans. "[NDEA] is a known carcinogen in laboratory animals; it is absorbed through the skin. The absorption rate is a function of the nature of the cosmetic; absorption is fastest in nonpolar vehicles".[17] Dermal absorption of NDEA was demonstrated by Lijinsky et al. In 1981.[18] As a fat-soluble chemical NDEA can be absorbed dermally in rats and humans.[19,20]

NDEA INCREASES CANCER RISK
There is substantial evidence of potent carcinogenicity of NDEA in a wide range of animal species.[21,22, 23, 24, 25, 26, 27, 28, 29] According to the International Agency for Research on Cancer (IARC).

There is sufficient evidence of a carcinogenic effect of N-nitrosodiethanolamine —. In view of the widespread exposure to appreciable concentrations of N-nitrosodiethanol-amine, efforts should be made to obtain epidemiological information.[30]

The National Toxicology Program similarly concluded: There is sufficient evidence for the carcinogenicity of N-nitrosodiethanolamine in experimental animals.[31] Of over 44 different species in which N-nitroso compounds have been tested, all have been susceptible. [32] Humans are most unlikely to be the only exception to this trend.

In 1978, the IARC concluded that "although no epidemiological data were available, nitrosodiethanolamine should be regarded for practical purposes as if it were carcinogenic to humans".[33]   In 1987 the IARC further confirmed the carcinogenicity of NDEA.

Based on early evidence of the carcinogenicity of NDEA and evidence of cutting fluid contamination, 20 years ago NIOSH recommended that action be taken to protect workers including elimination of nitrosamines from the fluids.[34] More recently, NIOSH published a hazard review of cutting fluids used in metal working that contain NDEA among other nitrosamines. This hazard review indicates that, based on epidemiological evidence in human beings, "Increased cancer risk has been generally attributed to worker exposure to nitrosamine or PAH (polyaromatic hydrocarbon) contaminants in metal working fluids".[35]

THE FAILURE OF THE FDA TO TAKE APPROPRIATE REGULATORY ACTION
In the Federal Register of April 10, 1979, the FDA called for industry "to take immediate measures to eliminate to the extent possible [NDEA] and any other N-nitrosamines from cosmetic products," and further insisted that "cosmetic products may be analyzed by FDA for nitrosamine contamination and that individual products could be subject to enforcement action."

FDA has taken no subsequent enforcement actions despite the limited compliance with this Federal Register order. According to the FDA officials Don Havery and Hardy Chou in 1994.

In the United States...the personal care industry has invested resources in understanding both the mechanisms of N-nitrosamine formation in cosmetic systems and the means of inhibiting N-nitrosamine formation. However, there is still room for improvement. New products containing nitrosatable amines with formaldehyde and nitrite-releasing preservatives are still appearing on the U.S. market. Manufacturers have a responsibility to be aware of the potential for N-nitrosamine formation and to take steps necessary to keep N-nitrosamine levels as low as possible as part of their good manufacturing practices.[36]

The goal of good manufacturing practices is to reduce "human exposure to N-nitrosamines to the lowest level technologically feasible by reducing levels in all personal care products. With the information and technology currently available to cosmetic manufacturers, N-nitrosamine levels can and should be further reduced in consumer products".[37]

The FDA has failed to act on the Federal Register recommendations made in 1979. More recently, the FDA has not fully recognized the consumer hazards of this carcinogen. Measurements have not been made to determine total daily exposure to nitrosamines and it is inappropriate to quantify exposures without such data.

COSMETIC INDUSTRY RESPONSE TO FDA ACTION

In response to the FDA Federal Register order, the Nitrosamine Task Force of the Cosmetics, Toiletries and Fragrance Association failed to eliminate the use of DEA, but rather, they investigated ways to inhibit the formation of NDEA. [38]

There are no known nitrosation inhibitors that eliminate nitrosamine contamination. Inhibitors have failed for the following reasons:

The compound a-tocopherol has been used as an inhibitor but this compound is useful only when the nitrosating agent is nitrite itself. It is not effective against nitrogen oxide, a gas found in polluted air. It has also been shown to be ineffective in some cosmetic systems. [39]

Many cosmetics make inhibition of nitrosamine formation more difficult. If they are two-phase emulsion systems the inhibitor must be soluble in both hydrophilic and hydrophobic media to be effective as an inhibitor. [40,41]

Ascorbic acid, sodium bisulfite, butylated hydroxyanisole (BHA), butylated hydroxytoluene (BHT) sodium ascorbated, ascorbyl palmitate and a-tocopherol have all been used in attempts to inhibit nitrosamine formation. None of these inhibitors have been adequate against all possible nitrosation agents to which a shelved cosmetic is exposed. [42]

Industry has had no success in reducing NDEA below 1984 levels. [43] As a result, in 1996 the Cosmetics, Toiletries and Fragrance Association stated in 1996, "These chemicals [Cocamide DEA, Lauramide DEA, Linoleamide DEA, and Oleamide DEA] should not be used as ingredients in cosmetic products containing nitrosating agents". [44]   Nevertheless, DEA is still widely used by major cosmetic manufacturers.

In contrast, some other manufacturers—have ceased to use diethanolamide soaps entirely. There are many alternative soap bases available without DEA that can be used by cosmetic manufacturers. In short, the removal of DEA does not pose a manufacturing problem to the cosmetic industry. [45] There is no reason for high levels of NDEA to be found in cosmetic products. With safe alternatives available, the elimination of DEA should not be an economic burden for the cosmetic industry.

RESPONSE OF NATIONAL INSTITUTE FOR OCCUPATIONAL SAFETY AND HEALTH

In striking contrast to the FDA's position on NDEA, The National Institute for Occupational Safety and Health (NIOSH) has issued two reports, one as early as 1976, stating that protective measures should be taken when workers are exposed to levels of NDEA similar to those found in cosmetics.[46, 47]

RESPONSE OF GERMAN INDUSTRY AND EUROPEAN UNION

The German Federal Health Office issued a request to eliminate all secondary amines from cosmetics in 1987 and in response, the German manufacturers' association has voluntarily complied and sharply reduced the use of secondary amines in cosmetics and toiletries.[48] Included in the specifications of the German Federal Health Office were that fatty acid diethanolamides contain as low as achievable contamination by unreacted diethanolamine. Eisenbrand et al. explained:

Commercially available products from the German market analyzed six to 18 months after the recommendation had been issued showed that only 15 percent were contaminated with [NDEA] or NDHPA. The overall results of this study demonstrate however, a strong downward trend in both levels and frequency of contamination. They prove that nitrosamine contamination of cosmetics can be minimized by simple preventive measures.[49]

The European Union has stated specific maximum allowable concentrations of inadvertently formed N-nitrosodialkanolamine. In legislation that was most recently amended in 1993, the European Union asserted that monoalkanolamines and trialkanolamines must be stored in nitrite free containers, cannot be used in nitrosating systems, must have purity of at least 99% and can contain no more than .5% secondary alkanolamine. With regards to N-nitrosodialkanolamine specifically, the maximum content that the EU allows is 50 micrograms per kilogram (50ppb).[50] In comparison, U.S. cosmetic levels for NDEA as high as 2,960 parts per billion were reported in 1992.[51]

CONCLUSION

There is strong evidence proving: the widespread use of DEA in cosmetics, nitrosation of DEA to form NDEA, contamination of cosmetics with NDEA, the potent carcinogenicity of NDEA, and the availability of alternatives to DEA. The FDA should take prompt action to require labels on all products containing DEA that reads: "Caution — This product may contain N-nitrosodiethanolamine, a known cancer-causing agent."

C. CLAIM FOR CATEGORICAL EXCLUSION

A claim for categorical exclusion is asserted pursuant to 21 CFR 25.24 (a)(11).

D. CERTIFICATION

The undersigned certifies, that, to the best knowledge and belief of the undersigned, this petition includes all information and views on which the petition relies, and that it includes representative data and information known to the petitioner which are unfavorable to the petition.

This petition is submitted by:

Samuel S. Epstein, M.D.
Cancer Prevention Coalition
520 N. Michigan Avenue, Suite 410
Chicago, IL 60611
312-467-0600 phone
312-467-0599 fax

Council to the Cancer Prevention Coalition
Center for Constitutional Rights
Michael E. Deutsch, Legal Director
666 Broadway
New York, NY 10012
212-614-6427

CITATIONS

1. Havery, Donald C. and Chou, Hardy J. "N-Nitrosamines in Cosmetics Product." Cosmetics & Toiletries, 109(5):53, May 1994.

2. Cosmetics, Toiletries and Fragrance Association. 1996 CIR Compendium, Cosmetic Ingredient Review, Washington, D.C., 1996.

3. NTP, Seventh Annual Report on Carcinogens. U.S. Department of Health and Human Services, Public Health Services, National Toxicology Program, National Institute of Environmental Health Sciences, Technical Resources Inc., Rockville, MD 1994.

4. Eisenbrand, G., M. Blankar, H. Sommer, and B. Weber. "N-Nitrosoalkanolamines in Cosmetics." In: Relevance to Human Cancer of N-nitroso Compounds, tobacco Smoke and Mycotoxins, Ed. I.K. O'Neill, J. Chen and H. Bartsch. International Agency for Research on Cancer, Lyon, 1991.

5. Havery, Donald C. and Hardy J. Chou. "Nitrosamines in Sunscreens and Cosmetic Products." Nitrosamines and Related N-nitroso Compounds, ACS Monograph No. 553. Ed. Richard N. Loeppky and Christopher J. Michejda. American Chemical Society, Washington, D.C., 1994.

6. Cosmetics, Toiletries and Fragrance Association. 1996 CIR Compendium, Cosmetic Ingredient Review, Washington, D.C., 1996.

7. Keefer, L.K. and P.P. Roller, "N-Nitrosation by nitrite ion in neutral and basic medium." Science 181:1245-1246, 1973.

8. Archer, M.C. and J.D. Okum. "Kinetics of nitrosamine formation in the presence of micelle-forming surfactants." Journal of the National Cancer Institute 58:409, 1977. (Cited In: National Institutes for Occupational Safety and Health. Draft Criteria for Recommended Standards: Occupational Exposures to Metal Working Fluids. U.S. Department of Health and Human Services, February 19, 1996.)

9. Davies, R. and D.J. McWeeny. "Catalytic effect of nitrosophenols on N-nitrosamine formation." Nature 266:657-658, 1977. (Cited In: National Institutes for Occupational Safety and Health. Draft Criteria for Recommended Standards: Occupational Exposures to Metal Working Fluids. U.S. Department of Health and Human Services, February 19, 1996).

10. Challis, B.D., A. Edward, R.R. Hunma, S.A. Kyrtopoulos, and J.R. Outram. "Rapid formation of N-nitrosamines from nitrogen oxides under neutral and alkaline conditions." IARC Scientific Publication, Lyon, France, 19:127, 1978. (Cited In: National Institutes for Occupational Safety and Health. Draft Criteria for Recommended Standards: Occupational Exposures to Metal Working Fluids. U.S. Department of Health and Human Services, February 19, 1996.)

11. Loeppky, R.N., T.J. Hansen, L.P. Keefer. "Reducing nitrosamine contamination in cutting fluids." Fd. Cosmet. Toxicol. 21(5):607-613, 1983. (Cited In: National Institutes for Occupational Safety and Health. Draft Criteria for Recommended Standards: Occupational

Exposures to Metal Working Fluids. U.S. Department of Health and Human Services, February 19, 1996.)

12. Havery, Donald C. and Hardy J. Chou. "Nitrosamines in Sunscreens and Cosmetic Products." Nitrosamines and Related N-nitroso Compounds, ACS Monograph No. 553, Ed. Richard N. Loeppky and Christopher J. Michejda. American Chemical Society, Washington, D.C., 1994.

13. Havery, Donald C. and Hardy J. Chou. "N-Nitrosamines in Cosmetic Products." Cosmetics & Toiletries, 109(5):53, May 1994.

14. Ibid.

15. Keefer, L.P. and P.P. Roller, "N-nitrosation by nitrite Ion in Neutral and Basic Medium." Science, 181:1245-46, 1973.

16. Havery, Donald C. and Hardy J. Chou. "N-Nitrosamines in Cosmetic Products." Cosmetics & Toiletries, 109(5):53, May 1994.

17. Havery, Donald C. and Hardy J. Chou. "Nitrosamines in Sunscreens and Cosmetic Products." Nitrosamines and Related N-nitroso Compounds, ACS Monograph No. 553. Ed. Richard N. Loeppky and Christopher J. Michejda. American Chemical Society, Washington, D.C., 1994.

18. Lijinsky, W., A.M. Losikoff, and E.B. Sansone. Journal of the National Cancer Institute 66:125-127, 1981.

19. Edwards, G.S., M. Peng, D. J. Fine, B. Spiegelhalder, and J. Kann. "Detection of N-nitroso-diethanolamine in human urine following application of contaminated cosmetics." Toxicol. Lett. 4:217-222, 1979. (Cited In: National Institutes for Occupational Safety and Health. Draft
Criteria for Recommended Standards: Occupational Exposures to Metal Working Fluids. U.S. Department of Health and Human Services, Feb. 19, 1996).

20. Preussman, R. "Occurrence and Exposure to N-nitroso Compounds and Precursors." In: N-Nitroso Compounds: Occurrence, Biological Effects and Relevance to Human Cancer. Ed. I.K.

O'Neill, R.C. Von Borstel, C.T. Miller, J. Long and H. Bartsch, IARC Scientific publications No. 57, IARC, Lyon, 1984.

21. Druckrey, H., R. Preussman, S. Ivankovic, and D. Schmahl. AOrganotrope Carcinogene Wirkungen Bei 65 verschiedenen N-Nitroso-verbindugen an BD-ratten. Z Krebsforsch 69:103-201, 1967. (Cited In: National Institutes for Occupational Safety and Health. Draft Criteria for Recommended Standards: Occupational Exposures to Metal Working Fluids. U.S. Department of Health and Human Services, February 19, 1996.)

22. Hilfrich, J., I. Schmeltz, and D. Hoffmann. "Effects of N-nitrosodiethanolamine and 1,2-diethanolhydrazine in Syrian golden Hamsters."Cancer Letters 4:55-60, 1978. (Cited In: National Institutes for Occupational Safety and Health. Draft Criteria for Recommended Standards: Occupational Exposures to metal Working Fluids. U.S. Department of Health and Human Services, February 19, 1996.)

23. International Agency for Research on Cancer, Monograph on the Evaluation of the Carcinogenic Risk of Chemicals to Humans: Some N-nitroso Compounds 17:77-82, 1978.

24. Lijinsky, W. M.D. Reuber, and W.B. Manning. "Potent carcinogenicity of nitrosodiethanolamine in rats." Nature 288:589-590, 1980.

25. Pour, P. and L. Wallcave. "The carcinogenicity of n-Nitrosodiethanolamine, An Environmental Pollutant, In Syrian Hamsters." Cancer Letters 14:23-27, 1981.

26. Preussman, R, M. Habs, H. Habs, and D. Schmahl. "Carcinogenicity of N-Nitrosodiethanolamine in Rats at Five Different Dose Levels."Cancer Research, 42:5167-5171, 1982.

27. Lijinsky, W. and M.D. Reuber, "Dose-response study with N-nitrosodiethanolamine in F344 rats." Fd. Cosmet. Toxicol. 22(1):23-26, 1984.

28. Lijinsky, W. And R.M. Kovatch. "Induction of liver tumor in rats by nitrosodiethanolamine at low doses." Carcinogenesis 6(12):1679-1681, 1985.

29. NTP, Seventh Annual Report on Carcinogens. U.S. Department of Health and Human Services, Public Health Service, National Toxicology Program, National Institute of Environmental Health Sciences, Technical Resources Inc., Rockville, MD 1994.

30. International Agency for Research on Cancer, Monograph on the Evaluation of the Carcinogenic Risk of Chemicals to Humans: Some N-nitroso Compounds 17:77-82, 1978.

31. NTP, Seventh Annual Report on Carcinogens. U.S. Department of Health and Human Services, Public Health Service, National Toxicology Program, National Institute of Environmental Health Sciences, Technical Resources Inc., Rockville, MD 1994.

32. Lijinsky, William. Chemistry and Biology of N-nitroso Compounds. Cambridge University Press, New York, 1992.

33. International Agency for Research on Cancer, Monograph on the Evaluation of the Carcinogenic Risk of Chemicals to Humans: Some N-nitroso Compounds 17:77-82, 1978.

34. NIOSH. "Nitrosamines in Cutting Fluids." Current Intelligence Bulletin, October 6, 1976.

35. NIOSH. Draft Criteria for Recommended Standards: Occupational Exposures to Metal Working Fluids, U.S. Department of Health and Human Services, Public Health Service, Center for Disease
Control and Prevention, National Institute for Occupational Safety and Health, Division of Standards Development and Technology Transfer. February 19, 1996.

36. Havery, Donald C. and Hardy J. Chou. "N-Nitrosamines in Cosmetics Products." Cosmetics & Toiletries, 109(5):53, May 1994.

37. Ibid.

38. Kabacoff, B.L., R. J. Lechnir, S.F. Vielhuber, and M.L. Douglass. "Formation and Inhibition of N-nitrosodiethanolamine in Anionic Oil-Water Emulsion." ACS Monograph. American Chemical Society, 1981.

39. Havery, Donald C. and Hardy J. Chou. "N-Nitrosamines in Cosmetic Products." Cosmetics & Toiletries, 109(5):53, May 1994.

40. Kabacoff, B.L., R. J. Lechnir, S.F. Vielhuber, and M.L. Douglass. "Formation and Inhibition of N-nitrosodiethanolamine in Anionic Oil-Water Emulsion." ACS Monograph. American Chemical Society, 1981.

41. Havery, Donald C. and Hardy J. Chou. "N-Nitrosamines in Cosmetic Products." Cosmetics & Toiletries, 109(5):53, May 1994.

42. Ibid.

43. Havery, Donald C. and Hardy J. Chou. "Nitrosamines in Sunscreens and Cosmetic Products." Nitrosamines and Related N-nitroso Compounds, ACS Monograph No. 553. Ed. Richard N. Loeppky and Christopher J. Michejda. American Chemical Society, Washington, D.C., 1994.

44. Cosmetics, Toiletries and Fragrance Association. 1996 CIR Compendium, Cosmetic Ingredient Review, Washington, D.C., 1996.

45. Hampton, Aubrey. Personal Communication, May 30, 1996.

46. NIOSH. "Nitrosamines in Cutting Fluids." Current Intelligence Bulletin, October 6, 1976.

47. NIOSH. Draft Criteria for Recommended Standards: Occupational Exposures to Metal Working Fluids, U.S. Department of Health and Human Services, Public Health Service, Center for Disease
Control and Prevention, National Institute for Occupational Safety and Health, Division of Standards Development and Technology Transfer. February 19, 1996.

48. Eisenbrand, G., M. Blankar, H. Sommer, and B. Weber. N-Nitrosoalkanolamines in Cosmetics." In: Relevance to Human Cancer of N-nitroso Compounds, Tobacco Smoke and Mycotoxins, Ed. I.K. O'Neill, J. Chen and H. Bartsch. International Agency for Research on Cancer , Lyon, 1991.

49. Ibid.

50. Council Directive of 27 July 1976, on the approximation of the Laws of the Member States Relating to Cosmetic Products (DIR. 76/768/EEC. DIR. Amendment 93/35/EC).

51. Havery, Donald C. and Hardy J. Chou. "Nitrosamines in Sunscreens and Cosmetic Products." Nitrosamines and Related N-nitroso Compounds, ACS Monograph No. 553, Ed.

Richard N. Loeppky and Christopher J. Michejda. American Chemical Society, Washington, D.C. 1994.

FDA RESPONSE (February 13, 1997)

FDA has not been able to reach a decision "because of the limited availability of resources and other agency priorities".

THE NEW YORK TIMES LETTER, FEBRUARY 16, 1994.
SO YOU CONSIDER HAIR DYES SAFE?

To the Editor:

Re "It's Safe to Hide the Gray, a New Cancer Study Says" (news article, Feb.2): The American Cancer Society-Food and Drug Administration study that finds "almost no connection between hair dyes and fatal cancers" is seriously flawed in design and interpretation. While a fourfold increase in mortality from relatively rare cancers, non-Hodgkin's lymphoma and multiple myeloma, was noted in some 1,100 women using permanent black dyes for more than 20 years, the study trivialized the significance of that increase as based on only very few cases.

Although the study, which was published in the Journal of the National Cancer Institute, concluded that hair dyes pose no overall cancer risk, it recommended "removal of carcinogens from hair dyes and appropriate labeling of hair coloring products."

This study was based on a group of women with an average age of 56 enrolled in 1982, when they were questioned on hair dye use, and followed until 1989, when their average age was 63. However, cancers are much more likely to develop beyond that age, reflecting the long latency following exposure to carcinogens. Rates for development of cancer in women older than 63 are up to 20 times higher for non-Hodgkin's lymphoma and multiple myeloma; 34 times for bladder cancer, and 8 times for breast cancer, which the study exculpated. The study would have missed the great majority of these.

The negative findings on breast cancer are further invalidated by the study's failure to analyze for other critical risk factors besides hair dyes, particularly duration of oral contraceptive use and age at onset; duration and dosage of estrogen replacement therapy, and history of mammography. The last is particularly important, as repeated mammography in healthy premenopausal women has been consistently associated with breast cancer mortality in some eight randomized controlled trials over the last decade.

The study also substantially underestimated hair dye exposure because it was based on only those women who had begun to use hair dye by 1982, without consideration of those who began later, but remained grouped among nonusers. Also missed were women using semipermanent dyes, about 20 percent of the market, which are chemically very similar to permanent dyes and probably pose similar cancer risks.

With these limitations, the striking discrepancy between the new findings and those of some six previous recent studies that provide strong evidence on the carcinogenicity of hair dyes is not surprising. For instance, a well-designed study in Nebraska, found that hair dye use would account for about 20 percent of all non-Hodgkin's lymphoma deaths in women; United States rates for this cancer have increased more than 100 percent since 1950. These and other studies also strongly incriminate multiple myeloma, leukemia and ovarian cancer, and suggest a relationship to breast cancer.

More recklessly misleading than the Cancer Society study is an accompanying editorial in the same journal that conclusively dismissed any cancer risk from hair dyes and recommended against any further studies.

There is substantial evidence on the carcinogenic hazards of petrochemical hair dyes. Their use represents a major class of avoidable cancer risks to some 50 million United States women. Legislative and regulatory action is now decades overdue. While waiting, women should switch to noncarcinogenic organic hair dyes.

Samuel S. Epstein, M.D.
Professor Environmental Medicine
University of Illinois School of Public Health, Chicago

STATEMENT OF SENATOR EDWARD M. KENNEDY (D-MA), ON HR 1411, SEPTEMBER 10, 1997

The 1997 FDA reform bill (HR 1411)—exempting cosmetics from state regulation is utterly irresponsible. The cosmetic industry has borrowed a page from the playbook of the tobacco industry, by putting profits ahead of public health. Once again, a special interest lobby is using its background muscle in the Republican Congress to obtain an unconscionable advantage.

Our message today is that cosmetics can be dangerous to your health. Yet this greedy industry wants Congress to prevent the American people from learning that truth.

Every woman who uses face cream, or hair spray, or lipstick, or shampoo, or mascara, or powder should demand that this arrogant and irresponsible power play by the industry be rejected.

A study by the respected, nonpartisan General Accounting Office (GAO) reported that more than 125 ingredients available for use in cosmetics are suspected of causing cancer. Other cosmetics may cause adverse effects on the nervous system, including convulsions. Still other ingredients are suspected of causing birth defects. A carefully controlled study found that one in sixty users suffered a cosmetic related injury identified by a physician.

Consumers have suffered painful, permanent injuries from hair treatment products that have caught fire. They have suffered serious urinary tract infections from bubble bath. They have suffered life-threatening allergic reactions to hair dyes, and severe chemical burns from skin creams and sun tan lotions. The GAO concluded that "cosmetics are being marketed in the United States which may pose a serious hazard to the public."

And these are only the acute injuries that require immediate medical care. The poisons in cosmetics can also cause long-term injuries and illnesses that do not develop for years after exposure. We don't know the full extent of the possible damage, and this bill tells us we can't even warn the public of the dangers. In fact, as Jill Ireland, the President of the National Organization for Women, stated this morning, this legislation might be aptly titled the "gag act," because it will effectively put a gag on states that want to make sure their citizens—and especially women—are aware of the dangers they may face.

Three specific products highlight the risks consumers face. Alpha-hydroxy acid one of the hottest selling cosmetic products on the market, with sales of roughly a billion dollars a year. It is sold to erase fine lines and tighten the skin. FDA has received numerous complaints of adverse effects from the use of these products. Alpha-hydroxy acids have been linked to severe redness, burning, blistering, bleeding, rash, itching, and skin discoloration. Most troubling, there is concern that alpha-hydroxy may promote skin cancer by increasing sensitivity to sun exposure. Yet these products are in the marketplace—with no warning labels and no limits on the concentrations that may be sold. Under this bill, every state would be prohibited from requiring these sensible warnings.

I ask unanimous consent that I may put a fact sheet laying the issues on alpha-hydroxy acid in the record. A critical point is that an industry-appointed panel itself set out safety tolerance levels for use of the product with regard to short term effects and warned that the product should not be used without a sunscreen. Yet, there is absolutely no binding requirement that manufacturers follow these recommendations—and virtually none of the products carry the information or warnings developed by the industry's own committee that would enable consumers to help protect their own safety. And, in point of fact, there has been no truly independent evaluation of the work of the industry panel. In fact, the FDA is belatedly so concerned about the safety of alpha-hydroxy acid that it has chosen it as its "top priority" for review by the prestigious National Toxicology Program.

A second example is feminine hygiene products, which have sales of $100 million a year. More than one-third of women use them—but they pose serious health hazards. They have been shown to cause upper reproductive tract infections, pelvic inflammatory disease, ectopic pregnancies and infertility. They may place women at additional hazard for cervical cancer. Women using these products should have the right to warning labels informing them of these hazards. But the FDA has done little to protect or warn women against these dangers, and this legislation will prohibit states from filling the gap.

There are a substantial number of studies on the safety of these products. The evidence that they are dangerous seems incontrovertible—but this legislation would prevent states from acting to simply warn women of the dangers. How outrageous it is that women should face illness and sterility without being warned of the danger of a seemingly harmless and beneficial product—and that states should be prohibited from taking steps to give them adequate warning.

A third example is talc, or talcum powder is widely used in popular bath and cosmetic products. But it is chemically similar to asbestos, and has long been suspected of causing cancer. A number of studies have suggested the possibility of a link to ovarian cancer, which afflicts 26,000 women annually. Under this legislation, states would be banned from even requiring warning labels. American women deserve better protection from their government.

These three issues have been carefully analyzed by Dr. David Wallinga, a physician and the Senior Scientist at the Natural Resources Defense Council. He points out the dangers of each of these three products based on studies in prestigious medical journals from researchers at institutions like Yale and the Mount Sinai Hospital in New York. I ask unanimous consent to enter his comments in the record, along with the articles analyzing these issues.

The language of pre-emption is broad and sweeping. States are totally pre-empted in their ability to regulate any aspect of labeling and packaging or any form of public communication by the manufacturer. States cannot even require a warning as simple as "keep out of reach of children." Think about that. States cannot even require a label saying "keep out of reach of children," even though 16,000 children per year suffer acute poisoning from artificial nail products alone.

The only reason preemption of cosmetic regulation is in the legislation is to increase the already swollen profits of this greedy industry. The American people deserve safe cosmetics. They have a right to full and fair information about the actual and potential dangers of the products they use every day. The last thing Congress should do in a bill called "FDA Reform" is to give the cosmetic industry a blank check to poison the American people with its products.

I will discuss this issue of the destruction of safeguards against dangerous cosmetics at more length later in my presentation.

The legislation we are debating today includes many positive elements. It reauthorizes the important Prescription Drug User Fee program, one of the most effective regulatory reforms ever enacted. It includes a number of other provisions that will significantly improve and streamline the regulation of prescription drugs, biologic products, and medical devices. I am pleased that through a long process of negotiation both prior to and subsequent to the markup of the legislation, many provisions that seriously threatened public health and safety were dropped or compromised.

But despite our best efforts, this legislation still includes at least four extremely damaging provisions—Trojan horses that could destroy all these positive proposals in this bill. FDA reform and reauthorization of the Prescription Drug User Fee program are too important to be used as a vehicle to advance selfish special interests. To be worthy of the name, FDA reform should improve the health of the American people, not jeopardize it. The pursuit of profit should not have a greater priority than protection of health.

A bill that includes these damaging provisions should not become law.

The provisions that make this bill unworthy of passage by the Senate include:

— preemption of state regulation of cosmetics and over-the-counter medicines;

— elimination of two important protections against unsafe or ineffective medical devices, including a provision that could undercut FDA's ability to regulate cigarettes; and

— a backdoor assault on one of our most important environmental protections.

As the Washington Post said in an editorial today, "This week's showdown on the FDA bill involves two "out of nowhere" provisions—an amendment that would exempt the FDA from a requirement in the new National Environmental Policy Act to provide environmental impact statements, at no particular cost to the FDA but great cost to the environmental regulation, and an amendment by Senator Judd Gregg (R-NH) to pre-empt state regulations on the labeling of cosmetics. Neither of these has any business in an FDA bill, particularly the "cosmetics provision." The editorial also points out the dangers in the two device provisions. I ask unanimous consent that the full text of the editorial be inserted in the Record.

The most egregious and unjustified provision in this whole bill would effectively pre-empt state regulation of over-the-counter drugs and cosmetics. These provisions were not included in the Chairman's original mark-up. They were not the subject of significant hearings. They have no place in a bill whose primary purpose is to reauthorize the Prescription Drug Users' Act. If this bill were serious about dealing with issues of over-the-counter drug and cosmetic regulation, it would undertake a serious reform of the whole regulatory structure to assure that consumers were adequately protected—not include a single provision designed to protect the profits of wealthy companies at the expense of the health of consumers.

This provision is opposed by the President, the National Women's Health Network, the National Organization for Women, the National Governor's Association, the National Council of State Legislators, the Association of State and Territorial Health Officers, the Attorneys-General of California and Massachusetts, the Environmental Defense Fund, the Natural Resources Defense Council, and by a broad coalition of consumer and health groups as well. The only support comes from the cosmetics industry—an industry that has consistently put profit ahead of consumer safety.

In fact, even some of the more responsible members of the industry—oppose this provision. I ask unanimous consent to place letters from these and other organizations in the record.

Pre-emption of cosmetic regulation is outrageous and shows a callous disregard for the health of American women, especially those who are pregnant. It shows a callous disregard for the likelihood of birth defects in newborn children. Cosmetics are broadly used—far more broadly than most prescription drugs, medical devices, or biologic products. In fact, cosmetics include: baby powder, bubble bath, toothpaste, deodorants, shaving creams, hair tonics, hairsprays, colognes, suntan lotions, mouthwashes, douches, baby shampoo, hand lotion, hair dyes, deodorants, moisturizing cream, as well as many other products.

Whether the issue is hair spray, or shampoo, or lipstick, or baby powder, suntan lotion, soap and toothpaste, American assume that the products they use are safe.

But this confidence is too often unjustified—because Federal oversight of this $20 billion industry today is extremely limited. The basic Federal law regulating cosmetics has not been updated since 1938. The FDA has less than 30 employees overseeing this huge industry—and only two employees dealing with the critical issue of packaging, labeling, and consumer warnings. The FDA has no authority to require manufacturers to register their plants and products. It cannot require manufacturers to file data on the ingredients in their products. It cannot compel manufacturers to file reports on cosmetics-related injuries. It cannot require that products be tested for safety or that the results of safety testing be made available to the agency. It does not have the right of access to manufacturers' records. It cannot require recall of a product.

In the Federal Food Drug and Cosmetics Act there are 126 pages devoted to the regulation of drugs and devices. Fifty five pages are devoted to foods regulation. A full eight pages of the Act is dedicated to definitions. But less than two pages are devoted to cosmetic regulation. (emphasis added)

In 1938, there was no requirement that industry show safety of drugs, medical devices, food additives, or cosmetics before they were marketed. Today, the public demands higher standards of protection, and they have been established for drugs, for medical devices, and for food additives—but not for cosmetics.

A study by the respected, nonpartisan General Accounting Office reported that more than 125 ingredients available for use in cosmetics are suspected of causing cancer. Twenty cosmetic ingredients may cause adverse effects on the nervous system, including headaches, drowsiness, and convulsions. Twenty cosmetic ingredients are suspected of causing birth defects. The GAO concluded that "cosmetics are being marketed in the United States which may pose a serious hazard to the public."

The cosmetics industry wants the public to believe that no effective regulation is necessary at either the state or federal level. They are masters of the slick ad and expensive public relations campaign. But all the glamorous pictures in the world cannot obscure the basic facts: this is an industry that is under-regulated and too often hazardous. A mother of a beautiful six year old girl in Oakland, California found this out when she used a hair product on her child that resulted in second degree burns on her ears and neck. A 59-year old California woman almost died from an allergic reaction to hair dye. A 47 year old woman had her cornea destroyed by a mascara wand. In another tragic case, a woman's hair caught fire as the result of an inflammable hair treatment gel. She lost her hair and was severely scarred.

In fact, for every one million cosmetic products purchased, there are more than 200 visits to the doctor to treat cosmetic-related illnesses. A 1987 study for the Consumer Product Safety Commission found that in one year alone, cosmetic products resulted in 47,000 emergency room visits. Another study found that between 1985 and 1987, more than 151,000 cosmetic-related injuries occurred. A carefully controlled study found that one in 60 cosmetic users over a three month period had an injury of some kind, verified by a physician as resulting from cosmetic use.

Let me read a dishonor roll of just a few of the complaints made to the FDA in the last few months.

- Eye problems such as rash, redness, swelling, and inflammation from Alberto Culver's "European Instant Hot Oil Treatment for Color Treated and Permed Hair."

- Clairol's Helene Curtis "Nice and Easy Natural Lite" causing problems such as pain and tissue damage.

- Proctor & Gamble "Cover Girl Make Up Master Sponge Puffs" causing such problems as rash, redness, swelling, sores.

- Maybelline "Great Lash Mascara": pain and rash.

- Proctor and Gamble "Pantene" shampoo: neck tissue damage.

- Personal Care Products "Personal Care Anti-Wrinkle Cream": eye infection.

- Neutrogena Corporation "Neutrogena Glow Sunless Tanning Spray", hand pain and tissue damage.

The list goes on and on.

These severe reactions are only the tip of the iceberg. As the GAO study points out: "Available estimates of cosmetic-related injuries do not accurately reflect the extent to which consumers are exposed to toxic cosmetic products and ingredients. Because symptoms of chronic toxic effects may not occur until months or years after exposure, injury estimates generally account for only acute toxic effects."

These potential dangers come into startling focus when we review the risks associated with just four widely-used products—risks unknown to the average consumer. Alpha-hydroxy acid used in face creams can be a potent contributor to skin cancer. Feminine hygiene products can cause pelvic inflammatory disease leading to infertility in young women. Talc used in baby powder and other products is a carcinogen. And mascara can cause blindness.

Alpha-hydroxy acid is one of the hottest selling cosmetic products on the market. This product is sold to erase fine lines and tighten the skin but has devastating health effects that are unknown to most consumers.

The agency has received 100 reports of adverse effects with alpha-hydroxy acid products, ranging from mild irritation and stinging to blistering and burns. More importantly, these products make users more sensitive to ultraviolet radiation from sunlight—which can cause skin cancer.

The cosmetic industry itself sponsored a study linking alpha-hydroxy acid to increased UV sensitivity and most likely skin cancer. An industry panel concluded that alpha-hydroxy acid cosmetics are "safe at concentrations less than or equal to 10 percent, at a pH of greater than or equal to 3.5 when directions for use include daily use of sun protection." But there has been no conclusive independent review of these findings. There is no mechanism for assuring that the industry is following its guidelines. And there is no required labeling to warn consumers that this product can cause skin cancer or to tell them whether the product they buy even meets the level the industry deems safe.

Many women would be surprised to find that an overwhelmingly majority of feminine hygiene products are regulated as cosmetics. These products have been shown to cause upper reproductive tract infections, pelvic inflammatory disease, ectopic pregnancies, and infertility with the most profound effect in young women. But the FDA has done little to protect or warn women against these dangers. And this legislation will prohibit states from taking action as well.

Talc is used in baby powder and other products. In 1992, the National Toxicology Program published a study of the effects of talc inhalation in animals and an epidemiology study on "Exposure to Talc and Ovarian Cancer Risk". The researchers reported an elevated risk of ovarian cancer associated with talc use. Workers at Columbia University have reported the detection of talc particles in the ovaries of patients undergoing surgery. The Cancer Prevention Coalition has submitted a citizen's petition to the FDA expressing their concern about the possible health risks posed by talc and requested the agency establish regulations to require carcinogen warning labels on cosmetics containing talc as an ingredient.

FDA is reviewing the information and may respond sometime in the future. If a State wanted to warn its consumers about this potential carcinogen, they would be prohibited under S. 830.

The FDA has received numerous reports of corneal ulceration associated with mascara products, some of which caused partial blindness of the infected eye. In addition, many other reports of conjunctivitis caused by contaminated mascara were received. In response, FDA published a notice asking the industry to provide information covering microbial testing methods and standards of performance suitable to assure that cosmetics do not become contaminated with microorganisms during manufacture as well as use. However, FDA's request for information resulted in little response from industry—and FDA has no power to require industry to provide the needed information.

Beauty parlor employees are particularly vulnerable to asthma and other diseases that result form exposure to chemicals in the products they use. In fact, their exposure to the chemicals in cosmetic products results in asthma rates twice as high as a comparison group.

In the fact of limited Federal authority to protect the public against these hazards, and the even more limited Federal resources devoted to preventing them, you would think that the Congress would want to encourage states to fill the regulatory vacuum. Instead, this bill entirely bars states from regulating packaging and labeling, and places severe limits on the states ability to establish other forms of regulation.

In fact, the language is so extreme that states are barred from establishing "any requirement relating to public information or any other form of public communication relating to the safety and effectiveness of a drug or cosmetic." No warning labels. No information that a product contains carcinogens or can cause severe allergic reactions. No " keep out of reach of children" labels. No notification that a product has been recalled because it is dangerous or adulterated. The cosmetic industry seems to believe that, for purchasers of their products, ignorance is bliss. In fact, what you don't know today can severely injure you, or even kill you tomorrow.

The prohibition on "keep out of reach of children labels" or "harmful if ingested" labels is particularly outrageous in view of the large numbers of children who have been harmed by these products. To cite just a few examples:

- A 13 month old girl was treated for chemical burns and poisoning after she ingested some permanent wave relaxer.

- A 16 month old toddler died of cyanide poisoning after swallowing a liquid used to remove artificial nails.

- A 2 year old boy in Utah was rushed to the emergency room for rigorous intensive care after his parents found him in bed vomiting, moaning and unresponsive, after swallowing another liquid used for removing artificial nails.

You would think that states should be entitled to require warning labels so that parents can be especially alert to these dangers—but not under this bill.

Some of the proponents of this provision have attempted to cloud the record by saying that states are free to act unless the Federal government has dealt with the problem. Let's describe what this bill really does.

Under the legislation, States would be totally banned from requiring manufacturers to provide any consumer safety warnings or other information regarding their products. The pertinent language in section 807 of the substitute amendment (establishing a new section 761 of the Food, Drug and Cosmetic Act) reads:

"no State or political subdivision of a state may establish or continue in effect any requirement . . . that relates wholly or in part to the packaging or labeling of a cosmetic" (Section 761(a)).

The scope of this preemption is further defined in Section 761(c): "a requirement that relates wholly or in part to the packaging or labeling of a cosmetic shall be deemed to include any requirement relating to public information or other form of public communication relating to the safety of a cosmetic."

This language clearly prohibits a state from taking any action requiring the manufacturer to communicate anything to the public, regardless of whether or not the FDA has taken any action.

States would be banned from requiring manufacturers to disclose that their product contains carcinogens, substance that could cause birth defects, or substances that are toxic. They would be barred from requiring warnings that a product should be kept out of reach of children, that it should not be ingested, or that a poison control center should be called if a child swallows it—even though a an estimated 19,000 children annually are poisoned by just by artificial nail solutions. They would even be banned from requiring a manufacturer to make an announcement that a product has been recalled or was contaminated.

The legislation does allow states to take regulatory actions not relating to packaging, labelling, and public communication " if there is no Federal requirement, or established under this Act, relating wholly or in part to the same aspect of safety of a cosmetic" or if the requirements are identical to the Federal requirements. In practice, however, the way most states act to protect their citizens is through requiring manufacturers to provide warning labels or other forms of consumer information. This would be entirely prohibited, even if the Federal government had taken no action whatsoever. Moreover, the language of the statute could prohibit the states from taking regulatory action in the face of any relevant Federal action, even if the Federal rules were vague, ineffective, or outdated.

Some states are already taking an active role in protecting consumers. Many more may do so in the future—but not if this bill becomes law. Minnesota has passed a hazardous product labelling bill, requiring a warning on all products that are ignitable, corrosive, reactive, or toxic. You would think that all consumers should be entitled to that kind of information about products they put on their faces, spray on their hair, or wash their bodies with. But the cosmetics industry disagrees.

California requires notification if products contain carcinogens, or reproductive toxins that can cause birth defects. You would think every consumer should be entitled to that information. But the cosmetic industry disagrees.

Texas is investigating hormone creams that may affect the reproductive health of young women. You would think that states should be encouraged to take this kind of action; but this law prohibits it. New York requires expiration dates on cosmetics, because products can break down or be subject to bacterial contamination after certain time periods. Most of us would think that this is basic, obvious information that every consumer should have—but not the cosmetic industry.

At least 25 states ban adulterated and misbranded cosmetic products, giving them broad authority to ban harmful ingredients or to require warning labels. This provision of the bill is an example of the worst kind of sweetheart deal for a special interest at the expense of the public interest. It is intolerable that it should be included in a bill that purports to be the "Food and Drug Administration Modernization and Accountability Act".

Every review of the issue by an independent authority has concluded that the cosmetics industry needs more regulation—not less. It defies logic that our single action in this important consumer product area is to preempt the States from acting where there is wide agreement that FDA has neither the authority or the resources to adequately fill the field.

It is especially ironic that critics of the FDA who often look abroad for guidance on how to regulate are notably silent on the issue of how we stack up to other countries on the issue of cosmetics. Although we often refer to FDA's regulation of drugs as the international gold standard, our country's regulation of cosmetics is more like a fool's gold standard. Cosmetic regulation in other countries is far superior to our own. The European Union requires full ingredient listing on packaging, documentary proof of good manufacturing practice and similar proof that extensive testing has been carried out on all products. Mexico recently adopted a regulation mandating expiration dates on all cosmetics. Although New York recently adopted such a rule, it may live a very short life—the bill before us would preempt that regulation even if FDA does not have its own regulation in place.

Let's continue our world tour: Canada requires that manufacturers submit data showing that a product is safe under normal use conditions. Sweden is initiating product registration for cosmetics and Denmark is considering a similar law. Malaysia requires mandatory registration of cosmetics. The list goes on and on, but the point is clear. Not only has our Federal regulation of cosmetics lagged far behind other countries, but this greedy industry now proposes to use its political muscle to ban state regulation as well.

This is unacceptable to the President, to the National Women's Health Network, to the National Governor's Association, the National Council of State Legislators, the Association of State and Territorial Health Officers, the Environmental Defense Fund, and to a broad coalition of consumer and health groups as well. When similar attempts to preempt state action were proposed a decade ago, they were even opposed by the Reagan Administration. The only group that supports it is the cosmetics industry—an industry with a consistent record of placing profits ahead of public health. And the Senate should have the courage to stand up to this corporate greed.

Another unacceptable part of this bill contains two provisions that is undermine FDA's ability to assure the safety of medical devices. One provision would ban the FDA from ever looking behind the manufacturer's proposed label in deciding whether a device is safe and effective, even if that label is false or misleading.

It ties the agency's hands for the benefit of a manufacturer that is unwilling to meet its obligation to the public. It is like requiring a policeman to take a robber's word that he is only wearing a mask and carrying a gun in order to attend a costume party. Even worse, this provision is drafted in such a way that it might seriously compromise FDA's ability to regulate cigarettes, since the FDA authority is based on treating them as drug delivery devices—a totally unacceptable outcome.

Another device provision is even more dangerous. It would require the FDA to approve a medical device, even if it knows that the manufacturing process is so flawed that the device cannot possibly be safe and effective. Recently, the FDA discovered that a surgical glove, which looked fine based on the specifications provided by the manufacturer, was being produced by defective machinery that actually punched holes in the gloves. The FDA refused to approve this product, and spared medical personnel and patients from a serious risk of infection by a host of dangerous blood-born illnesses. Under this legislation, the FDA would have been forced to allow these defective gloves to be sold— because it would be barred from considering the quality of the manufacturing process in approving the product.

A further unacceptable element of this bill is an assault on the basic environmental protections contained in the National Environmental Protection Act. That Act is a key Federal environmental statute which regulates the government's own actions by requiring "environmental impact statements." Under the Act, Federal agencies must undertake a comprehensive environmental planning process for every major action they take. This law is a crucial statutory assurance that steps taken by the government and the actions of regulated industries are consistent with the guiding principle of environmental protection.

Yet, Section 602 of the bill broadly exempts the FDA's activities from environmental impact assessments under the Act. This week, I spoke with the Vice President, who expressed his serious concerns about this provision. In just a few sentences, this bill opens the door to weakening basic environmental protections. It lays down a welcome mat down for future exemptions and future attacks on an effective and essential environmental statute. This is an act of anti-environmental extremism which should have no place in this or any other bill.

We all agree on the importance of FDA reform. The reauthorization of the Prescription Drug User Fee Program is tremendously important to assure that the FDA will have adequate resources to review new drugs and biological products quickly and effectively. This legislation contains many significant reforms that can streamline the regulatory process and codify improvements that FDA has already taken administratively. I compliment Senator Jeffords, the Chairman of our Committee, and many other colleagues who have worked hard on this bill and have been willing to work together to eliminate many other troublesome provisions in the bill as originally introduced.

I hope that in the days ahead a similar spirit of negotiation will result in eliminating these serious remaining unacceptable provisions, so that the Senate can consider a bill that merits its support and that can be passed and signed into law by the President. But until these problems are addressed, this legislation should not go forward. The health of the American people is too important to put at risk simply because the cosmetic industry or any other industry can enjoy even larger profits. I urge my colleagues on the other side of the aisle to work together to improve this bill.

USA TODAY, FEBRUARY 28, 1998

C A N C E R   P R E V E N T I O N   C O A L I T I O N   O F F I C E S

INTERNATIONAL OFFICES AND DIRECTORS

COUNTRY/NATIONAL OFFICE	NATIONAL DIRECTOR	E-MAIL ADDRESS
AUSTRALIA/NEW ZEALAND **Total NO's = 1 ~ Total Members = 20**	Lalita Claff	lalita@nor.com.au
JAPAN **Total NO's = 1 ~ Total Members = 28**	Atsuko Nakano	a-nakano@mc.neweb.ne.jp
KOREA **Total NO's = 1 ~ Total Members = 2**	Sunny A. Kim	sunnyakim@hanmail.net
MEXICO **Total NO's = 1 ~ Total Members = 2**	Vicente Escobar	
SINGAPORE **Total NO's = 1 ~ Total Members = 2**	Karen Jordan Heng	jcis@pacific.net.sg
UNITED KINGDOM **Total NO's = 1 ~ Total Members = 30**	Jane Webster	janew@neways.co.uk
UNITED STATES & CANADA **Total LO's = 142 ~ Total Members = 1,255**	Margie Aliprandi	margie@crowndiamond.net

NO = National Office
LO = Local Office

REGIONAL OFFICES IN USA AND CANADA

States in Region (# Local Offices)	Region Coordinator	E-mail Address
California 19 LO's ~ 125 members Hawaii 1 LO ~ 5 members **Total LO's = 20 ~ Total Members = 130**	Region 1 / June Milich	Liveyoung8@aol.com
Washington 7 LO's ~ 36 members Oregon 3 LO's ~ 50 members Idaho 6 LO's ~ 20 members Montana 1 LO ~ 8 members Wyoming 1 LO ~ 6 members North Dakota 3 members South Dakota 1 member **Total LO's = 18 ~ Total Members = 124**	Region 2 / Julia Meek	info@cancernomore.org
Utah 3 LO's ~ 30 members Colorado 4 LO's ~ 33 members Arizona 5 LO's ~ 51 members Nevada 10 members New Mexico 6 members **Total LO's = 12 ~ Total Members = 130**	Region 3 / Beverly Eves	Eves4neways@qwest.net
Texas 8 LO's ~ 66 members Louisiana 1 LO ~ 4 members Kansas 3 LO's ~ 15 members Missouri 4 LO's ~ 16 members Mississippi 1 LO ~ 6 members Arkansas 1 member Alabama 2 members **Total LO's = 17 ~ Total Members = 110**	Region 4 / Jim Trammell	ke6dre@worldnet.att.net
Minnesota 7 LO's ~ 50 members Iowa 1 LO ~ 8 members Illinois 1 LO ~ 232 members Wisconsin 2 LO's ~ 15 members **Total LO's = 11 ~ Total Members = 305**	Region 5 / Billy Jo Fiege	fig@discover-net.net
Michigan 1 LO ~ 20 members Indiana 2 LO's ~ 15 members Ohio 4 LO's ~ 50 members Kentucky 1 LO ~ 6 members Tennessee 3 LO's ~ 15 members West Virginia 2 members Virginia 1 LO ~ 10 members **Total LO's = 12 ~ Total Members = 112**	Region 6 / Pat Alves	Alves12345@aol.com
North Carolina 6 LO's ~ 45 members South Carolina 3 LO's ~ 21 members Georgia 3 LO's ~ 26 members Florida 6 LO's ~ 50 members **Total LO's = 18 ~ Total members = 142**	Region 7 / Jim & Barbara Murphy	buildtheimage@ghpc.net

States in Region (# Local Offices)	Region Coordinator	E-mail Address
Maryland 3 LO's ~ 30 members Delaware 1 LO ~ 2 members Pennsylvania 1 LO ~ 11 members Rhode Island 2 members Connecticut 3 LO's ~ 26 members Massachusetts 10 members New York 4 LO's ~ 40 members Vermont 1 member New Jersey 10 members New Hampshire 3 members Maine 2 members **Total LO's = 12 ~ Total Members = 137**	Region 8 / Kim Hicks	KB2FREEDOM@aol.com
CANADA (Western) Alberta 3 LO's ~ 16 members British Columbia 6 LO's ~ 34 members **Total LO's = 9 ~ Total Members = 50**	Region 9 /Junae Sinclare	jbs@paralynx.com
CANADA (Eastern) Ontario 3 LO's ~ 15 members **Total LO's = 3 ~ Total Members = 15**	Region 10 /Eileen Cedroff	cedroff@nbnet.nb.ca

Total LO's = 132 ~ Total Members = 1,255

COUNTRY / State / # Local Offices	Region Coordinator	E-mail Address
CANADA (Western) ~ Region 9 Alberta (3) British Columbia (7) **Total LO's = 10**	Junae Sinclare	jbs@paralynx.com
CANADA (Eastern) ~ Region 10 Ontario (3) **Total LO's = 3**	Eileen Cedroff	cedroff@nbnet.nb.ca
AUSTRALIA North South Wales (1) **Total LO's = 1**	Lalita Claff	lalita@nor.com.au
JAPAN **Total LO's = 1**	Nakano Atsuko	a-nakano@mc.neweb.ne.jp
KOREA **Total LO's = 1**	Sunny A. Kim	sunnyakim@hanmail.net
MEXICO Puerto Vallarta (1) **Total LO's = 1**	Ana Vlasic	cpcinfous@yahoo.com
SINGAPORE **Total LO's = 1**	Karen Jordan Heng	jcis@pacific.net.sg
UNITED KINGDOM **Total LO's = 3**	Larry Brooks	larrybrooks@onetel.net.uk

LOCAL OFFICES IN USA AND CANADA

Director's Name	E-Mail Address	City	State	Country
Donna Hudson	donnahu@telusplanet.net	Red Deer	AB	Canada
Brenda Keenan	keenanb@telusplanet.net	Calgary	AB	Canada
Yvonne Evans	yevans@telusplanet.net	Medicine Hat	AB	Canada
Faye Condon	fayec@home.com	Surrey	BC	Canada
Tracey De Paoli	tpdd@home.com	Pt Coquitlan	BC	Canada
Jeanne Shaw	jshaw@netidea.com	Kootenays	BC	Canada
Junae Sinclare	jbs@paralynx.com	White Rock	BC	Canada
Bill Morrison	bill.morrison@3web.net	Burnaby	BC	Canada
Faye Rowe	ayobaby@rslnet.net	Abbotsford	BC	Canada
Christine Rogers	stingray@awink.com	Montney	BC	Canada
Carol Parks	healthful.insight@sympatico.com	Sutton West	ON	Canada
Kevin Rath	plana@on.aibn.com	London	ON	Canada
Shirley E.Whitely	Swhitely@aol.com	Ajax	ON	Canada
Larry Brooks	larrybrooks@onetel.net.uk			UK
Helen Harracott	hn@oliverandstoddard.com			UK
Peter & Mary MacDonald	No E-mail	Hampton	Mddx	UK
Piers Whitley	pierswhitley@wwaltd.com	Steep Petersfield		UK
Cathy McFall	cm2888@prodigy.net	Phoenix	AZ	USA
Sharen Halonen	sdhalonen@juno.com	Prescott Valley	AZ	USA
Karl & Signe Nichols	signes@qwest.net/knic4@qwest.net	Phoenix	AZ	USA
Nancy Kerbs	kerbserv@whitemtns.com		AZ	USA
Claudia Proto	proto@theriver.com	Tucson	AZ	USA
Kuldip/Rebekah Sandhu	krs@itsup2you.com	Sacramento	CA	USA
Shelley Sarason/Kathryn Angel	sarason@snowcrest.net	Siskiyou County	CA	USA
George Gluck	ggluck@exl.com	Bay Area	CA	USA
Sunny Hand	FTHsunnyhand@aol.com	San Francisco	CA	USA
Michael McCright	bodymind1@home.com	S. San Diego Cnty	CA	USA
Steve Walker	walker1@silcom.com	Santa Barbara	CA	USA
Ray Mena	mena4096@mindspring.com	Huntington Beach	CA	USA
June Milich	Liveyoung8@aol.com	Stanislaus County	CA	USA
Dawn Birch	Y2KWASDOTCALM@aol.com	Fremont	CA	USA
Steven Hadar	antiaging@home.com	N. San Diego Cnty	CA	USA
William (Bill) Johnson	stpcncr@aol.com	Orange County	CA	USA
Shelley Kramer	Helthcom@aol.com	Malibu	CA	USA
Linda Taylor	TACMKT@aol.com	Laguna Niguel	CA	USA
M'Lou Keller	SKP2MLOU@aol.com	Ventura	CA	USA
Richard Red Barber	richardredbarber@earnware.net	San Rafael	CA	USA
Elizabeth Hyde	mbh@psin.com	Susanville	CA	USA
Beth Schultz	bsphs@aol.com	San Mateo	CA	USA
Irene Oliver	irenedell@peoplepc.com	LaMesa	CA	USA
Maureen Parker, M.A. M.P.T.	reverseaging@home.com	LaMesa	CA	USA
Lance Jones	LanceJ1s@hotmail.com	Goleta	CA	USA
Susan E. Hayes	No E-mail	Milk Valley	CA	USA
Beverly Eves	Eves4neways@earthlink.net	Aurora	CO	USA
Frances McDaniel	bob-fran@webtv.net	Parachute	CO	USA
Shirlee Davis	No E-mail	Platteville	CO	USA
Ron Vigard	RONVIGARD@aol.com	Evergreen	CO	USA
Al Rickenbrode	No E-mail	Denver	CO	USA
Rosemarie Candelora	healthgood@webtv.net	Hartford	CT	USA
Joel B. Singer	jsingerplast@msn.com	Westport	CT	USA

Cathy Lok	cathysllok@msn.com	Norwalk	CT	USA
Jeanne Sisk	No E-mail	Rehoboth Beach	DE	USA
Nancy Werner	unlimited@home.com	Sarasota	FL	USA
Rita Czanko	provisions@mindspring.com	Temple Terrace	FL	USA
Fredrico A. Dixon III DDS	safemove@newaysonline.net	High Springs	FL	USA
Dan Auger	pbdan@eudoramail.com	Palm Beach Gardn	FL	USA
Belva Flegle	Belvaflegle@compuserve.com	Fruitland Park	FL	USA
Mike & Sandy Quast	quastteam@aol.com	N. Fort Meyers	FL	USA
Randy Smith	r2smith@mail.atl.bellsouth.net	Atlanta	GA	USA
Patricia Gibson	pgibson@zwallet.com	Marietta	GA	USA
Carol Shelnut	carol@insuringamerica.com	Athens	GA	USA
Renee Bonds	ReneeBonds@yahoo.com	Atlanta	GA	USA
Dennis Fukushima	(808) 573-1154	Pukalani	HI	USA
Amy Bierstedt	bierent@netins.net	Iowa City	IA	USA
Melissa Timmerman	HBKSECRET@aol.com	Boise	ID	USA
Sharlene Williams	srdist@ida.net	Idaho Falls	ID	USA
Treva Burnside	No E-mail	Rexburg	ID	USA
David & Jackie Klingler	D3JKLIFAM@email.msn.com	Rexburg	ID	USA
Debbie Dalrymple	hedranews@juno.com	Nampa	ID	USA
Kate Raczek	kater@daily-journal.com	Kankakee	IL	USA
Tina Stodgell	stodgell@comteck.com	Peru	IN	USA
Donna Kindrick	cdkindrick@email.msn.com	Terre Haute	IN	USA
Michael Shaver	mwshaver@kscable.com	Wichita	KS	USA
Bobbie Hulse	healthyaltmc@mpks.net	Mcpherson	KS	USA
Thomas Hampton	michampton@yahoo.com	Little River	KS	USA
Della J. Hall	dhall@aggressiveonline.net	Leitchfield	KY	USA
Belinda Tuminski	betboys@aol.com	Walker	LA	USA
Marie Patin	Kjuntweeti@aol.com	Lafayette	LA	USA
Florence Shanko	fshanko@erols.com	Baltimore	MD	USA
Ronnie Fulkersin/Dan Creedon	ROFOACN@yahoo.com	Germantown	MD	USA
Kim B. Hicks	kb2freedom@aol.com	Odenton	MD	USA
Gail J. Weissert	davew@goeaston.net	Denton	MD	USA
Bob Blank	Rblank8944@aol.com	Detroit	MI	USA
Lynnae Stamy	DiamondStamy@aol.com	Apple Valley	MN	USA
Sharon J Erickson	No E-mail	White Bear Lake	MN	USA
ARI/International	ari@tcinternet.net	Inver Grove Heights	MN	USA
Joyce Ciffra	pfingcif@clear.lakes.com	Owatonna	MN	USA
Patrice DeGray	sownreap@pinenet.com	Grasston	MN	USA
Wallace E. Tilander	wilander@norshore.net	International Falls	MN	USA
Lisa Peterson/Dave Gabrielson	prevention99@aol.com	Cambridge	MN	USA
Bill/Fran Ryan	Rytecent@aol.com	St. Louis	MO	USA
Jean Coash	JJCC770@socket.net	Fulton	MO	USA
Sally Grate	sgrate@gte.net	Branson	MO	USA
Tina L. Hecke	tlhecke@peoplepc.com	Kansas City	MO	USA
Steve Hardman	sch@tecinfo.com	Cleveland	MS	USA
Kevin Rollins	rollinsfam1@home.com	Billings	MT	USA
Barbara Murphy	buildtheimage@ghpc.net	Charlotte	NC	USA
Anita Bender	Aebbus@aol.com	Raleigh	NC	USA
Bear & Deborah Shutt	YourLongevity@msn.com	Raleigh	NC	USA
Donna Wood	donnaw@ttinational.net	Asheville	NC	USA
Teresa Ramsey	No E-mail	Lincolnton	NC	USA
Virginia R. Kelly	blackjb@bellsouth.net	Charlotte	NC	USA
Joe Jolly	jolyeagle@aol.com	Charlotte	NC	USA
JoAnn & Charles Williamson	(607) 797-5717	Johnson	NY	USA

Khaleelah Ziyad	Kziyad@hotmail.com	New York City	NY	USA
Dick Cumming	mentorgroupdc@visto.com	Wallkill	NY	USA
Charles E. Skinner	pskinner@netsync.net	Cassadaga	NY	USA
Paula/Jennings Hall	PJHJAH@aol.com	Canton & Akron	OH	USA
Anita Belfi	anita@ncweb.com	Painsville	OH	USA
Fury Rusinow	furyus@gateway.net	Cleveland	OH	USA
Susanne Woodbury	woodburysj@yahoo.com	Mentor	OH	USA
Pat Alves	Alves12345@aol.com	Chardon	OH	USA
Kalyn Gibbens	kalyng@ecopax.com	Eugene	OR	USA
Karen Van Cleef	support@HealthnBeauty.com	Oregon City	OR	USA
Dr. Bob Doughton	Eeye@teleport.com	Portland	OR	USA
Donna Tsiknas	tsiknas@epix.net	Towanda	PA	USA
Virlyn ""Todd"" Waters	virg@mindspring.com	Columbia	SC	USA
John/Nell Hadley	LCHEOHEE@aol.com	Greenville	SC	USA
Teresa Carter	tcarter@beachaccess.net	Myrtle Beach	SC	USA
Mason B. Collins	masonbc@aol.com	N. Myrtle Beach	SC	USA
Lucille Allensworth	Lallenswor@aol.com	Nashville	TN	USA
Rita Montesi	ritamontesi@email4u.com	Memphis	TN	USA
Dr. Alan White	Alanite@juno.com	Nashville	TN	USA
Raquel Cardenas	ke6dre@worldnet.att.net	Rio Grande Valley	TX	USA
Bob Gannett	bgannett@austin.rr.com	Austin	TX	USA
Jim/Eileen Trammell	ke6dre@worldnet.att.net	Corpus Christi	TX	USA
Charles L. Whittom	cwhittomjr@hot.rr.com	Killeen	TX	USA
Tammy Alvaredo	SALINASDONOVAN@CS.COM	San Antonio	TX	USA
Bill & Betty Kelleher	billk@mcia.com	Houston	TX	USA
Sherry L. Schaat		S. Houston	TX	USA
Ted Thedford	profit@newayoflife.com	Dallas/Ft. Worth	TX	USA
Vanessa Baker	rebvanbaker@hotmail.com	Lubbock	TX	USA
Colleen Lenhart	Colleen@touchfon.com	Riverton	UT	USA
Marianna Pugmire	motherpug@juno.com	Springville	UT	USA
Corinne Selk	tselk1@home.com	Provo	UT	USA
Ron Adams	No E-mail	Sandy	UT	USA
Allison Hague	allison@allicat.com	Sandy	UT	USA
Lori Lenhart	lorilenhart@sisna.com	Sandy	UT	USA
Sheila H. Rivera	No E-mail	Sandy	UT	USA
Desiree' Nedved	Britiabri@juno.com	Centreville	VA	USA
Diana Bublitz	rbublitz@whidbey.net	Greenbank	WA	USA
Julia Meek/Shelley Grimes	info@cancernomore.org	King County	WA	USA
Leslie Burke/Koni Seaberg	leslieb@olynet.com	Thurston County	WA	USA
Patricia Van DeGrift	healthnaturally@webtv.net	Sedro Woolley	WA	USA
Konda Kearton	konda_kearton@hotmail.com	Clinton	WA	USA
Celeste Mergens	mergens@whidbey.com	Freeland	WA	USA
Teresa E. Welch	neways2000@yahoo.com	Langley	WA	USA
Billy Jo Fiege	fig@discover-net.net	Menomonie	WI	USA
Sherry Williams	rwill@wctc.net	Wisconsin Rapids	WI	USA
Lisa/Richard Booth		Glenwood City	WI	USA
Linda Reinbold	lreinbol@union-tel.com	Hanna	WY	USA

REFERENCES

1. Cancer Prevention Coalition (CPC) website: www.preventcancer.com

2. Cosmetic, Toiletry and Fragrance Association (CTFA). Technical Guidelines: Safety Testing Guidelines. 1991.

3. CTFA. Annual Report, 2000.

4. CTFA. Cosmetic Ingredient Review (CIR) Compendium 2000.

5. CTFA. International Regulatory/Resource Manual, 2001.

6. Davis, D. and Hoel, D. (eds) Trends in Cancer Mortality in Industrial Countries. Ann. New York Acad. Sci. 609:November 21, 1990.

7. Epstein, S.S. Polluted Data, The Sciences, 18:16-21, 1978.

8. Epstein, S.S. Corporate Crime: Why We Cannot Trust Industry-Derived Safety Studies. Int. J. Health Services, 20(3):443-458, 1990.

9. Epstein, S.S. The Politics of Cancer, Revisited. East Ridge Press, Fremont Center, NY, 1998.

10. Epstein, S. S. American Cancer Society: The World's Wealthiest 'Non-Profit' Institution. Int. J. Health Services 29, 565-578, 1999.

11. Epstein, S.S. Legislative Proposals for Reversing the Cancer Epidemic and Controlling Run-Away Industrial Technologies. Int. J. Health Services, 30(2):353-371, 2000.

12. Epstein, S.S. and Gross, L. The High Stakes of Cancer Prevention. TIKKUN 15(6):33-39, 2000.

13. Food and Drug Administration (FDA), Industry Programs Branch, Center for Food Safety and Applied Nutrition. Cosmetic Handbook, June 1989.

14. General Accounting Office (GAO), Report of The Comptroller General of the United States, Before the House Committee on Interstate and Foreign Commerce on the Food and Drug Administration's Regulation of Cosmetics, February 3, 1978.

15. IARC (International Agency for Research on Cancer, World Health Organization, Lyon, France). Monographs. IARC Press, Geneva, Switzerland (See latest monograph, Volume 78, 2001 for index of all chemicals, industrial products and processes, and radiation, published since 1972).

16. IARC/WHO. Cancer Incidence in Five Continents. Scientific Publications Nos. 884 & 143, Lyon, France, 1997.

17. International Fragrance Association (IFRA), Geneva, Switzerland, 2001.

18. Kennedy, D. Creative Tension: FDA and Medicine. <u>New Eng. J. Med.</u> 298(15):846, 1978.

19. Kennedy, Edward M., Senator (D-MA). Statement on the "Food and Drug Administration Modernization and Accountability Act", September 10, 1997.

20. Lichtenstein, P., et al. Environmental and Heritable Factors in the Causation of Cancer: Analysis of Cohorts of Twins from Sweden, Denmark and Finland. <u>New Eng. J. Med.</u> 343(2):78-85, 2000.

21. Morris, L.A., Mazis, M.B., Barofsky, I., eds. Banbury Report No. 6, Product Labelling and Health Risks. Cold Spring Harbor Laboratory, 1980.

22. Nielsen, G.D. et al. Effects of Industrial Detergents on the Barrier Function of Human Skin. <u>Int. J. Occup. Med.</u> 6(2):138-142, 2000.

23. Nielsen, G.D. Effects of Four Detergents on the In-Vitro Barrier Function of Human Skin. <u>Int. J. Occup. Med.</u> 6(2):143-147, 2000.

24. SEER (1973-1998) Cancer Statistics Review (Surveillance, Epidemiology and End Results), National Institutes of Health, National Cancer Institute.

25. Sorensen, T.G. et al. Genetic and Environmental Influence on Premature Death in Adult Adoptees. <u>New Eng. J. Med.</u> 318:727-732, 1988.

26. Walker, M. Sir Richard Doll: A Questionable Pillar of the Cancer Establishment. <u>The Ecologist</u> 28, 82-92, 1998.

27. <u>WHO Data Bank, WHO Mortality Data Bank Japan 1998: All Malignant Neoplasms</u>, WHO Data Bank, 1950-1997.

RECOMMENDED READINGS

Clinard, M.B. and Yeager, P.C. Corporate Crime: <u>The First Cmprehensive A ccount of Legal Practices Among America's Top Corporations</u>. The Free Press, Macmillan Publishing Co., New York, NY, 1980.

Conry, T. et al. The Science Action Coalition, <u>Consumer's Guide to Cosmetics</u>. Anchor Press/Doubleday, Garden City, NY, 1980.

Epstein, S.S. and Grundy, R.D. <u>The Legislation of Product Safety</u>: Volume 2, Consumer <u>Health and Product Hazards/Cosmetics and Drugs, Pesticides, Food Additives</u>. Nader, R. Chapter 2, p. 73-141 The Regulation of the Safety of Cosmetics. The MIT Press, Cambridge, MA, 1974.

Epstein, S.S., Steinman, D. and LeVert, S. <u>The Breast Cancer Prevention Program</u>. Paperback Edition, Macmillan, New York, 1998.

Epstein, S.S. <u>Got (Genetically Engineered) Milk! The Monsanto BGH/BST Milk Wars Hand Book.</u> E-Book Edition, Seven Stories Press, New York, 2001.

Erickson, K. <u>Drop Dead Gorgeous: Protecting Yourself from the Hidden Dangers of Cosmetics.</u> Contemporary Books, McGraw Hill, 2001.

Gresser, J. Fujikura, K. and Morishima, A. <u>Environmental Law in Japan</u>. The MIT Press, Cambridge, MA, 1981.

Gresser, J., Fujikura, K. and Morishima, A. <u>Environmental Law in Japan</u>. The MIT Press, Cambridge, MA, 1981

Hawken, P., Lovins, A., and Lovins, H. <u>Natural Capitalism: Creating the Next Industrial Revolution</u>, Little Brown, Boston, 1999.

Iijima, N. ed. <u>Pollution Japan: Historical Chronology</u>. Asahi Evening News, Tokyo, Japan, 1979.

Moore, T.J. <u>Prescription for Disaster: The Hidden Dangers in Your Medicine Closet</u>. Simon & Schuster, New York, NY, 1998.

Natural Resources Defense Council. <u>Intolerable Risk: Pesticides in Our Children's Food</u>. February 27, 1989.

Rampton, S. and Stauber, J. <u>Trust-Us, We're Experts. How Industry Manipulates Science and Gambles with Your Future</u>. Center for Media & Democracy, Madison, WI, 2000.

Rechelbacher, H. <u>Aveda Rituals: A Daily Guide to Natural Health and Beauty</u>. An Owl Book, Henry Holt and Company, New York, 1999.

Steinman, D. and Epstein, S.S. <u>The Safe Shopper's Bible</u>. Macmillan, New York, 1995.

Winter, R. <u>A Consumer's Dictionary of Cosmetic Ingredients</u>. Fifth Edition, Three Rivers Press, New York, 1999.

Samuel S. Epstein, M.D., D.Path., D.T.M&H, Professor of Environmental and Occupational Medicine at the School of Public Health, University of Illinois Medical Center Chicago, is an internationally recognized authority on the mechanisms of carcinogenesis, the causes and prevention of cancer, and the toxic and carcinogenic effects of environmental pollutants in air, water, soil and the workplace, and of ingredients and contaminants in consumer products—food, cosmetics and toiletries and household products. He has published some 260 peer reviewed scientific articles, and has authored or co-authored ten books: the 1971 Mutagenicity of Pesticides; the 1971 Drugs of Abuse: Genetic and Other Chronic Non-Psychiatric Hazards; the 1974 The Legislation of Product Safety: Consumer Health and Product Hazards; the prize-winning 1978 The Politics of Cancer; the 1982 Hazardous Wastes in America; the 1983 Cancer in Britain: The Politics of Prevention; the 1995 Safe Shopper's Bible; the 1997 Breast Cancer Prevention Program; the 1998 The Politics of Cancer, Revisited; and the 2001 Got (Genetically Engineered) Milk! The Monsanto rBGH/BST Milk Wars Handbook (Internet book). He has also contributed numerous editorials and letters to leading national newspapers.

Dr. Epstein's past committee and society involvements include: chairman of the Air Pollution Control Association Committee on Biological Effects of Air Pollutants; President of the Society of Occupational and Environmental Health; Founder and Secretary of the Environmental Mutagen Society; advisor to a wide range of public interest, environmental, citizen activist and organized labor groups; Co-Chairman of the Commission for the Advancement of Public Interest Organizations (CAPIO); and President of the Rachel Carson Council, Inc. He is currently Chairman of the nation-wide Cancer Prevention Coalition.

Dr. Epstein's activities in the interface between science and public policy include: consultant to the U.S. Senate Committee on Public Works; drafting Congressional legislation; frequent invited Congressional testimony; and membership of key federal agency advisory committees including the Health Effects Advisory Committee of EPA, and the 1973 Department of Labor Advisory Committee on the Regulation of Occupational Carcinogens. He was the key expert involved in the banning of hazardous products and pesticides, including DDT, Aldrin and Chlordane. He is the leading international expert on the public health hazards of the biosynthetic bovine growth hormone (rBGH) used for increasing milk production, and of sex hormones used for fattening cattle in feedlots on which he consulted for the E.C., testified on their behalf at the January 1997 World Trade Organisation hearings, and presented testimony to the EU Parliament in May, 1997. More recently, he presented draft "Legislative Proposals for Reversing the Cancer Epidemic" to the Swedish Parliament in December 1998 and to the U.K. All Parliamentary Cancer Group in June 1999.

Dr. Epstein's numerous honors include: medals and prizes in the U.K. Royal Army Medical Corp.; the 1957 British Empire Cancer Campaign (now the CRC) Fellowship at The Hospital for Sick Children Great Ormond Street and the Chester Beatty Cancer Research Institute, London; the 1969 Society of Toxicology Achievement Award; the 1977 National Conservancy Award of the National Wildlife Federation; the 1981 Yale University Henry Kaiser Family Foundation Award; the 1989 Environmental Justice Award; the 1990 Rachel Carson Legacy Award, for "Significantly Advancing Medical Research Into Effective Toxic Chemicals And Bringing His Knowledge Forcefully To World Attention"; the 1998 Right Livelihood Award (the Alternative Nobel Prize) for International Contributions To Cancer Prevention; the 1999 Bioneers Award; and the 1999 Project Censored Award (the Alternative Pulitzer Prize for Investigative Journalism) for an article exposing the American Cancer Society. Dr. Epstein is also a member of the National Writers Union, AFL-CIO, and the National Association of Science Writers.

Dr. Epstein has extensive media experience involving numerous invited appearances on major national TV networks including Sixty Minutes, Face the Nation, Meet the Press, McNeil/Lehrer, Donahue, Good Morning America, and the Today Show. He has also made frequent appearances on Canadian, European, Australian and Japanese T.V.